Wittgenstein's Philosophy of Language

International Library of Philosophy and Scientific Method

Editor : Ted Honderich

A Catalogue of books already published in the
International Library of Philosophy and Scientific Method
will be found at the end of this volume.

Wittgenstein's Philosophy of Language

Some Aspects of its Development

James Bogen

Pitzer College,
Claremont, California

London

ROUTLEDGE & KEGAN PAUL

New York : Humanities Press

First published 1972
by Routledge & Kegan Paul Ltd
Broadway House, 68–74 Carter Lane
London EC4V 5EL
Printed in Great Britain by
Willmer Brothers Limited, Birkenhead
Copyright James Bogen 1972

ISBN 0 7100 7264 3

CONTENTS

This book is for Amy and Aubrey,
Edith and David

It is dedicated to the memory of
Emil Bogen

The 'Codex' (first so-called by Bassett in his monumental *De Selby Compendium*) is a collection of some two thousand sheets of foolscap closely hand-written on both sides. The signal distinction of the manuscript is that not one word of the writing is legible. Attempts made by different commentators to decipher certain passages which look less formidable than others have been characterized by fantastic divergencies. . . . One passage described by Bassett as being 'a penetrating treatise on old age' is referred to by Henderson (biographer of Bassett) as a 'not unbeautiful description of lambing operations on an unspecified farm'. (Flann O'Brien)

ACKNOWLEDGMENTS

What little gets done in this book would have been impossible without the generosity of David Shwayder and Elizabeth Anscombe. Professor Shwayder introduced me to the *Tractatus* and allowed me to consult his unpublished dissertation, which is and will remain the definitive work on that subject. My book began as a dissertation written under his supervision. I am indebted to him for exhaustive comments and invaluable suggestions on a number of drafts of it. Miss Anscombe allowed me to consult the unpublished Wittgenstein material she holds as Wittgenstein's literary executrix, and gave generously of her time to talk to me about Wittgenstein's philosophy. I am sorry not to have a better book in which to thank them.

I am indebted to Professor G. H. von Wright and Brian McGuinness for giving me access before their publication to the *Zettel* and Wittgenstein material from the *Wienerkreis,* to Morton Beckner, Daniel D. Merrill, Robert Grimm, James Griffin, Jaakko Hintikka, and H. R. G. Schwyzer for conversation on various points discussed in this book, and to David Pears and Brian McGuinness for allowing me to attend a seminar on the *Tractatus* which they gave in Oxford in 1964, and to read there a preliminary draft of part of chapter I.

My work was also helped in various ways by Dr Pedro Junjent-Font, Mr and Mrs Henry Mayers, Dr and Mrs Richard Barnes, and Professor Stuart Friebert. Parts of it were financed by a James Sutton Memorial Traveling Fellowship from the

Acknowledgments

University of California at Berkeley, and a research grant from Pitzer College.

I was fortunate to be able to work on this book in two remarkably congenial places, Oberlin College and Pitzer College. I am grateful to my colleagues and students at these institutions for having made them congenial. An early draft was typed by Mrs Harriet Reynolds; later drafts were typed by Mrs Barbara Benton. Both of them are patient women who can read illegible writing. And finally, I am indebted to Susan Burt who helped with the index.

J.B.

ABBREVIATIONS

TITLES OF WITTGENSTEIN'S WORKS

B R. Rhees (ed.), *Philosophische Bermerkungen,* Blackwell, 1965.

BB and *BRB* R. Rhees (ed.), *The Blue and Brown Books,* Blackwell, 1958.

NS G. E. M. Anscombe and G. H. von Wright (eds.), *Notebooks 1914–16,* trans. by G. E. M. Anscombe, Blackwell, 1961.

OC G. E. M. Anscombe and G. H. von Wright (eds.), *On Certainty,* trans. by D. Paul and G. E. M. Anscombe, Blackwell, 1969.

PI G. E. M. Anscombe and R. Rhees (eds.), *Philosophical Investigations,* trans. by G. E. M. Anscombe, Blackwell, 1953.

RFM G. H. von Wright, R. Rhees, and G. E. M. Anscombe (eds.), *Remarks on the Foundations of Mathematics,* trans. by G. E. M. Anscombe, Blackwell, 1956.

RLF 'Remarks on Logical Form', in C.

TS D. F. Pears and B. F. McGuinness (trans.), *Tractatus Logico-Philosophicus,* Routledge & Kegan Paul, 1961.

UPN Unpublished notebooks.

Z G. E. M. Anscombe and G. H. von Wright (eds.), *Zettel,* trans. by G. E. M. Anscombe, Blackwell, 1967.

Abbreviations

Citations of *B, BRB, PI, RFM, TS,* and *Z* give section numbers unless otherwise indicated. I am deeply indebted to Miss G. E. M. Anscombe for allowing me to read the unpublished notebooks she keeps as an executrix of Wittgenstein's literary estate, and to G. H. von Wright who did me a great kindness in letting me read the galleys of *Z* before its publication.

OTHER ABBREVIATIONS

A *Analysis*

APQ *American Philosophical Quarterly*

C Irving Copi and Robert Beard (eds.), *Essays on Wittgenstein's Tractatus,* Routledge & Kegan Paul, 1966.

I *Inquiry*

M *Mind*

P George Pitcher (ed.), *Wittgenstein: The Philosophical Investigations,* Macmillan, 1968.

PAS *Proceedings of the Aristotelian Society*

PASS *Proceedings of the Aristotelian Society (Supplementary Volume)*

PM B. Russell and A. N. Whitehead, *Principia Mathematica,* Volume I, Cambridge University Press, 1910.

PR *Philosophical Review*

R *Review of Metaphysics*

INTRODUCTION

(1) After completing the *Tractatus Logico-Philosophicus*, Ludwig Wittgenstein retired from philosophical work for a period of ten or eleven years during which he taught in a school, designed a dwelling in the style of the *Bauhaus* for his sister, worked as a gardener, contemplated joining a monastery, and spoke only occasionally to philosophers. In the meantime the *Tractatus* came to be considered a classic or near-classic text. In 1929 he returned to Cambridge. Wittgenstein had begun to believe some changes had to be made in the doctrines of the *Tractatus*.[1] He was dissatisfied with his account of colour imcompatibilities, and seems to have believed his work on this topic could not be patched up without a relatively drastic revision of the *Tractatus* account of elementary propositions. Nevertheless, one would have expected his work to proceed along lines more or less congenial to the *Tractatus*. It did not. By 1930 he was devoting serious attention to topics he had seldom considered before and whose connection with philosophy could even seem problematic from the standpoint of the *Tractatus*. The *Brown Book* (1934–5) involves new topics, a new jargon, and doctrines which seem to exclude positions which were central to the *Tractatus*. More surprisingly, there appears to be a lack of concern with what had gone on in the *Tractatus*, whose doctrines seem to have been not so much rejected or argued against, as simply ignored. By 1945 when Wittgenstein wrote the Preface to the *Philosophical Investigations* he appeared to be so far from his early thought that his

suggestion that the *Investigations* should be published together with the *Tractatus* because it can be 'seen in the right light only by contrast with and against the background of my old ways of thinking' can be cause for legitimate puzzlement (*PI* p.x). One can feel that Wittgenstein's inquiries into language had become redirected in such a way as to make it impossible to set the considerations of the later work up against the *Tractatus* for comparison (*PI* 108).

However, I believe that in certain respects, the *Tracatus* and the later work are mutually illuminating, and have undertaken a study of points of contact between them. This topic recommends itself on the following grounds. Firstly and most obviously, the *Tractatus* is an important as well as an influential and historically interesting treatise on language. If it really contains grave errors exposed by Wittgenstein in his later works, one would like to know what they are and how they were corrected. Secondly, one would like to know how 'the axis of our examination' was rotated, and to be able to appreciate the differences between its old and its new orientation (*PI* 108).

Thirdly, I think that it is difficult to begin reading works like the *Brown Book* or the *Investigations* without experiencing doubts about their relevance to traditional philosophical problems. Readers experiencing this kind of doubt have vacillated between feeling that the later Wittgenstein's work was seriously wrong-headed, and offering suspiciously exaggerated praise of it at the expense of previous philosophy. An extreme reaction was the suspicion voiced by Russell and Broad that Wittgenstein was practising a kind of intellectual seduction and fraud in his later period.[2] Russell and Broad are not stupid men, and their reactions should be considered seriously. I believe this kind of qualm can be allayed by comparing aspects of the *Tractatus* to the later work.

(2) Commentators tell us the chief errors Wittgenstein uncovered in his own and other previous theories of language were, for example, that they sought to discover the essence of language, and were guided by 'a basic human tendency ... to seek unity in diversity'.[3] If this is so, little would be gained in the way of understanding Wittgenstein's later thought by a close comparison of the details of the early and later work. Since that is what I am about to attempt, I must oppose this view. It

is hard to believe that a man who promised us a perspicuous representation of our grammar (*PI* 122) did not crave order and unity as much as the rest of us. And it demeans Wittgenstein's later work to think that when he seemed to be responding (even if in an odd way) to traditional problems, he was really just telling us elaborately and at great length to stop seeking unity in diversity. If Wittgenstein wanted us to stop looking for the essence of language, it is hard to explain why he urged us to realize that his later investigations were directed towards what is essential in language (*PI* 92) and that our need to find the essence stems from disquietudes whose significance 'is as great as the importance of our language' (*PI* 92, 111).

Wittgenstein said 'the axis of our examination must be rotated ... about the fixed point of our real need' (*PI* 108). We who have the need are philosophers, and our need is not to stop looking for, but to 'understand the essence of language— its function, its structure' (*PI* 92). Our mistake is to look for this in the wrong way. Wittgenstein thinks we could understand the essence, etc., of language if we could give a perspicuous representation of what lies open to our view—features of language with which we are already acquainted as native speakers (*PI* 122, 92). But something makes us think the essence is hidden from us and, therefore, that we cannot appeal to what is open to view. To understand the essence and function of language would be to understand 'how propositions really work'. But we are unable 'simply to look and see how propositions really work' because 'the forms that we use in expressing ourselves about propositions and thought stand in [our] way' (*PI* 93).[4] The 'enormous importance attaching to the proposition and .... a misunderstanding of the logic of language' lead us to think the proposition must be 'something remarkable' able to achieve 'something extraordinary, something unique' in virtue of hidden mechanisms and powers which an examination of the familiar facts of language with which we are already acquainted will not reveal to us (ibid). Against the popular view which interprets these remarks as saying that traditional philosophy of language is mistaken in general because it seeks unity and essence, I suggest that Wittgenstein had in mind *specific* mistaken doctrines (some of which are to be found in

3

the *Tractatus*) stemming from *specific* and independently criticizable misinterpretations of *specific* facts about language.

In particular, Wittgenstein holds that some of the mistaken doctrines he criticizes are responses to problems generated by an apparent paradox which can be expressed by saying, '*Thought* can be of what is *not* the case' (*PI* 95). The special source of the illusion that the proposition must be something queer is a misunderstanding which makes us think this is paradoxical when in fact it is merely truistic (*PI* 95–6). The problems arise because of misunderstandings of the logic or grammar of 'thought can be of what is not the case' and of other statements which Wittgenstein offers as alternative formulations of the same seeming paradox (for example, 'when we say that *such and such* is the case . . . we mean *this is so*' (*PI* 95)). It is these misunderstandings (whose explanation will take up a good bit of the discussion which follows) and not a craving for order, generality, essence, etc. which Wittgenstein thought misled traditional theorists. Crucial doctrines he criticizes were supposed by him to be attempts to solve problems arising from these misunderstandings.

I take *PI* 95–6 to be serious attempts on Wittgenstein's part to locate the source of important philosophical difficulties because their topic figures so importantly in the works which precede the *Investigations*. When Wittgenstein first hit on the idea of treating propositions on the model of pictures, he wrote, 'This must yield the nature of truth straight away (if I were not blind).' If a proposition is a picture, it 'can be true and false. It has a sense independent of its truth or falsehood.' The importance he attached to explaining this is indicated by his saying, 'It must be possible to demonstrate everything essential' from the case of a proposition set out in picture writing (*Notebooks 1914–1916*, p. 7). The picture theory is, of course, central to the *Tractatus,* and many of its details are supported on the grounds that they allow us to see how the sense of a proposition can be independent of its truth value. The same topic was taken up again and again in the *Bemerkungen* (section III), the unpublished notebooks of 1929–32, and the Cambridge lectures reported by G. E. Moore.[5] In these works and in the *Blue Book* Wittgenstein developed arguments in which the Tractarian picture theory and related theories were rejected because they do not explain how we can believe or assert what is not the case (*BB* p. 31 f.).

The chief contention of this study is that the picture theory of the *Tractatus* and the ontological doctrines which frame it were largely shaped by Wittgenstein's strategy for trying to explain how contingently false assertion is possible, and that some of the more striking disparities between his earlier and later work can be explained by considering how he came to abandon his early account of false belief. Accordingly, I deal mainly with the development of Wittgenstein's views concerning contingent assertions. Other aspects of Wittgenstein's philosophy of language will be discussed only as they arise' in connection with the picture theory, its demise, and the discussions of language use which finally replaced it. Those which receive the most attention are the theory of simple objects and facts, the topic of intentionality, the thesis that the sense of an assertion must be perfectly determinate, and aspects of the later account of logical necessity, rules, and rule-following. This, of course, does not even begin to exhaust the subject-matter of the early or the later works. For example, I have very little to say about the notion of 'criteria', and almost nothing concerning private languages. An excuse for these omissions is that more than enough has already been written on these topics. But more importantly, I believe that despite its narrowness, the subject-matter I have selected is central enough to Wittgenstein's development to shed considerable light upon it. I think an emphasis upon his treatment of false assertion places his interests and the changes in his thought in a much less distorting perspective than accounts which treat the later Wittgenstein as a reformed solipsist obsessed with the notion of a private language, or a Zen-masterly figure who wallowed about in familiar details of language use without sullying them by looking for order.

A cautionary note—the discussion which follows is not to be taken as an essay in intellectual biography.[6] I have often found it necessary simply to ask whether arguments can be extracted from Wittgenstein's texts which would have provided good grounds for the abandonment or modification of a given doctrine because there seemed to be no chance of finding a text which shows clearly what *the* argument was that *actually*

5

led Wittgenstein to change a given view. In such cases I can only claim that the argument is justifiably extractable from a Wittgensteinian text and that it *could* have been used to do the job I present it as doing.

(3)   Why should the truisms

(1) When we say and mean that such and such is the case, we mean that this is so, and

(2) Thought can be of what is not the case

appear to be paradoxical?

Here is an argument suggested by Buridan's discussions of the sophisms 'every spoken proposition is true', 'a man is an ass', and 'you are an ass'.[7] I will refer to it as 'Buridan's argument', BA for short.

(I) If a man thinks or asserts, he must think or assert something; hence there must be something which he thinks or asserts.

(II) Suppose he thinks or asserts that such and such is the case. If it were not the case, no existing thing (fact, state of affairs, etc.) would be the such and such he thinks or asserts. If so, there is nothing which is what he thinks or asserts. Therefore, he could not be said to have thought or asserted something.

(III) But it is impossible to assert or think without asserting or thinking something and hence, if such and such were not the case, no man could assert or think it. Therefore, no man can think or assert what is not the case, and whatever is asserted or thought must be the case. Hence whatever a man thinks or asserts must be true and nothing a man thinks or asserts is false.

If BA were cogent, (1) and (2) would clearly be paradoxical. According to (2) thought can be of what is not the case, but BA purports to show that to think what is not the case is to think nothing at all. (1) becomes paradoxical if we consider that normally (excluding, for example, what Austin called 'verdictive' uses of language in which saying something makes it so) there is a distinction between making and confirming an assertion.[8] If saying is not confirming, we must be able to say and mean that such and such is the case when it is not. But according to BA this is impossible; when such and such is not the case there is no such and such to say or mean and a man who tried to say it would say nothing.[9] Thus when we say and mean that such and such is the case, we say and mean just that—that such and such is the case—only if saying is confirming.

The considerations which underlie BA can be traced back far beyond the time of Buridan to the *Sophist* and *Theaetetus* of Plato.[10] Wittgenstein knew the passages on false belief from the *Theaetetus* and considered them important enough to quote in the *Zettel* (Z69) and the *Investigations* (PI 518).

(4) The questionable steps in BA occur in stages (ı) and (ıı). First there is the move in (ı) from (ıa) 'if a man thinks or asserts he must think or assert something' to (ıb) 'there must be something which is what he thinks or asserts.' Some instances of this kind of inference are clearly outrageous. If Andrew wants something, it does not follow that there is a thing which is what he wants. Suppose he wants a wife. But there are other instances which are correct. If Aubrey kicks something, there must be a thing which she kicks. The following passage (*BB* p.31) has led commentators to say that Wittgenstein thought that the move from (ıa) to (ıb) depends upon a false analogy between 'thinking' or 'asserting' and such words as 'kicking'.

> 'If I think that King's College is on fire when it is not on fire, the fact of its being on fire does not exist. Then how can I think it? How can we hang a thief who doesn't exist?' Our answer could be put in the form: 'I can't hang him when he doesn't exist; but I can look for him when he doesn't exist.'
>
> We are here misled by the substantives 'object of thought', and 'fact' and by the different meanings of the word 'exist'.

The plausibility of the move from (ıa) to (ıb) depends upon an analogy which Wittgenstein does not reject: a man cannot hang unless there is a true answer to 'what does he hang?' and a man cannot think or assert unless there is a true answer to 'what does he think (assert)?' Wittgenstein's point is that it is harmless to say that a true answer gives the object of thought or assertion (and hence that if there is a true answer there is something thought or asserted) as long as we do not misunderstand these uses of 'there is' and 'object'—as long as we can give a correct account of the truth conditions for 'there is something which he thinks (asserts).' What Wittgenstein thinks *is* a mistake is to model an account of the truth conditions for 'there is something which he thinks (asserts)' after 'there is a thief which he hangs.' But the move from (Ia) to (Ib) does not offer or presuppose any account of 'there is something which he thinks (asserts)', and hence is not necessarily incorrect taken by itself. The confusion in BA must be located in the direction the argument pushes us if we grant stage (I) and then go on to try to give an account of 'there is something which he thinks.' We shall not diagnose this if we stop the argument at stage (I).

What looks more sinister is the manoeuvre accomplished in (BA II) by the claims (IIa) 'if such and such were not the case, no existing thing (fact, state of affairs, etc.) would be the such and such which the man (who asserts or thinks that such and such) asserts or thinks' and (IIb) 'if this were so, a man who asserted (thought) that such and such is the case could not be said to have asserted (thought) anything.'

(IIa) appears to be true, if we take 'no existing state of affairs' to mean no state of affairs which obtains and 'no existing fact' to mean nothing which happens to be the case. If it is not the case, for example, that King's College is on fire, then the state of affairs (or situation), King's College being on fire, does not obtain, and there is no fact that King's College is on fire, that is, whatever happens to be the case is not King's College being on fire. Someone might say 'King's College is on fire' signifies an existing thing, King's College. But a college is not a college on fire, at least when there is no fire.

Accordingly we should look to (IIb) to see where BA goes wrong. The import of (IIb) is that if no existing thing, no obtaining state of affairs, situation, etc., and no fact is the such and such which X asserts, then he cannot assert that such and such is the case because there is nothing for him to assert. There are two ways in which this suggestion might be resisted. Both attempt to show that the conditions for the truth of 'there is something which X thinks (asserts)' are not the same as the conditions for the truth of his assertion (thought).

(A)   'A thief' answers the question 'what is X looking for?', without committing the speaker to the claim that any thieves exist. By analogy, we could say that in answer to 'What does X assert (think)?', 'King's College is on fire' gives a description which *could* be true of a fact (or obtaining situation or state of affairs) but does not commit the speaker to the claim that there actually is any fact, etc., to fit the description. On this view, if the assertion or thought is true there is an individual which fits the description, just as there is an individual fitting the description 'thief' if the search succeeds. If the assertion or thought is false, no individual fits the description 'King's College is on fire'. But even so, there is something to assert as long as King's College being on fire is a *possible* fact or a situation which *could* obtain—as long as it is possible for King's College to be on fire. X has something to assert as long as there is a true answer to 'what did he assert?' And there is, as long as there is a possible fact or situation for 'King's College is on fire' to signify.

But what is it for there to be a possible fact or for there to be a state of affairs which could obtain? The answer to this depends upon what account is to be given of 'fact' or 'state of affairs' or 'situation'. A very old account, whose adherents included some of Wittgenstein's contemporaries and teachers, treats facts or states of affairs as complexes whose constituents are referred to by the constituents of ordinary language assertions or analysed versions of them. To say that such and such is the case is to say that certain things, *a, b, c,* etc., stand in a certain relation.[11] When they do not so stand, there is a possible fact to assert as long as *a, b, c,* etc., exist or subsist and are capable of standing in the relation in question. Then it does not follow from the fact that no obtaining situation or fact is the such and such a man asserts that he asserts nothing, because what is asserted is a possible state of affairs or fact which is available for assertion as long as *a, b, c,* etc., exist and can stand in the asserted relation. Theories of type A seem intuitively to represent the most direct response which can be made to BA. In part 1 of this discussion, we shall see that the *Tractatus* picture theory is essentially a theory of this kind.

The most serious difficulty with A-theories arises from their treatment of facts as individual pieces of ontological furniture.[12] In sketching the problem which arises from this assumption, it will be convenient to introduce conventions for using single and double quotes to distinguish between assertions and signs. The same sign (mark or sound) can be used by the same or different speakers on different occasions to make different assertions. If Wittgenstein produced the signs 'I wrote the *Trac-*

tatus', he would have made an assertion which is true because Wittgenstein was the author of the *Tractatus Logico-Philosophicus*. In the mouth of Spinoza the same signs make a different assertion which is true because a different man wrote a different *Tractatus*. I will use double quotes in connection with signs and single quotes in connection with assertions. Thus 'p' is an assertion which can be made by producing or exhibiting the sign "p". I will sometimes use 'p*' as an abbreviation for 'the fact that p is the case' to signify the fact that the situation (state of affairs) which 'p' says obtains, obtains.

A-type theories treat 'p' (the assertion) and p* (the fact which makes it true) as individuals. If they are individuals, they are existentially independent. It can be the case that p whether or not anyone has ever asserted that p is the case, and we can make the assertion 'p' even though it is not the case that p. If two individuals are existentially independent, they must also be numerically different; and so an A-theorist must say that 'p' and p* are numerically different individuals. But it is a necessary truth that:

(T1) 'p' is true if and only if it is the case that p, and

(T2) 'p' is false if and only if it is not the case that p.

From (T1) we can conclude that no fact which fails to verify 'p' is p* and that no assertion which is not verified by the existence of p* is 'p'. From (T2) we can conclude that no fact whose non-existence would fail to falsify 'p' is p* while no assertion which would not be falsified by the absence of p* is 'p'. It is an *essential* feature of 'p' that its truth depends upon p*, and of p*, that its presence or absence determines the truth value of 'p'. There must therefore be a necessary connection between the two.

The difficulty with (A) lies in the question how two existentially independent and numerically different individuals can be essentially connected in this way. In chapter II of this book I argue that Wittgenstein abandoned the *Tractatus* picture theory over this point.[13] B-type responses to BA recommend themselves as ways of avoiding the conclusion that false assertion is impossible without assuming that facts and assertions are individuals. The sketch which follows is suggested primarily by the later Wittgenstein. Related doctrines are to be found in Ramsey and Strawson.[14]

(B) Suppose we assume that facts and possible facts are not individuals. Then, asserting or thinking that p cannot be treated as involving a connection between one thing called an assertion, and another thing called a fact or possible fact. B-theories treat asserting as something we do with a sign; assertion is a kind of activity (a thing done) and the assertion that p as an activity of that kind. Since facts are not treated as individuals, asserting that p can no more be treated as something done to or with p* than scoring a goal can be treated as something done to or with a thing called a goal, or giving a straight look as something done to or with a thing called a look. On this view the question 'what did he assert?' asks which assertion-type act X performed (for example, was his act an asserting-that-p sort of assertion as opposed to an asserting-that-q sort of assertion?) instead of asking which individual (fact or possible fact) was asserted. Thus to say he asserted something means that he performed an act of a certain kind, and 'there was something for him to assert' means only that the act was possible—that there is a performable activity called asserting-that-p.

How then can a man assert that King's College is on fire when it is not? According to (B), asserting that King's College is on fire requires only that there be words to use in making the assertion, and a procedure for using them. If we answer the question 'what did X assert?' by saying he asserted that King's College is on fire, the phrase "King's College is on fire" is used to indicate what X accomplished by using the words he used. That this phrase signifies or expresses something requires only that X's words have a use and not—as (IIb) claims—that King's College is on fire. The same account can be applied to thinking that King's College is on fire on the assumption that to think is to use signs (overtly or covertly).[15]

Thus the B-theorist's programme for combating BA calls for giving an account of the uses of signs to assert and an explanation of what it is for there to be such a use for a given sign or signs. This is an important part of the programme which Wittgenstein pursued in the *Brown Book* and the works which followed it.

(5) My account of the development of Wittgenstein's views concerning contingent assertions relies heavily upon the identification of his worries about false assertions with the problems

raised by Buridan's argument, and upon connections I claim to be able to establish between doctrines from the picture theory and the later work and A- and B-type responses to this argument. My account may be outlined as follows.

The Tractarian picture theory of language is essentially an A-theory. My reasons for thinking this are developed in chapter I below (see ch. I.1, I.2 (2.5, 2.6, 2.7)). The main difficulty with A-type accounts of false belief is the problem of explaining how two existentially independent individuals (an assertion and the fact—if there is one—which makes it true) can be essentially connected. In chapter II, I argue that this kind of difficulty led Wittgenstein to abandon the picture theory (ch. II.1) and that his abandonment of the picture theory led to his adoption of a B-type theory (ch. II.2, II.3).

B-theories explicate 'there is something which a man who asserts falsely asserts' as claiming that there is an activity (asserting that such and such is the case) which a man can perform whether or not his assertion is true. In order to carry out his programme, the B-theorist must tell us what it is to use words to assert. For some time after his return to Cambridge, Wittgenstein believed that to assert is to use signs as projections according to fixed and strict rules. I refer to this conception of language as 'the calculus theory'. Chapter III explicates this account and Wittgenstein's reasons for abandoning it. In chapter III.1, I discuss this view as a bridge between the Tractarian and the later theory. The Tractarian conception of the proposition partly anticipates the transitional theory that the use of language is the construction of rule-bound projections. The notion of a projective use of signs together with the idea that meaningful uses of signs are rule-bound figures importantly in the *Tractatus*. Thus the calculus theory of use originates in the *Tractatus*. But at the same time it was used by Wittgenstein, during the transitional period at least, to combat psychologistic accounts of the use of words whose rejection is typical of his later work. This application of the calculus theory is discussed in chapter III.1. Chapter III.2 discusses the investigations of the notions of rule and rule-following which led Wittgenstein to reject the calculus theory. This aspect of the development of Wittgenstein's thought may roughly be described as involving the transition from one variety of B-theory to another, the differences between them being constituted by differing conceptions of what it is to use signs. My account thus pictures the relation between the later work and the Tractarian picture theory as a complex one. One of the characteristic doctrines of the picture theory was that propositions are individuals which are internally connected to possibly non-existent facts. In this respect, the picture theory was an A-theory and as such was rejected after 1929. But the early Wittgenstein also treated propositions as signs in use as projections, their use governed by systems of projection rules (ch. II.3, (3.2, 3.3)). In this respect, the picture theory was rejected as an incorrect B-theory instead of as an A-theory.

This account is opposed to the theory (advanced by Pitcher) that Wittgenstein rejected the picture theory as a consequence of his arguments against the theory of simple objects. Against Pitcher I hold that the theory of simple objects was postulated by Wittgenstein to shore up the picture theory and that it gains its plausibility largely from the way in which it supports the picture theory (ch. I.2. and I.3). In order to give up the Tractarian theory of simples (together with other aspects of the early ontology) Wittgenstein had to develop arguments against the picture theory which do not depend upon his complaints against the theory of simples. To establish this, I consider the *Investigations* discussion of the theory of simples and argue that the arguments advanced in it are inconclusive by themselves and presuppose an independent refutation of the picture theory (ch. I.4). Although this discussion may appear to be a digression, it is required to clear the way for the account of the rejection of the picture theory presented in chapter II.

I

THE PICTURE THEORY AND
THE *TRACTATUS* ONTOLOGY

1 A SKETCH OF THE PICTURE THEORY
OF LANGUAGE

(1.1)   Wittgenstein wrote that he first became interested in the
picture theory when someone gave him a newspaper report of
a trial 'in which it said that in Paris an investigation of a street
accident was carried out with the use of dolls, model omnibuses,
etc.' (UPN 1930). What attracted him to the theory was his
feeling that it 'must yield the nature of truth straight away
(if I were not blind)' (*NS* p.7). 'Yielding the nature of truth'
meant explaining how a proposition can have 'a sense independent of its truth or falsehood' (ibid). What led him to think
a consideration of pictures could yield an account of truth is
that a picture shows something whether or not it is an accurate
representation of its model.

In order to see why the question of how the sense of a proposition can be independent of its truth value is difficult, consider
the theory that the sense of a proposition is something whose
existence is independent of the proposition—something which is
there to be said or expressed whether or not there is a proposition to express it—and that the proposition names or refers to
its sense. Let us call this the 'name-theory' of the proposition.[1]
It is the simplest account that can be given of the relation of a
proposition or assertion to its sense; because it is oversimplified
it will allow us to consider the problem of false assertion in a
clear and uncomplicated form.

On the name-theory, we might say that a proposition has a sense because it refers to something and that it is true just in case what it refers to exists. But then, a false assertion or proposition would have no referent and would, therefore, have no sense.

To avoid this difficulty, Meinong and others held that what a false proposition signifies does not exist but has being in some other mode.[2] If this provides a way out, it is a tortuous one. The Meinongian must distinguish the various modes of being in such a way as to allow just the right degree of reality to the referent of a false proposition. If he allows too little, the false proposition will be senseless; if he allows too much, the referent will exist full-bloodedly enough to make the proposition true. Furthermore, the postulation of things (the senses of false propositions) which subsist without existing involves the theorist in questions concerning the identity of non-existents analogous to those raised in connection with possible fat men by Quine.[3] These difficulties may not be insurmountable, but they are serious enough to make Meinongian accounts highly unattractive.

A second way of trying to save the name-theory is to hold that the true assertion 'p' and the false assertion '–p' are names which refer to one and the same existent, p*, but which refer to it in different ways. The difference between their truth values would be that 'p' signifies in the true way what '–p' signifies in the false way. But on the name-theory, no matter how differently they may refer to it, both 'p' and '–p' refer to p*. A name-theorist must hold that two propositions or assertions which signify the same thing have the same sense. But assertions with different truth values cannot have the same sense. If '–p' expresses the same sense as 'p' and 'p' is true, then what '–p' says is true, not false (*TS* 4061–2).

Wittgenstein's comparison between propositions and pictures replaced the name-theory of meaning by treating the proposition as if it were a representational picture instead of a name. By 'representational picture' I mean a picture which, like a map or a portrait, has a real subject to which it can be compared for accuracy. The picture theory is an analogy between the sense of a proposition and the features which a representational picture shows its subject as having. On this view, checking the truth of a proposition is analogous to checking the correctness of a representational picture by comparing it to its subject. Truth and falsity correspond to the correctness and incorrectness of representational pictures.

Much of the attractiveness of this model derives from the fact that a representational picture can depict its subject as having features it actually lacks. An example of this is a picture whose elements correspond to things to be found in its subject but which shows them in arrangements which do not obtain. Suppose that a map of Northern Ohio includes the letters "O", "E", and "K" used to stand for the towns Oberlin, Elyria, and Kipton, all of which are in fact located in Northern Ohio. The map is correct if it shows these towns as in arrangement (1).

$$(1) \quad \begin{array}{c} (K) \\ (O) \longrightarrow \text{North} \\ (E) \end{array}$$

It is incorrect if it shows any other arrangements, for example, arrangement (2).

$$(2) \quad (O) \quad (K) \quad (E) \longrightarrow \text{North}$$

The actual deployment of the three towns determines only that map (1) is correct and that map (2) is incorrect. It does not determine whether the map represents something or what it represents. That is why (2) shows a putative arrangement of towns in Northern Ohio just as surely as does (1).

The elementary propositions of the *Tractatus* (upon which all other propositions depend) present possible concatenations of objects whose existence—or subsistence—is guaranteed by the *Tractatus* ontology.[4] More specifically, the elementary proposition asserts (*behauptet*) the obtaining of a state of affairs (*das Bestehen eines Sachverhalte*) (*TS* 421).[5] The obtaining of a state of affairs is the obtaining of a concatenation of objects. The sense (*Sinn*) of a proposition or a picture is what it presents (*TS* 2221, 2202, 2203, 4021, 4031, 404) or what the proposition has (*TS* 33) or expresses (*TS* 42, 4431).[6] It is not clear whether these characterizations of the sense of a proposition are consistent, but presumably we can conclude from them together with *TS* 421 that the sense of an elementary proposition involves '*das Bestehen eines Sachverhalte*', the obtaining of a concatenation of objects.

But it would seem that if the sense of a proposition is what

16

it asserts (*TS* 421), the sense of an elementary proposition could not be the obtaining of a state of affairs. What a proposition asserts should be true or false. The phrase 'that a certain relation obtains among such and such objects' gives us what could be true or false while 'the obtaining of such and such a relation among such and such objects' does not; we can say it is true that a certain relation obtains, but not that the obtaining of a certain relation is true. Nor can the sense be equated with an obtaining state of affairs. False elementary propositions have a sense just as much as true ones, but if an elementary proposition is false there is no obtaining state of affairs. The phrase 'such and such relation between such and such objects' signifies a state of affairs but not what is true or false. Nor does it give what an elementary proposition *asserts,* for as it stands, the phrase is not an assertion or even an indirect discourse report of an assertion. It is most natural, I think, to take the senses of propositions in general to be possible facts and to treat the sense of an elementary proposition as the possible fact that such and such a state of affairs obtains. As Shwayder observes, this interpretation appears to conflict with passages in which Wittgenstein suggests that the sense of a proposition is shown (for example, *TS* 4022).[7] The trouble is that the sense of a proposition is something said, and saying is different from showing. But since Wittgenstein suggests that what is said by a proposition is shown by it as well, this need not be a serious objection (*TS* 4461).

Non-elementary propositions are truth functions of elementary propositions (*TS* 44, 5). If the sense of an elementary proposition is that a certain state of affairs obtains, then the simple case of representational picturing illustrated above by the maps of Northern Ohio may be seen to have been central to Wittgenstein's account. If elementary propositions are pictures there would be no more reason for thinking that only a true proposition can have a sense than for thinking that only a perfectly accurate map can show an arrangement of towns. A possibly obtaining state of affairs could be set forth simply by arranging proposition elements in a way that shows how the objects would be arranged if the proposition were true—just as the setting forth of a possible arrangement of small Ohio towns required nothing more than the arrangement of the letters "O",

"E", and "K". "O" would not be significant if Oberlin did not exist, but there is no reason to think a putative arrangement of towns could not be shown unless the arrangement existed. Similarly the use of signs to stand for objects might be impossible were there no objects, but in order to picture the obtaining of a state of affairs the objects need not be concatenated as the picture shows. And if the senses of elementary propositions are independent of their truth value, it should be easy to establish the independence of truth and sense for their truth functions as well.

(1.2) The aesthetic side of Wittgenstein's assimilation of propositions to pictures is not nearly as attractive as its linguistic side. Pictures are not the kind of thing Wittgenstein held propositions to be, and the analogy between what a representational picture shows and the sense of a proposition goes lame if pressed.

(1) Wittgenstein held that a picture is not a thing but a fact, the fact 'that its elements are related to one another in a determinate way' (*TS* 214). Even if propositions were facts, representational pictures like road maps and portraits are not. A representational picture can be moved from place to place; a fact cannot. A picture can be constructed and taken apart; a fact cannot. A picture can change; a fact cannot. 'Picture' belongs to an entirely different grammatical category from the gerundive and 'that . . .' phrases which express facts. The fact that the elements of a picture stand to one another in certain relations is what makes the picture the picture it is. Thus in analysing or criticizing a painting we may note, for example, what the obtaining of a certain relation between certain elements does to the picture and how the picture or its composition would be different if the fact were otherwise. But this is not to say that a picture consisting of certain painted figures arranged in a straight line from left to right *is* the fact that the painted figures stand in a straight line. Mundane, representational pictures are not facts; we state facts about them.

(2) What a proposition says is that such and such is the case. Thus the assertion or proposition 'Errol is fencing with Douglas Junior' says *that* Errol is fencing with Douglas Junior. But consider the picture of a fencing match.[8]

Suppose the figure on the left is Errol and the figure on the right is Douglas Junior. The picture shows *a* fencing match, Errol fencing with Douglas Junior, or a fencing match between Errol and Douglas Junior. It does not show *that* Errol is fencing with Douglas Junior or *that* a fencing match is going on. Nor does it show a possible fact; if anything, it shows a possible fencing match whose occurrence would make it a fact that Errol is fencing with Douglas Junior.

There are cases in which it would be natural to say that a representational picture shows that such and such is the case, but they lend no support to Wittgenstein's analogy between pictures and propositions. Suppose Errol has made a habit of drawing a picture of himself fencing with someone before he goes out to fence. On finding such a picture, we could say 'this shows that Errol fenced today'. But this does not mean that the picture says anything or that the picture is true or false. What it means is that from the picture we can infer or conclude that Errol is fencing. If it turns out that he was not fencing, we would have to say that the picture did not show that he was fencing after all. A proposition, on the other hand, presents a putative fact whether or not it is true, and in saying that a proposition asserts that such and such is the case, Wittgenstein cannot have meant that such and such being the case is to be inferred or concluded from the proposition.

In order to say that propositions are representational pictures in the ordinary sense (*TS* 4011), Wittgenstein must have stretched the notion of a picture to fit his conception of the proposition instead of merely noting similarities between the two. If the theory of the proposition is linguistically satisfactory, all we can conclude from the above is that the picture theory is aesthetically unsatisfactory. It need not follow from this that it is unsuitable for the purposes of philosophy of language which were much more important to Wittgenstein than aesthetic considerations. One analogy between propositions and pictures seems to hold: we can tell what a picture shows without checking to see if it is accurate and we can tell what a proposition asserts before we know whether it is true. This is the analogy which is crucial for the picture theory of language. (1.3) What does the proposition represent? What corresponds to the geographical region against which we check a map for accuracy? Wittgenstein says 'a picture is a model of reality' (*TS* 212). But as he observed years later, 'If one means by a picture the correct or incorrect representation of reality, then one must know of which reality or of which part of reality' (UPN *circa* 1931). According to Stenius, the reality which a given proposition represents is a single fact:[9]

> From 212 it seems to follow that Wittgenstein always thinks of a picture as having a *real* prototype, which it represents. What we form pictures of are *facts* according to 212. Since by 'reality' Wittgenstein means 'a real state of affairs' what a picture is a model of according to 212 is also a fact. I think that Wittgenstein must be understood literally here: that a picture has a real prototype means in his terminology that it is either a 'true' or a false representation of a fact.

But TS 212 can also mean that each proposition represents *the totality* of facts. This is a more satisfactory interpretation.

Suppose the proposition 'aRb' says that an object, a, stands in a certain relation, R, to another object, b.[10] Suppose the proposition is false because in fact a stands in some other relation, R', to a different object, c, while b stands in yet another relation, R'', to another object, d. What is the *fact* which 'aRb' represents, and against which 'aRb' is to be checked for truth on Stenius's interpretation? Clearly it is not the fact that aRb. The proposition is false because there is no such fact. If we still wanted to say that aRb is the prototype for 'aRb', we should have to revert to the Meinongian view and say that aRb, though non-existent, is somehow there to compare the proposition to.

Stenius steers the picture theory past the Meinongian Scylla only to swamp it on a Charybdis. He thinks Wittgenstein would have said that 'aRb' pictures falsely a fact which another proposition pictures truly.[11] This cannot have been Wittgenstein's own view. *TS* 4061 includes a *reductio ad absurdum* argument against the notion that the sense of a proposition depends upon what is the case. The argument is that if the sense of a proposition depends upon what happens to be the case then 'true and false are relations of equal status between signs and what they signify. One could then say that "p" signifies in the true way what "–p" signifies in the false way.' Wittgenstein supposed this to be so obviously false that it could figure as the absurdity in a *reductio ad absurdum* argument.

The view Stenius ascribes to Wittgenstein is also unsatisfactory philosophically. A consequence of it is that we cannot check the truth of a proposition or assertion unless we already know whether it is true. 'aRb' is such a perfect picture of the fact that aRb, that if it is the case that aRb, I cannot see what other fact could possibly be called the prototype of 'aRb'. But we could not determine whether the fact that aRb is the prototype of 'aRb' without determining first that there is such a fact —without determining that the proposition is true. Similarly, we could have no justification for calling some other fact the prototype for 'aRb' unless we knew that the proposition is false and hence that the fact that aRb is not available as a prototype. But on Stenius's account, we cannot tell if a proposition is true except by comparing it to its prototype and in order to do this we must know what the prototype is. Hence we cannot tell whether 'aRb' is true without first determining whether or not it is true.

There is a second difficulty brought out by considering the case in which the fact is that aR'c and bR''d and asking which fact is the prototype for the false proposition 'aRb'. Since it is not the case that aRb, the prototype would have to be the fact that aR'c, that bR''d, that—(aRb) or that a-Rb. Which of these is the fact that 'aRb' represents? What would justify our choosing one rather than any of the others? Consider a real picture. Suppose it shows Thelonius sitting at the piano. Suppose that in fact Thelonius is not sitting at a piano but is eating a banana split in a booth while Hildegarde sits *on* the piano. In this example, Thelonius, Hildegarde, the piano, and the booth correspond to the objects *a, b, c,* and *d* of the previous example, while sitting at, sitting on, and sitting in correspond to the relations *R, R',* and *R''*.

Are we to say that the picture of Thelonius sitting at the piano is a *bad* or *incorrect* picture of Thelonius sitting in the booth, of Hildegarde sitting on the piano, or of any combination of these? Clearly not, for what it shows is either Thelonius who is not a fact or situation at all, or else the putative fact or situation which involves Thelonius sitting at the piano. Nothing in the picture makes it reasonable to say it represents the situation which actually obtains—Thelonius not sitting at the piano. If someone called the picture 'Thelonius not sitting at the piano', 'Thelonius in the booth', etc., the title would be incomprehensible. Here Stenius's interpretation obliterates the distinction between X's being an inaccurate representation of Y and its not being a picture of Y at all.

In the notebook mentioned earlier, Wittgenstein sketched a Stenius-like account of what the proposition represents if it is a picture (UPN *circa* 1931):

> 'The proposition is a picture.' A picture of what? Can one
> say: of the fact that makes it true if it is true, and of the
> fact that makes it false if it is false; and that in the first
> case it is a correct picture, in the second an incorrect one?

He rejects this, and observes: 'I can represent this space correctly or incorrectly, but in order to find out whether the representation is correct or incorrect, I must know that this space was intended' (ibid).

Stenius's view does not provide for this. In the *Tractatus,* Wittgenstein took greater care over this than Stenius gives him credit for. He did hold that the proposition is a picture or model of reality (*TS* 401, 212), but he did not equate 'reality' with '*a* fact'. Wittgenstein explained what he meant by 'reality' in terms of the notions, 'world', 'positive fact', and 'negative fact' in the course of the ontological disquisition which runs from *TS* 1 to *TS* 2063.

The world is the totality of facts.... (*TS* 11.)

What is the case—a fact—is the obtaining of states of affairs. (*TS* 2.)

The totality of obtaining states of affairs also determines which states of affairs do not obtain. (*TS* 205.)

States of affairs are concatenations or possible concatenations of simple objects (*TS* 201). The obtaining of a state of affairs is the fact that such and such objects stand in such and such a relation to one another. But not every fact is the fact that a state of affairs obtains. Facts correspond to clauses of the form 'that such and such' in locutions of the form 'it is the case that such and such'. The clause which follows 'that' in a locution of this kind specifies a situation or state of affairs whose obtaining or non-obtaining would make it a fact that such and such is the case. The clause which follows the 'that' may mention complexes, and when it does, the putative fact is not the obtaining of a single state of affairs. Nor is it the obtaining of a state of affairs if the 'that . . .' clause occurs in the context 'it is the case that not. . . .' However, every fact involves the obtaining or non-obtaining of (one or more) states of affairs (*TS* 206).

If we know that such and such relations do obtain among such and such objects *and also* that these are *all of* the states of affairs which obtain, we may conclude for every other state of affairs that it does not obtain and that its obtaining is not part of the world. This is why Wittgenstein said the totality of obtaining states of affairs determines which states of affairs do not obtain (*TS* 111, 1206).[12]

> The obtaining and non-obtaining of states of affairs is reality. (We also call the obtaining of states of affairs a positive fact and their non-obtaining a negative fact.)

Thus reality is not a single fact and *a fortiori* not the putative fact asserted by the proposition, the negative fact which is a fact in case the proposition is false, or any other single fact in which the objects mentioned by the proposition actually figure. Reality—what the proposition represents, what we check the proposition against—is the totality of positive and negative facts.

The only passages which appear to count against calling reality the totality of positive and negative facts are *TS* 2063 ('The sum total of reality is the world') and *TS* 2171 ('A picture can depict any reality whose form it has'). The 'any' in the latter passage suggests that there is more than one reality, and presumably there is only one totality of positive and negative facts. But what is at present the totality of facts is one of many possible realities. If so, *TS* 2171 is a way of saying that every possible reality can be represented by any picture which has the required form. Wittgenstein must say this if he believes that we can tell what a proposition represents (what to check it against) without first checking to find out what the facts are. Wittgenstein does not talk about possible realities in the *Tractatus,* but he allows for possible and imagined worlds (*TS* 2022). If reality is the totality of positive and negative facts and if the world comprises the positive facts and determines the negative facts, it follows that if different worlds are possible, different realities are also possible.

It is much more difficult to understand exactly what Wittgenstein could have meant by saying that the sum total of reality is the world (*TS* 2063). He cannot mean that 'world' and 'reality' are synonymous or co-extensive, for he explicitly identifies the world with 'the totality of obtaining states of affairs' (*TS* 204) and reality with 'the totality of obtaining *and non-obtaining* states of affairs' (*TS* 206). Instead of equating 'world' and 'reality' the function of the passage appears to be to secure the doctrine that we can verify or falsify a proposition by comparing it to the world, that is, that we can determine the truth value of a positive or negative proposition by considering which states of affairs do obtain (*TS* 2063 and elsewhere). Without an account according to which we can determine that such and such is *not* the case by considering that so and so *is* the case, it would be difficult to explain how we discover what the negative facts are. And it would be difficult to do justice to the fact that we very often verify a negative assertion (for example, 'Kate is not walking') by verifying a positive one (for example, 'Kate is riding'). If the sum total of reality (including the totality of negative facts) is (in some sense of 'sum total') the world, we can determine the non-obtaining of states of affairs by determining which states of affairs do obtain. If this was Wittgenstein's purpose in saying the sum total of reality is the world, *TS* 2063 does not give 'the world' in answer to the question 'what do propositions represent?' Instead, it says that the world is what we look at to see if a proposition is true; this is compatible with the doctrine that a proposition represents reality. It is not clear how one is supposed to go about 'adding up' the positive and negative facts which comprise reality in order to arrive at 'the world' as a total, but even so, it is clear that *TS* 2063 does not support Stenius's equation of reality with a single fact and his conclusion that a single fact is what a proposition represents.

(1.4) If reality is the prototype to which a proposition is compared for truth, we must distinguish between the connection between the proposition and reality on the one hand, and the proposition and what it asserts to be a fact on the other. Reality stands to the proposition as a mapped region stands to a map, while the putative fact stands to the proposition as a possible arrangement of towns shown on the map stands to the map. We determine the accuracy of the map by comparing it to the geographical region of which it is a map, not by comparing it to the possibly non-existent arrangement of towns which it shows. Similarly, we compare the proposition to reality and not to the putative fact which it asserts. If the putative arrangement of towns does not exist (if the towns do not stand as the map shows them) the map is an inaccurate picture of a certain region. But if there were no such region, the map would not be a picture (not even an inaccurate one) of anything. Similarly, the proposition is a false picture of reality if what it shows as a fact is not a fact. But if there were no reality, it would not be a representational picture at all. I will use the words 'represent' and 'present' as technical terms under the stipulation that what is *represented* by a representational picture is the prototype which must exist in order for the picture to be either accurate or inaccurate, and against which the picture is to be checked for accuracy. What is *presented* by a representational picture is what the picture portrays its prototype as including. Thus a picture can *present* something (X) whether or not any existing thing is X; but if there is no X, the picture cannot *represent* it.[13] The picture theory holds that the proposition *represents* reality and *presents* a possible fact. With this in mind, we can see why the picture theory has a better chance of enabling us to disentangle the notions of truth and sense than any of the alternative theories considered so far. Let us compare it first to the name-theory, and then to the theory which Stenius ascribes to Wittgenstein.

(1) The trouble with the name-theory was that it treated the existence of the sense of a proposition as a condition for its truth and its non-existence as a condition for its falsehood. On the picture theory the truth value of a proposition depends

upon whether a certain putative fact belongs to reality (the totality of facts), but the proposition presents and does not refer to the putative fact.

But isn't this just another Meinongian theory? Wittgenstein holds that the sense of 'p' is a putative fact. Doesn't that commit him to the doctrine that p* must subsist even when 'p' is false and p* does not exist? In order to answer this question, let us consider the case where 'p' is an elementary proposition and ask which existence or subsistence conditions must be met if 'p' asserts the obtaining of a state of affairs.

Suppose that 'p' asserts that aRb. In order to do so, elements of the proposition must refer to the objects *a* and *b*. Wittgenstein held in the *Tractatus* that reference presupposes the existence or subsistence of what is referred to.[14] Thus if 'p' has a sense, *a* and *b* must subsist. But to require this is not to require the existence or subsistence of p* (the fact that aRb). If we call the elements which figure in a fact its constituents, all that has been required so far is the subsistence of the constituents of what would be a fact if aRb, not the subsistence of the fact itself.

In addition to making reference to *a* and *b*, 'p' must indicate the relation *R* and present it as obtaining between *a* and *b*. This does not presuppose the existence or subsistence of *R* because Wittgenstein did not treat relations as real constituents of obtaining states of affairs. In a state of affairs the objects hang together like the links of a chain (*TS* 203). The relevant feature of a chain is that its constituent parts are all links; there are no special elements whose function it is to connect one link with another: 'the chain consists only of its links, not of the links and their spatial relations. . . . The fact that these links hang together in such and such a way does not *consist* of anything' (*B* 303). Part of what Wittgenstein means here is that the connections between the links are not elements or things out of which the chain is composed. The spatial relations between the links are the ways in which the links hang together, and not connections which tie them together. Similarly, there is no element in an obtaining state of affairs which can be called the relation between the objects. If the state of affairs obtains, *a* is concatenated with *b* in a certain way, but the state of affairs contains only two constituents, *a* and *b*. Hence the assertion that

aRb presupposes the subsistence of a and b, but not the subsistence of a relation to connect them (*TS* 20121–20141).

A final condition for making the assertion 'p' is that aRb be a state of affairs which could possibly obtain. If a could not stand in the relation R to b, 'p' would not express a possible fact and hence would have no sense (*TS* 302). The possibility that aRb does not require the subsistence of any entity called 'the possible fact that aRb'. It requires only that a and b subsist and that they be capable of standing to one another in the way 'p' says they do. This presupposes that a and b are objects of certain kinds—that is, that they are suitable for a particular kind of concatenation—but the requirement does not call for the subsistence of p* any more than does the requirement that a and b subsist.

We have exhausted the relevant existence and subsistence conditions for 'p'. The assertion that aRb presupposes the subsistence of objects (a and b) capable of a certain concatenation, but not the subsistence of p*. Thus it avoids the difficulties of the name-theory without resorting in any obvious way to the postulation of subsisting non-existent facts in order to provide senses for false assertions or propositions. In saying this we have been considering only the case in which 'p' is an elementary proposition. But since non-elementary propositions are simply truth functions of elementary propositions, there is no reason to think that Meinongian shades of facts need to be invoked to secure senses for non-elementary propositions.[15]

(2) The difficulty with Stenius's account was that it failed to provide anything which could clearly be identified as the prototype represented by a false proposition. In contrast to Stenius, Wittgenstein held that 'p' represents reality as including the putative fact that p is the case. Reality is the totality of positive and negative facts (or, perhaps, the facts comprising the totality) and it is clear that its existence does not depend upon its being the case that p. Even if 'p' along with every other elementary proposition were false, there would still be a reality consisting of the negative facts that a is not related to b, that c is not related to d, etc., etc. Thus the picture theory secures that there will always be something against which 'p' can be checked for truth regardless of whether 'p' is true.

This clears the picture theory of some versions of the charge

I lodged against Stenius's account. In particular, it eliminates the difficulty of explaining why a given fact should be designated the prototype of 'p' when 'p' is false. But to say that reality (as opposed to one particular fact) is what a proposition represents, raises the question what entitles us to say that a false proposition is a representation of the *totality* of facts. This question will be taken up in the next chapter (2.2). Before considering it, it will be necessary to introduce some further details of the picture theory, and this is what I propose to do now. (1.5) Assuming for the time being that Wittgenstein had a way of justifying the claim that even a false proposition could represent reality, what kind of picture did he suppose the proposition to be?

TS 311 says we use the proposition sign (the spoken or written sentence) as a projection of a possible situation (*Sachlage*). The language of this passage suggests an analogy with geometrical projections. The following diagram illustrates one of the simplest kinds of projection.

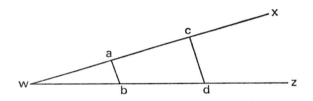

The line *cd* is a projection of the line ab produced by cutting the rays *wx,* and *wz.* The procedure for cutting the rays in order to construct the projection once the line *ab* is given could be called a rule of projection; it determines how the line *cd* is to be constructed and read off as a projection of the line *ab* (cp. *TS* 40141). The procedure used in the diagram calls for drawing *cd* parallel to *ab.* But we could imagine alternative procedures for different purposes in which the projection of *ab* would have to be drawn through different points so as not to be parallel to the line being projected.

Suppose that different methods were used for projecting the line *ab* into various planes as in the following diagram.

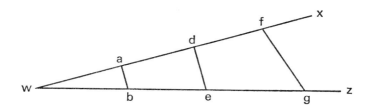

If *ab* were analogous to the sense of a proposition we could compare the lines *de* and *fg* to sentences (*Satzzeichen*) in different notations or tongues and the methods by which they are used as projections to the rules by which different signs can be used to express the same sense. The point of this analogy is that different signs may be used to express the same thing, that what they express depends upon the way in which they are employed, and that apart from the rules of projection, the signs are simply noises or marks—just as the lines *de* and *fg* are merely lines and not projections of anything apart from their use according to methods of projection. It is not intended to suggest that a sense (possible fact) exists or subsists all ready to be expressed in anything like the way in which *ab* is given for projection before the rays are cut further. In order to avoid this suggestion, we could have considered plans or work diagrams for the construction of machines or buildings which have yet to be built and so cannot be thought of as objects from which the diagrams were copied (cp. *PI* 291). Very different drawings consisting of strikingly dissimilar configurations of lines can serve as plans or work diagrams for the construction of the same machine or building. Here the diagrams are analogous to sentences and the machine, etc., they picture to a sense which can be expressed by different signs under different linguistic conventions.

In the *Tractatus,* Wittgenstein described two fundamentally different kinds of projection method. In methods of the first kind, what correspond to the rules by which the rays are cut and the work diagrams constructed and read off are conventions under which signs are used as names to stand for simple objects and arranged to show possible configurations of the objects. In propositions constructed in this way, 'one name stands for one object, and another for another, and they are combined with one another' (*TS* 40311). The fact that the signs are arranged as they are and are so arranged under the conventions of a projection method shows how the objects would stand if the proposition were true (*TS* 215). I will call methods of this kind 'methods of elementary projection' because elementary propositions (propositions which assert the obtaining of single states of affairs) are constructed according to them. The difference between two elementary methods of projection could be, for example, that in one of them the sign 'a' is used to stand for a certain object, while in the other, a different sign is used for the same purpose.

A proposition constructed in this way can assert no more than the obtaining of a single state of affairs. The elementary methods for projection include no mechanisms for negation or for the expression of disjunction, conjunction, implication, etc. The signs 'v', '—', etc., do not function as names according to Wittgenstein (*TS* 40312, 54–54611). If an elementary proposition were to express the non-obtaining of a state of affairs, it would have to register negation by means of the arrangement of the signs used to name the objects. Suppose we wanted to assert that *a* does not stand to *b* in the relation *R*. In order to show *which* relation does not obtain between which objects, we should have to write "*a b*", spacing the letters in the way required to indicate the relation. But if we follow the elementary conventions by which an arrangement of signs shows objects as related, we would thus assert that *a*R*b* when we were trying to assert just the opposite. If we placed the signs in a different relation to make it clear that we were not arranging them to show *a* as related to *b* (for example, if we wrote " $\frac{a}{b}$ ") it would not be clear that *R* is the relation we claim not to obtain. And if we tried to avoid making the assertion '*a*R*b*' by omitting the letters "a" and "b" we would succeed only in asserting that some other state of affairs obtains or in asserting nothing at all. Thus elementary propositions cannot be negative (cp. *PI* 520). Related considerations apply to conjunction, disjunction, and implication. For example, we could write, "*ab cd*", but we could not make it clear (confining ourselves to the use of an elementary method of projection) whether we were asserting the conjunction '*ab* & *cd*' or simply asserting '*ab*', '*cd*'.[16] If we employed a convention according to which a space between "*ab*" and "*cd*" is used to indicate conjunction while another kind of spacing is used for the unconjoined assertion of '*ab*' and '*cd*', etc., we would in effect have introduced spacings to function in the same way as the sign "&". Then the notation would include a sign (a space) which does not refer to an object, and would no longer comprise an elementary method of projection. That is why 'the simplest kind of proposition, the elementary proposition, asserts the obtaining of states of affairs' (*TS* 421; cp. *NS* p. 130); one obtaining of one state of affairs for each elementary proposition—no more. Non-elementary propositions are constructed by what may be called 'truth-functional methods'. Non-elementary propositions express their senses by registering agreement and disagreement with truth possibilities of elementary propositions (*TS* 44). They assert the non-obtaining of states of affairs, the obtaining of two or more states of affairs, and they present putative facts involving the obtaining of some and the non-obtaining of other states of affairs. If follows that the truth conditions of any given non-elementary proposition must correspond to the truth possibilities of elementary propositions.

The rules of a truth-functional method of projection are conventions by which signs are used to indicate the joint negation of sets of elementary propositions and to specify the sets which serve as bases for this operation (*TS* 6).[17] A language which includes non-elementary propositions need not produce them perspicuously; its speakers may be unaware that they are producing truth functions of elementary propositions and there need be nothing in the language which explicitly indicates that its assertions or propositions are produced from elementary propositions. According to Wittgenstein, the most striking examples of this are the tongues which comprise ordinary colloquial speech. When Russell rightly observed that Wittgenstein was 'concerned with the conditions which would have to be fulfilled by a logically perfect language' (*TS* p. ix) he was wrong to conclude from this that Wittgenstein's treatise was not concerned with ordinary language (*TS* p. x).

In fact, all the propositions of our everyday language, just as they stand, are in perfect logical order.—That utterly simple thing, which we have to formulate here, is not an image of the truth, but the truth itself in its entirety.

(Our problems are not abstract, but perhaps the most concrete that there are.)

The best commentary on this passage (*TS* 55563) comes from Wittgenstein himself (*PI* 98):

On the one hand it is clear that every proposition in our language 'is in order as it is'. That is to say, we are not *striving for* an ideal, as if our ordinary vague propositions had not yet got a quite unexceptionable sense, and a perfect language awaited construction by us.—On the other hand it seems clear that where there is sense there must be perfect order.—So there must be perfect order even in the vaguest proposition.

If the picture theory covers the assertions of ordinary language, they must have been treated by Wittgenstein as non-elementary propositions; in ordinary speech we do not speak about Tractarian simples and assert the obtaining of relations between them. Thus when Wittgenstein claimed we express senses without 'having any idea of how each word has meaning or what its meaning is—just as people speak without knowing how the individual sounds are produced', he meant that we produce truth functions of elementary propositions without realizing that this is what we are doing. The enormously complicated 'tacit conventions on which the understanding of everyday language depends' are conventions for jointly negating sets of elementary propositions (*TS* 4002).

The distinction between elementary and truth-functional methods of projection renders the *Tractatus* immune to a criticism raised against the picture theory by Daitz:[18]

Consider . . . the notion that elements of the proposition sign stand for elements in the signified. Take the phrase 'the river' in 'the river is long'. For what could it stand? The river? But then since all words in the sentence stand for an object, for what does 'long' stand? The river too? . . . Clearly a 'stand for' account of the function of the words in a sentence will not do. . . . And how can it apply at all to conditional sentences or negative sentences? Does 'not' name an element in the world? If it does, how odd an element; if it doesn't, how do we describe the difference between 'this is red' and 'this is not red'?

By 'stand for' theory Daitz means the theory that each word in a sentence is used to stand for something. It is clear that in the *Tractatus,* only elementary propositions can fit this characterization of the uses of words in a sentence. But elementary propositions contain nothing but words used to signify simple objects. Thus it is no objection to the *Tractatus* to point out that 'long' and 'not' do not stand for or name individual things. These words do not name simples and therefore do not figure in elementary propositions. It is true that elementary propositions are fundamental to fact-stating discourse on the *Tractatus* theory. This is because non-elementary propositions depend upon them for the expressions of their senses. But this is not to say that all propositions are elementary projections as the Daitz criticism assumes.

2 THE THESIS THAT THE MEANING OF A NAME IS ITS BEARER, AND THE DETERMINACY OF SENSE

(2.1) Now I will consider two of the most characteristic doctrines of Wittgenstein's early period and argue that they are consequences of the picture theory. My view is that the thesis that the meaning of a name is its bearer was stipulated to secure the possibility of the representation of reality by the proposition, and that the determinacy thesis is required because the picture theory is a version of the correspondence theory of truth.

(2.2) The correspondence theory holds that truth is or depends upon correspondence between an assertion and something to which it is compared. A correspondence theorist must tell us *why* the comparison should have anything to do with the determination of truth value. If he has the kind of theory Stenius ascribed to Wittgenstein (so that 'correspondence' means correspondence with a particular fact) he must tell us why comparison with this rather than that fact is crucial. Wittgenstein does not have to worry about this, but he does have to tell us why the state of reality should have anything to do with the truth value of a proposition. His answer is that each proposition is a representational picture of reality and purports to represent it correctly. But then, what makes a proposition (even a false one) a representation of reality? Well —according to the *Tractatus* we produce propositions by employing signs according to projection methods to picture reality. But *TS* holds also that the possibility of this employment of signs rests on an isomorphism between elements of language and of reality. To see why, it is helpful to consider the following facts about the use of ordinary pictures as representations.

In many cases we can make something into a picture of a certain person or thing by simply giving it a title and treating it as a picture of that thing. A painter might, for example, make a painting drawn from one girl, A, into a portrait of her twin sister, B, by giving it the title 'Portrait of B'. (And he can also turn it into a genre picture by giving it the title 'A Country Girl'.) But there are limits to what an artist's intentions can accomplish (or perhaps, to what he can intend) and they are given in part by what is on the canvas on the one hand, and by facts about what is to be represented on the other. Suppose the drawing shown here were called 'The Battle of Waterloo'.

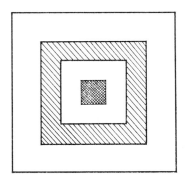

Unless the artist can tell us *how* this can be used as a portrayal of the battle, we can dismiss the title. Perhaps it can be taken as an evocation or comment on the battle, but not as a representational picture; A *represents* B only if it can be checked against B for accuracy, and so far, there is no possibility of that. But can't we supply a projective scheme under which this or *anything at all* can represent anything we choose? Clearly not. Suppose that B is complex (for example, a battle with soldiers, guns, horses, a scene composed of various objects, a person's face with features, etc.) and A is a uniformly black canvas. A cannot represent B (it cannot, for example, show the narrowness of B's eyes, how far apart they are set, the wart on the nose, etc.) because it lacks sufficient complexity. It does not divide into distinct parts which can be employed to show distinct features of the face. No projective scheme which required the correlation of parts of the picture with parts of the face could be applied to it unless we altered the canvas to provide distinguishable parts. Thus:

(1)   where the complexity of B is essential to what a representational picture of it might portray, A cannot represent it unless it is sufficiently complex. Let us call this the 'multiplicity requirement'. With regard to it, Wittgenstein's dictum that 'there must be something identical in a picture and what it depicts to enable the one to be a picture of the other at all' (*TS* 2161) is unexceptionably correct.

At least two further requirements must be met by A if it is to serve as a representative picture of B.

(2)   It must be possible to understand the elements of A as standing for or depicting what at least *could have* figured among the elements of B. Wittgenstein's face could have had a different sort of nose, eyes, and mouth from those which it actually had, but it could not have had rocks and trees for features. A picture (because of facts about it, or facts about the projective scheme under which it is to be read off) which had to be seen as showing only rocks and trees could not be a picture of Wittgenstein's face. Finally:

(3)   we could not understand A as a representational picture of B even if its elements showed what could have been elements of B unless we could see it as showing possible arrangements or relations among relevant elements of B. Suppose A is a cubist picture of a face which could not be taken as a literal portrait without being seen as showing the facial features in physically impossible positions. Such pictures can show us much about their models (they can, for example, evoke the sitter's mood, or features of his personality) but they cannot purport to show us the model in the sense in which maps and literal portraits can.

We could not say what it would be to call a picture intentionally constructed in this way accurate or inaccurate (although we could talk about how successful it is in evoking its subject, and about its being 'true to' its subject in the sense in which a genre picture can be 'true to' a region or kind of person).

The failure of a picture to meet these conditions can be due to defects in a projection method, as in cases where a map fails because its legend is defective. Or it can be due to the thing used as a picture, as in the case of the uniformly blank canvas which no projective schema could turn into a representation of a face. In the case of portraits, photographs, landscape drawings, etc., as opposed to maps, and other depictions in which there is a clear distinction between a projective scheme (for example, a legend) and what is used as a projection, we may not want to characterize the failure in either of these ways. Instead, we may simply say the picture cannot be, or cannot be seen as a representation of the putative subject. But even in these cases, I think the conditions just sketched are, with suitable refinement, plausibly called necessary conditions for representation.

Wittgenstein's account of what makes a proposition a representation of reality has the effect of securing the satisfaction of conditions analogous to those just outlined. The features ascribed to propositions and reality at *TS* 217–30321 and elsewhere could plausibly be treated as results of a sort of transcendental deduction which begins with the premises that the proposition pictures reality and that 'there must be something identical in a picture and what it depicts to enable the one to be a picture of the other' and proceeds on the assumption that the requisite similarity is required to guarantee the satisfaction of conditions related to (1)–(3) (p. 35). The 'transcendental deduction' would ascribe to the proposition and to reality whatever is necessary to constitute the proper sort of similarity between the two.

Wittgenstein identified what is shared in common by a picture and reality as 'The Form of Representation' (*Form der Abbildung*) (*TS* 217). Form of Representation is initially characterized as the possibility (*Möglichkeit*) of the connections between picture elements which constitute the picture (*TS* 214–215). Following Schwyzer, I take this to mean that the Form of

Representation is what *makes it possible* for the elements of a picture to stand in the arrangement which goes to make up the picture. Thus part of what is meant by *TS* 217 is that what makes possible the facts which constitute reality is also what makes possible the arrangements of elements in pictures. This follows from the thesis that pictures are facts (*TS* 214–2141, etc.). The Form of Representation is the form of reality (*TS* 218–22) and thus it is what makes possible all facts—including pictures.

What Wittgenstein goes on to say is less clear: 'The Form of Representation is the possibility that things are related to one another in a particular way, like the elements of the picture' (*TS* 2151). This may mean (as *TS* 215 seems to suggest) that the Form is the possibility that objects are related in the same way as the propositional elements. But the ability to stand in a certain relation to a given object is an essential feature of the objects which can so stand (*TS* 2011, 2012, 20121, 20123, 20141). The objects referred to by propositional elements could not be concatenated in the same way as the propositional elements unless they were essentially similar, and presumably they could not be unless the propositional elements were themselves simples. But it is hard to see how they could be simples. We may suppose Wittgenstein meant instead that the *Form of Representation* is the possibility that objects are related as the picture *shows* them related. This sounds more plausible, and it follows from the stronger thesis that they stand in the same relations as the propositional elements. Thus what I have to say that depends on the weaker interpretation will stand even if Wittgenstein intended the stronger thesis.[19]

Now we said that a picture must show things as they could have stood in what the picture represents. If the Form of Representation and the form of reality make it possible for the things which the propositional elements stand for to be related as the proposition shows them, it guarantees that whatever the proposition represents as a fact could occur in reality. Thus it satisfies a condition analogous to (2), p. 35, for if p* can occur in reality, so can its constituents—the objects shown as related to one another by 'p'. Similarly, if what is pictured is always a possible fact, propositions cannot violate condition (3), p. 35 by presenting elements in impossible combinations.

37

But what is the Form of Representation, and how can it be identical to the Form of Reality? Wittgenstein associates the form of the world with the objects whose concatenations are states of affairs (*TS* 2024–20271). The reason for this is as follows. The structure of a state of affairs is the way its elements are concatenated (*TS* 2032). The form of the state of affairs is whatever makes the concatenation possible (*TS* 2033). This must have to do with the objects which constitute the state of affairs. For one thing, a concatenation of n objects would be impossible unless there were n objects to concatenate. For another, there could be no concatenation unless the objects were able to hang together. As noted in connection with *TS* 2171, the essence of a Tractarian object is just its ability to concatenate with other objects (*TS* 20123). Hence the number and nature of objects are what make states of affairs possible. But every fact is the obtaining or non-obtaining of states of affairs, and reality is the totality of positive and negative facts (*TS* 206, 20272, 2032, 2033, 2034). Hence the multiplicity of simple objects and their abilities to concatenate are what make facts in general possible. That is why the form of reality is connected with the totality of objects (*TS* 2024–206). Can we find something in this which could be shared by and considered to be the form of proposition pictures? We need only consider the case of elementary propositions since whatever makes them possible will also constitute the possibility of non-elementary ones.

If the identity between the form of reality and the Form of Representation secures that elementary propositions present nothing except possible facts, each name in an elementary proposition must refer to a simple object (a putative state of affairs presented by names without bearers could not obtain), and each elementary proposition must contain the proper number of different names. That is because every state of affairs contains at least two objects and it is conceivable that some objects are capable of concatenating with no less than two others. What is common to a proposition with a given number of names and the state of affairs it presents as obtaining is their multiplicity, the number of names and objects respectively (*TS* 404). We have seen that multiplicity is (part of) what makes facts possible. It therefore seems plausible to equate the forms of representation and reality with the multiplicity shared by names in the language and simple objects in reality.

But it looks as though the form of reality and of representation must involve more than the multiplicity of its elements. If there are two objects, *a* and *b,* which cannot concatenate with each other, but only with other objects, or which cannot concatenate in the same way with each other as with other objects, nothing short of syntactical restrictions governing the arrangement of their names can preclude the possibility of their being combined to present an impossible state of affairs. The mere number of names (and its correspondence to the number of objects) cannot provide the typal distinctions between names thus required. At this point it becomes difficult to see how the forms of reality and representation could be literally identical. Unless the names are simple objects, they cannot be connected in the same way as their bearers. Syntactical rules could guarantee that every permissible combination of names corresponds to a (different) possible arrangement of objects, but not that the structures of the proposition and the state of affairs it presents can be identical. If the structures of propositions differ from those of presented facts and if form is what makes structure possible (*TS* 2033, etc.), then the form of representation would have to be different from the form of the reality which propositions are supposed to represent. It is difficult to see what differences between forms could amount to unless the impossibility of similar arrangements of the elements of two systems reflected a dissimilarity in their forms. I do not believe the *Tractatus* provides any coherent way of reconciling the thesis that the proposition shares its form with reality with the presumption that the elements of a proposition which refer to objects would have to be different from the elements of what the proposition presents as a fact.

Be that as it may, the theory that propositions represent reality depends to a great extent upon the logical properties Wittgenstein ascribed to the names whose arrangements are elementary propositions. This is why Wittgenstein held that what makes a proposition a picture of reality is the correlation of the names it contains with the constituents of states of affairs (*TS* 21513–21514), and it helps to explain why 'the possibility of propositions is based on the principle that objects have signs as their representatives' (*TS* 40312). What makes a proposition a representational picture of reality is (1) the cirumstance that even if the proposition is false, the objects correlated with its names are elements to be found in reality as constituents of positive and negative facts (*TS* 2024–20271), and (2) the circumstance that the syntactical rules which govern the arrangements of names in elementary propositions prevent configurations of names (elementary propositions) which do not correspond to possible configurations of objects and hence to possible facts (*TS* 2021, 2022–2023, 215–2151, 302, etc.).[20] These provisions fulfil the conditions that a representational picture must meet if its subject is complex and is importantly characterized by its complexity. They ensure that picture elements correspond to elements which belong to reality and that what is shown by the picture is something which could be a fact. This is analogous, for example, to ensuring that a representation of a face shows what could be arrangements of its features.

(2.3) Let us consider one further contribution Tractarian names make to the appropriateness of considering propositions as representational pictures of reality. A is a representational picture of B only if A can be compared to B for accuracy.

> If one means by picture the correct or incorrect representation of reality . . . one must have a means for comparing the proposition with reality in a definite way. (UPN *circa* 1931.) It makes sense to declare the length of an object only if I have a method for locating the object. For otherwise I cannot lay the measuring stick upon it. What I formerly called simples amount to no more than what I can refer to without fear that perhaps they don't exist . . . that means: that about which we can speak no matter what is the case (*B* section III, 36, par. 1).

If the proposition (or—in the case of a non-elementary proposition—the propositions of which the proposition is a truth function) did not contain names, we would not know *how* to go about comparing the proposition to reality to check its truth value even if we did somehow know that it was a representational picture of reality.

The proposition 'lies against reality like a ruler. Only the end points of the graduation lines actually *touch* the object to be measured' (*TS* 21512, 215121).[21] If there were no names the proposition would be like a ruler without graduating marks. If the names were not correlated with objects to be found in reality as the constituents of facts, reality would be like an object which could not be measured because it lacked clearly demarcated edges to match with the marks on the ruler. Very roughly speaking, comparison must involve looking to the objects named in the proposition (or the propositions whose truth function it is) to check their actual deployment (the concatenations which obtain between them) against the deployment shown by the arrangement(s) of names. This requires a fixed correlation between names and the constituents of states of affairs.

(2.4) When we consider how the claim that reality is represented by false as well as true propositions depends upon the thesis that names refer to the constituents of states of affairs, we can see reasons for Wittgenstein to assume that the meaning of a name is its bearer. The representation of reality by the proposition requires the stipulation that no name shall be without a bearer. The simplest way to satisfy this stipulation is simply to say that the meaning *is* its bearer (*TS* 3203). When Wittgenstein wrote the *Tractatus* he was exposed to long-standing precedents for the assumption that the meaningfulness of a name depends upon the existence or subsistence of its bearer, and even for the more radical thesis that its meaning *is* its bearer. I do not wish to deny this, or to deny that the doctrine may have appealed to him for reasons other than those I have mentioned. Nevertheless, I think the place of the doctrine in the Tractarian theory is best understood in the way I have been suggesting. It serves to underpin the thesis that propositions represent reality, and the Tractarian account of what it is to compare a proposition to reality. It accomplishes this by guaranteeing that no name can be without a bearer, thus securing the connection between propositions and reality which the picture theory depends upon.

(2.5) The second Tractarian thesis to be introduced in connection with the picture theory is the claim that the sense of a proposition is determinate (*TS* 323). I hold that the determinacy thesis was required to shore up the Tractarian account of the connection between a proposition and the putative fact it presents against difficulties which arise from Wittgenstein's account of facts.

Although the early Wittgenstein's appeal to the determinacy thesis is an argument for simple objects and the later Wittgenstein's extended polemics against the thesis leave little room to doubt its importance in the *Tractatus,* Wittgenstein's writings contain no clear explanation of what the 'requirement that sense be determinate' actually required (*TS* 323). Accordingly, I must ask at some length what the determinacy thesis amounts to.

Anscombe and Griffin take it to require nothing more than that propositions have truth conditions.[22] But the *Tractatus* says that 'What a proposition expresses it expresses in a determinate manner which can be set out clearly; a proposition is articulated' (*TS* 3251). Judging from this, a proposition whose sense is determinate must also be articulated and must express its truth conditions clearly. Unfortunately, we are not told by what standard clarity is to be judged, to what degree a proposition must be articulated, or what—if there could be such a thing—an unclear or unarticulated proposition would be like. For this we must consult the *Notebooks.* In an entry dated 1915, Wittgenstein wrote (*NS* pp. 67–8):

> But could it be possible that the propositions in ordinary use have, as it were, only an incomplete sense? ... When I say 'the book is on the table' does this really have a clear sense? (An extremely important question.) But the sense must be clear, for after all, we mean *something* by the proposition, and as much as we certainly mean must be clear.
> If the proposition 'the book is on the table' has a clear sense, then I must, *whatever is the case,* be able to say whether the proposition is true or false. There could, however, be *cases* in which I should not be able to tell straight off whether the book is on the table. And then—? Is it here a case of my knowing exactly what I want to say but then of making mistakes in expressing it? Or can this uncertainty be included in the proposition as well?

The last lines of this passage suggest a distinction between the proposition expressed by a speaker and the speaker's expression of it. Presumably 'proposition' has to do with the assertion or statement the speaker wants to make, while 'expression' has to do with the sentence he uses or his use of the sentence to make the assertion.

The proposition has truth conditions ('I must be able to say . . . whether the proposition is true or false') whose specification sets out exactly what the speaker intended to say. And a proposition can be given a more or less complete expression by a speaker. In some cases, the expression may fail to give us the complete proposition, and if this happens, we need another expression in order to see what the speaker meant to say.

Wittgenstein thought that if we know what is the case, we must be able to say straight away whether the proposition 'the book is on the table' is true or false. If there is any uncertainty (aside from lack of knowledge of the facts) over whether a given situation verifies or falsifies the proposition, the uncertainty must be due to an incompleteness in its expression and not to any incompleteness in the proposition or to any unclarity in its sense. Before he completed the *Notebooks* Wittgenstein vacillated on this point, but more often than not he inclined toward the view expressed in the following passage (*NS* p. 68):

> It seems clear that what we *mean* must always be 'sharp'.
> Our expression of what we mean can in its turn be right or wrong. And further, the words can be applied consistently or inconsistently. There does not seem to be any other possibility.

This excludes the possibility that the uncertainty belongs to the proposition. If the proposition can be expressed correctly, its best expression should leave no doubt as to whether any relevant state of affairs satisfies or fails to satisfy its truth conditions.

The kinds of case Wittgenstein worried about were borderline cases. He gives no examples but we can imagine, for example, that the book lies half on one table and half on another, or that the book and the table have been chopped up and pieces of the book are scattered over pieces of the table. If the sense of 'the book is on the table' is 'sharp', a proper expression of the proposition should enable us to decide straight away whether it is true or false even here. There will also be situations which have nothing to do with the truth value of the proposition (for example, the circumstance that the book is older than the table). If the proposition has a 'sharp' sense, its full expression should also determine which situations are thus irrelevant to its truth value.

> If a proposition tells us something, then it must be a picture of reality just as it is, and a complete picture at that. There will, of course, also be something that it does *not* say— but what it does say it says completely and must be susceptible to a sharp definition. (*NS* p. 61)
> If possibilities *are left* open in the proposition, just *this* must be *definite*: what is left open. . . . What I do not know I do not know, but the proposition must show me *what* I know. (*NS* p. 63; cp. *TS* 5156)

And so the proposition flatly determines for any situation whether it verifies, falsifies, or leaves entirely open the truth value of the proposition. In border-line cases the proposition does not really have an indefinite truth value. Its truth value seems indefinite only because its expression is incomplete.

The *Tractatus* contains no mention of border-line cases. This is not because Wittgenstein had abandoned the idea that sense must be perfectly sharp; it is because the *Tractatus* theory collapses the distinction between the completeness or clarity of a speaker's expression and a proposition. According to the *Tractatus*, the use of a proposition-sign is its employment according to a projection method as a representational picture of reality, and the proposition itself is nothing more than the proposition-sign in use according to rules of projection (*TS* 311, 312, 35–4). Therefore, the proposition-sign is a sentence. Thus the proposition can say no more and no less than any expression of it because, *inter alia,* the proposition *is* an expression. Furthermore, every picture (hence every proposition) has a single, well-defined sense (*Sinn*) (*TS* 323, 325); it follows that propositions with different senses are different propositions. While two different expressions can constitute different propositions with different senses, there cannot be two different expressions for the same sense such that one expresses the sense less completely than the other. Lacking the distinction between a proposition and its expression which the *Notebooks* account of border-line cases presupposes, the *Tractatus* view is that there can be no such thing as a border-line case. 'A proposition must restrict reality to two alternatives: yes and no' (*TS* 4023). No matter what is the case, there are no maybes. This is what the determinacy requirement requires: an utterance has a determinate sense only if a complete description of the state of reality (an enumeration of all of the facts) determines the truth value of the utterance straight away; the utterance itself must be *flatly* true or *flatly* false. Since reality is constituted by the obtaining of some and the non-obtaining of other states of affairs the requirement is also that each possible combination of obtainings or non-obtainings must leave the truth value of the utterance completely open or else must flatly verify or falsify the utterance.

Is an utterance whose sense is not determinate (an utterance which fails to rule out border-line cases) a proposition? In the *Notebooks,* Wittgenstein says: 'Every proposition that has a sense has a *complete* sense, and it is a picture of reality in such a way that what is not said in it simply cannot belong to its sense' (*NS* p. 61). I believe this is the doctrine of the *Tractatus.* An utterance which has a sense has a complete sense. What fails to express a complete sense has no sense whatever. And what lacks a sense is not a proposition at all. If this is correct, the doctrine Wittgenstein criticizes at *Investigations* 99 ('The sense of a proposition—one would like to say—may of course leave this or that open, but the proposition must nevertheless have *a* definite sense. An indefinite sense . . . would really not be a sense *at all*') is the *Tractatus* doctrine of determinacy.

There are two passages in the *Tractatus* which may seem to count against this. The one which presents the least difficulty is a remark from *TS* 5156 made in the course of a discussion of probability: 'A proposition may well be an incomplete picture of a certain situation, but it is always a complete picture of *something.*' If no proposition lacks a perfectly determinate sense, how can a proposition be an incomplete picture? The answer to this is given in a passage I quoted earlier: 'If a proposition tells us something, then it must be a picture of reality just as it stands, and a complete picture at that.—There will, of course, also be something that it does *not* say—but what it does say it says completely' (*NS* p. 61; cp. *PI* 99, 465, etc.). No proposition needs to say everything that could be said (by a different proposition or by more propositions) and that is all it means to say that a proposition can be incomplete. The determinacy thesis requires that no proposition be incomplete in the sense of leaving the possibility of border-line cases; it does not require every assertion to be complete in the sense of saying all there is to say.

A much more difficult passage is the following from *TS* 324:

> When a proposition element signifies a complex, this can
> be seen from an indeterminateness in the propositions in
> which it occurs. In such cases we *know* that the proposition
> leaves something undetermined.
> (In fact, the generality sign *contains* a prototype.)

So much in this is obscure that I cannot pretend to offer a definitive interpretation. But the following speculation is at least plausible.

The parenthetical remark about the generality sign suggests that propositions which mention complexes are or can be re-formulated in existentially or universally quantified form. If this were not Wittgenstein's view, the parenthetical remark would be completely irrelevant. That it was his view is indicated by a 1915 version of this passage (*NS* p. 69):

> It can be seen that a name stands for a complex thing from
> an indefiniteness in the proposition in which it occurs.
> This comes from the generality of such propositions. We
> *know* that not everything is determined by this proposition.
> For the generality notation contains a protopicture.

This says explicitly that a proposition about a complex is general. It agrees with something else Wittgenstein said at *TS* 324. The reason that 'a proposition which mentions a complex will not be nonsensical if the complex does not exist, but simply false' is that such propositions assert the existence of the complexes they mention. In this passage Wittgenstein registers general agreement with Russell's theory of descriptions; that makes it plausible to say he treated assertions which mention complexes as existentials.

If propositions mentioning complexes are or are reducible to existentials, their indeterminacy can be explained by appeal to an analogy between assertions of the form $(\exists x)\ (\o x)$ and unquantified disjunctions. Suppose we had an assertion ana-lysed into disjunctive normal form and the disjuncts were all elementary propositions. Since possible worlds differ from one another with respect to the elementary propositions true in them, we could have possible worlds which differed only in that one of them verified some while another verified other members of the disjunction. If all of the disjuncts express their truth conditions exhaustively, the disjunction itself will have a determinate sense; someone who understood it would be able to say for any possible obtaining or non-obtaining of states of affairs whether it verified, falsified, or left open the truth value of the assertion. But even so, there is something the assertion leaves open. If *all* we knew was that the disjunction 'pvqvrvs' was true, we would not yet know *which* possible world was actual. It could be the one characterized by the truth of 'p' and 'q', but it could be another instead (for example, the one characterized by the truth of 'r' and 's'). Someone could thus assert a proposition in disjunctive normal form without asserting of any *single* possible world that it was actual, even though his assertion would have a perfectly determinate sense. Similarly, we can know that an assertion of the form $(\exists x)(\emptyset x)$ is true without knowing whether it is the case that øa, øb, or øc, etc. This is a kind of indeterminacy which does not violate the condition that the proposition must exclude border-line cases. My speculation is that Wittgenstein thought propositions which mention complexes are existentials and that their indeterminacy is of the harmless kind which characterizes disjunctions.[23]

A final piece of evidence for my account of the determinacy requirement is the fact that Wittgenstein's treatment of propositions as truth functions of elementary propositions (*TS* 5, 6) guarantees the fulfilment of the conditions, (1) that the proposition express its sense in such a way as to determine for every possible reality whether the proposition is true or false in that reality, and (2) that the proposition express its sense in such a way as to determine for every possible situation whether its obtaining verifies, falsifies, or is indifferent to the truth of the proposition. These were the conditions I suggested in explication of the thesis that the sense of every proposition is determinate. Let us see how these conditions are secured by the *Tractatus* account of propositions as truth functions.

Suppose we could construct a truth table with one column for each of the elementary propositions. Following Shwayder, let us call this the Ultimate Truth Table.[24] Each row of the Ultimate Truth Table can be filled in with "T"'s and "F"'s to show a different combination of truth possibilities for the elementary propositions. If the squares in the rows are properly marked, there will be one row for each of the possible combinations of truth possibilities for elementary propositions.

The world is the totality of facts consisting of the obtainings of single states of affairs (*TS* 204) and there is one elementary proposition for every state of affairs which could possibly obtain. Thus 'if all true elementary propositions are listed, the world is completely described' (*TS* 426). It follows that the "T" and "F" marks in any given row of the Ultimate Truth Table would comprise an exhaustive description of one possible world, and that each possible world would be described in one of the rows of the Ultimate Truth Table. Reality is determined by the obtaining states of affairs and by their being the only states of affairs which obtain (*TS* 205–2063). Thus each row also characterizes a possible reality.

As Shwayder observes,[25]

> a picture presents that such and such truth conditions are satisfied. So we fix the *Sinn,* say what the picture presents, by specifying the truth conditions (*TS* 4431). We do that by listing all the possible worlds in which the picture would be true.

The truth conditions which fix the sense of a proposition are expressible by writing "T" in the far right-hand column of the Ultimate Truth Table to mark each possible world (hence reality) in which the proposition would be true, and "F" to mark each possible world (hence reality) in which the proposition would be false (*TS* 43–4442). This applies to elementary as well as to non-elementary propositions. '*Elementarsätze*', Wittgenstein says, assert '*das Bestehen eines Sachverhaltes*', (*TS* 421). Shwayder comments:[26]

> We can say that an *Elementarsatz* presents precisely those truth possibilities in which a particular *Sachverhalt besteht,* it agrees with just those truth possibilities and no others. According to this an *Elementarsatz* is a truth function of itself (*TS* 5).

The truth conditions of an elementary proposition are satisfied by every possible world in which a certain state of affairs obtains, and can, therefore, be specified by marking a 'T' against the rows which show those possible worlds and an 'F' against all of the others.

Notice that propositions are expressions of agreement and disagreement with truth possibilities of the elementary propositions (all of them!) (*TS* 4431, 42, 43, 5, 501). The expression of the truth conditions of a proposition requires that *all* of the elementary propositions be given. We have already observed that the proposition is the expression of its sense (of *all* of its truth conditions) no matter what sentence in which notation is used. Since the sense of a proposition is fixed by nothing short of a complete specification of its truth conditions, we must conclude, incredible though it seems, that according to the *Tractatus,* even the propositions produced by the use of ordinary language say as much as could be said by their expression through the use of the Ultimate Truth Table or any other notation which explicitly sets out all the elementary propositions and marks agreement and disagreement with their various truth possibilities. 'A proposition is the expression of its truth conditions' (*TS* 4431). All of them! The moral of this is that every proposition exhaustively determines which possible realities verify and which falsify it. That satisfies the first of the conditions identified with the determinacy thesis (p. 47).

We can characterize the kind of thing I have been calling a situation as what corresponds to any portion of a row on the Ultimate Truth Table. A situation is what is characterized by the "T"s and "F"s marked in any selection of squares from any one of the rows. Each situation will (1) belong to some possible realities in which a given proposition is true and also to some in which it is not, (2) belong *only* to possible realities in which the proposition is true, or (3) belong *only* to realities in which the proposition is false. Since the proposition expresses all that could be indicated by marking "T"s and "F"s in the right-hand column of the Ultimate Truth Table, the proposition may also be said to determine for every situation whether its obtaining or non-obtaining verifies, falsifies, or is indifferent to the truth of the proposition. Situations of type (1) leave its truth value open while type (2) situations verify and type (3) situations falsify it. This satisfies condition (2), the second condition I identified with the determinacy requirement.

(2.6) Although something like the determinacy thesis could be true of an artificial language whose molecular propositions are truth functions of a finite number of atomic propositions, it seems incredible that Wittgenstein should have ascribed determinacy to ordinary language. Nevertheless, the later Wittgenstein thought that although the doctrine is false, it represented something we might easily and naturally be led to think must be true (*PI* 97–107). He felt it was a *compelling* idea—so, much so that if there is such a thing as genuinely moving passage in recent 'linguistic' philosophy, it is the section of the *Investigations* (97–107) in which Wittgenstein struggles to exorcize the demand for determinacy.

Typically, Wittgenstein does not tell us just what led him down the primrose path to the determinacy thesis. Part of it must have been the way in which the determinacy thesis fits the Tractarian account of probability (*TS* 515–5156). But I think the temptation results more importantly from features of the correspondence theory of truth together with an assumption about facts which is characteristic of the *Tractatus* ontology— the assumption that facts are real, numerically different individuals. Before elaborating and defending this suggestion, I think I must say that I do not find it wholly satisfactory. I believe it fits the *Tractatus* and agrees with the criticism which finally led Wittgenstein to abandon the picture theory (see chapter II). It also captures all that I can find in the *Tractatus* which strikes me as a plausible and compelling reason for holding that sense must be determinate. But I do not think it does full justice to the spirit of *Investigations* 97 and the sections which follow it. There is more to be said and I have not been able to say it.[27]

(2.7) The correspondence theory of truth may amount to the truism (C1): 'p' is true if and only if it is the case that p, and 'p' is false if and only if it is not the case that p. So understood, the theory is every bit as compatible with pragmatist and coherence accounts of truth as with accounts like that of the *Tractatus*. Well-developed versions of all of these theories interpret ' 'p' is true' and 'it is the case that p' in such a way as to preserve the equivalences of (C1).[28] The correspondence theory can also mean (C2) that the truth value of an assertion or a proposition depends upon how things are. When so taken, it contrasts with some accounts of truth, (for example, some versions of pragmatism and coherence theory) and tells us what was sometimes disregarded by theorists as diverse as Locke, James, and Kierkegaard.

On both of these interpretations, the theory comes as close to being unexceptionable as any philosophical theory can. But so interpreted, it fails to provide any substantive account of *what* makes an assertion true, what truth is, or what it is to verify or falsify an assertion; (C1) and (C2) are free from ontological and epistemological commitments. I shall call these two interpretations of the correspondence theory 'truistic correspondence theories'. Strictly speaking they are less theories than results which any adequate theory of truth should ensure; they fare better as criteria to judge theories of truth than as theories. The *Tractatus* commits Wittgenstein to much more than these truisms. In particular, it commits him to the view that facts are discrete entities of which reality is a collection.

The world is the totality of facts, not of things. (*TS* 11.)
The world divides into facts. (*TS* 12.)

And reality is the totality of positive and negatives fact—the obtainings and non-obtainings of states of affairs (*TS* 206). I assume that Wittgenstein intended this sort of talk to be taken literally. It cannot be so taken unless we assume that facts are discrete individuals which differ from one another. We cannot speak of a *totality* or collection of things unless the things are distinct enough to be counted. If the world *divides* into facts, the facts must be numerically different from one another. Wittgenstein's account of truth holds that the proposition presents *a* possible fact: we determine the truth value of a proposition by determining whether the totality of facts (reality) includes *the* fact in question. This too would seem to presuppose that facts are real individuals. Looking for one particular fact would be impossible unless the fact (if there is one) is distinct from other facts. Finally, what Wittgenstein says at *TS* 427 suggests the possibility of counting states of affairs and hence that we can

count possible or actual facts. For n states of affairs there are
$$Kn = \sum_{v=0}^{n} \binom{n}{v}$$ possibilities of obtaining and non-obtaining
(*TS* 427). Obtainings and non-obtainings of states of affairs are
facts (*TS* 206). Only individuals which obey the laws of
identity can be tabulated in this way.

Consider the proposition which asserts that the cat is on the
mat. We should want to call it true if we found the cat standing on the middle of the mat, and also if the cat were sitting
on the upper left-hand corner, lying near the right edge, or
occupying any number of other positions. 'The cat is on the mat'
should be a truth-functional proposition whose truth conditions
can be expressed by ticking off all the worlds in which the
proposition would be true on the Ultimate Truth Table. If
more than one possible world (row on the table) makes the
proposition true, the fact that the cat is on the mat may be
characterized by each of these rows taken together as its composite picture. For example, if it is a disjunctive fact, it would
be characterized by one situation from one of the worlds in
which the proposition is true, another from another, etc.[29]
Thus the obtaining of a certain situation (what is pictured by
the 'T's and 'F's in a selection of squares from one row of the
Ultimate Truth Table) may verify 'the cat is on the mat' even
though the fact that the cat is on the mat could require the
consideration of features of other possible worlds for its complete characterization.

Let us call the various relations which could obtain between
the cat and the mat 'C-M situations'. The obtaining of some
C-M situations will flatly verify the proposition. Call these
'positive C-M situations'. Others will flatly falsify it. Call these
'negative C-M situations'. Others (common to worlds in which
the proposition is true and worlds in which it is false) will leave
its truth value open. Call these 'neutral C-M situations'. For
example, the situation whose obtaining makes it a fact that the
cat is standing in the middle of the mat would be a positive
C-M situation. The situation whose obtaining would make it a
fact that the cat is standing outside the room in which the mat
lies would be a negative C-M situation. The situation whose
obtaining would make it a fact that the cat is older than the
mat, or the same colour as the mat, would be neutral.

Each proposition presents *one* putative fact (*TS* 211, 4032, 404). If facts are individuals which obey the laws of identity and contradiction, we shall have to treat the obtaining of any one positive C-M situation as an 'instance' of the *same fact* as the obtaining of any other positive C-M situation. But there could be no justification for calling the obtaining of any C-M situation the same fact as the obtaining of any other unless *all* of them were explicitly specified as included in the possible worlds in which the proposition is true. To give such a specification would be to satisfy the determinacy requirement and I submit that this is at least *a* major reason for Wittgenstein's stipulation that sense must be determinate.[30]

Now, suppose that in trying to determine the truth value of 'the cat is on the mat', we discover the cat straddling two mats. The plain man would probably say the assertion is not quite true (in a way, the cat is not on the mat) but also that it is not quite false (in a way, the cat *is* on the mat). But all the same, the straddling-two-mats situation is not simply irrelevant as is the fact that the cat is older than the mat. If we *had* to say that the assertion is either true or false, we could not ignore the two-mat situation as we could if it were irrelevant.

The early Wittgenstein could not have said what the plain man would say. According to the *Tractatus* ontology, the obtaining of the two-mat situation constitutes a fact, and facts are real individuals which obey the laws of identity. Had Wittgenstein said that the two-mat situation can just as well verify, falsify, or leave open the truth value of the assertion, he would have to have treated the obtaining of the two-mat situation as comprising a fact which neither is nor is not the fact that the cat is on the mat. This would be overwhelmingly repugnant. A reality whose contents were like this would be like a room containing a chair which neither is nor is not numerically identical to the chair I am now sitting on. If reality is a collection of facts, then facts are discrete, and discrete individuals cannot be indeterminate in this way. The sense of a proposition is (or corresponds to) a possible fact. Thus if propositions do not have determinate senses, indeterminate facts are possible. But Wittgenstein believed that facts are real individuals, and on this assumption, indeterminate facts are impermissible because they violate the laws of identity. Thus the determinacy

E

thesis is an inevitable consequence of the *Tractatus* picture theory together with the ontology which accompanies it.

(2.8) While Wittgenstein's early writings contain no arguments explicitly set out in support of the determinacy thesis, the 1914–16 notebooks contain isolated passages which are symptomatic of the line I have just been sketching.

In 1914 Wittgenstein wrote, 'The truth or falsity of every proposition makes some difference to the structure of the world' (*NS* p. 20). This is so because 'The proposition is true when what it pictures exists' (*NS* p. 26). The structure of a thing is the way in which its elements are put together (*TS* 2032) and the way in which a thing is put together depends in part upon what it is put together out of. When a proposition is true, the world contains one more fact, and this makes a difference to its structure. Further, although a proposition can be false, its being a proposition guarantees that what it presents could be a fact (*NS* p. 27; *TS* 2203). It follows that what kind of structure the world can have depends upon which declarative utterances are meaningful.

In 1915, Wittgenstein said, 'My *whole* task consists in explaining the nature of the proposition. That is to say, in giving the nature of all facts whose picture the proposition is' (*NS* p. 39). Since the possibilities for propositions determine the possibilities for facts, he might just as well have said that to explain the nature of facts would be to explain what propositions are. And later on, he did say just this (*TS* 54711; cp. *PI* 90, etc.).

Now, Wittgenstein thought the world must have a determinate structure: 'The world must be just what it is, it must be definite. Or in other words, what vacillates is our determinations, not the world. . . . The world has a fixed structure' (*NS* p. 62). The structure of the world can be no more determinate than the facts which are its constituents, and a fact can be no more determinate than the sense of the proposition which presents it. Any indeterminacy in the proposition's expression of its sense makes possible an indeterminacy in reality. Thus it would have been impossible for Wittgenstein to give up the determinacy thesis without giving up either the theory that reality is a collection of facts or the notion that reality has a fixed structure.

54

3 NAMES AND SIMPLE OBJECTS

(3.1) None of the ontological doctrines of the *Tractatus* seem more obviously stipulated to meet the needs of Tractarian linguistic theory than the theory of simple objects. Hence the best introduction to the theory is a consideration of Wittgenstein's account of names, the parts of speech he claimed to be connected with objects.

> In a proposition a thought can be expressed in such a way that elements of the proposition-sign correspond to objects of the thought. (*TS* 32.)
> I call such elements 'simple signs', and such a proposition 'fully analysed'. (*TS* 3201.)
> The simple signs employed in propositions are called names. (*TS* 3202.)

If names are simple, they cannot be divided into parts. But what kind of division is Wittgenstein excluding and what kind of simplicity did he have in mind? He cannot have meant physical simplicity because he says the features of a word which 'result from the particular way in which a proposition sign is produced' are accidental (*TS* 334). If so, the fact that a proposition is composed of physically simple signs (assuming that we have a standard for physical simplicity) would not determine whether or not it contains names. Nor can he mean merely that a name has no parts which are themselves significant signs. This criterion would distinguish names from propositions or from sentences and phrases, but Wittgenstein wanted also to distinguish names from defined words. A defined sign need not contain separate words and thus cannot be distinguished from a name just by saying that a name is not composed of words. Nor does Wittgenstein mean by 'simple sign' exactly what Russell once meant by 'simple symbol', a word 'directly designating an individual which is its meaning and having this meaning in its own right, independently of the meanings of all other words'.[31] A name has meaning 'only in the context of a proposition' (*TS* 33) and so it would have no meaning unless there were other meaningful words to combine with it in order to construct propositions; the name does not therefore have 'a meaning in its own right independently of the meanings of all other words'.

To see what kind of simplicity does characterize a name, we must consider Wittgenstein's later (and more careful) treatment of a name as a symbol (*TS* 424). A symbol or expression (Wittgenstein used '*Ausdruck*' and '*Symbol*' interchangeably) is 'any part of a proposition which characterizes its sense. (A proposition itself is an expression.) Everything essential to their senses that propositions can have in common with one another is an expression' (*TS* 331). Propositions can share signs in common but, *qua* mark or sound, a sign is not a symbol because its occurrence is not essential to their senses (*TS* 3322):

> Our use of the same sign to signify two different things
> can never indicate a common characteristic of the two, if
> we use it with two different *modes of signification*. For the
> sign, of course, is arbitrary. So we could choose two different
> signs instead, and then what would be left in common on
> the signifying side?

A sign is 'what can be sensibly perceived of a symbol' (*TS* 332). It is a mark or sound which can be used in the expression of a sense. A proposition is a proposition-sign (sentence) 'in its projective relation to the world' (*TS* 312). Judging from this, a symbol should be either *the use* of a sign, or a sign *in use* as a projection or projection element to say something. Out of the context of a proposition, a sign is not a symbol; it is simply a mark or sound which has a symbolic use (cp. *TS* 33).[32]

In calling names simple signs (*TS* 3201) Wittgenstein must have meant that a name is a 'simple use' of a sign.

> A name means (*bedeutet*) an object. The object is its
> meaning (*Bedeutung*). (*TS* 3203.)
> A name cannot be dissected any further by means of a
> definition: it is a primitive sign. (*TS* 326.)
> Every sign that has a definition signifies *via* the signs that
> serve to define it; and the definitions point the way. (*TS* 3261.)

Signs used to name are assigned directly to objects. This sets them off from defined signs which 'signify *via*' the signs which define them (*TS* 3261). A defined sign is a contraction of or abbreviation for its definition (*TS* 324) while a name is a primitive. What is simple then is not the sign used as a name, but its mode of reference. It is simple in the sense that it cannot be analysed.

Wittgenstein's terminology is misleading. Although he calls them 'simple signs', a name is not just a sign. In essence, it is what all symbols signifying the same object have in common (*TS* 33411). What all symbols signifying the same object have in common is the contribution they make to the senses of the propositions in which they occur (*TS* 331). Presumably their contribution, and hence the name proper, is not a sign but reference to an object achieved by the employment of a sign in a proposition.[33] At the same time, it is misleading to call Tractarian names 'names'. What we ordinarily call names, for example, 'Ludwig Wittgenstein', 'Wellington Square', etc., do not refer to simple objects and are not therefore Tractarian names. Accordingly, I will use the term 'ordinary name' in connection with the signs we use as proper names, and will call Tractarian names 'simple symbols'.

(3.2) Before going on, we should attend to two questions raised by the passages quoted so far in connection with simple symbols. First, Wittgenstein says that an object is the *Bedeutung* of a name. Did he really mean that the object is the meaning of a simple symbol? Second, Wittgenstein suggests that 'simple signs' occur *only* in the fully analysed versions of propositions. How are simple symbols connected with unanalysed propositions?

(1) The text of *TS* 3203 ('*Der Name bedeutet den Gegenstand: Der Gegenstand ist seine Bedeutung*') *could* be taken to mean nothing more than that an object is the *referent* of a name. If so, a name without an object would be meaningless, but it does not follow from this that the object *is* the meaning of the name. However, meaning in the *Tractatus* is always either *Sinn* or *Bedeutung*, and Wittgenstein held that only propositions have *Sinn*. Presumably that means that a name can have only *Bedeutung*, and Wittgenstein does explicitly identify the *Bedeutung* of a name with the object to which it refers. Wittgenstein's later objections to the doctrine that the meaning of a name is its bearer are, therefore, very likely directed against the *Tractatus* (*PI* 38–43).

(2) If Wittgenstein thought that all of the propositions of

'everyday language are in perfect logical order just as they stand' (*TS* 55563), he must have thought that ordinary language assertions share the general form of the proposition with all other propositions (*TS* 45, 6). If so, ordinary language assertions would have to be truth functions of elementary propositions. Moreover, Wittgenstein believed that in essence, a truth function of the elementary propositions is the result of their successive joint denial (*TS* 6001, 54711, 53, etc.). In order to deny jointly, we must indicate the set of propositions upon which the operation of joint denial is being performed. Thus if ordinary language assertions are genuine propositions, they must involve simple symbols which figure in them as the constituents of the elementary propositions. The notion that we somehow employ Tractarian names in everyday speech must seem incredible to any native speaker who, like Wittgenstein himself, is unable to produce a simple example of a simple symbol (*NS* p. 68). Furthermore, 'simple signs' are introduced in the *Tractatus* as the constituents of fully analysed propositions, and the fully analysed version of an assertion would require a special notation which we do not employ in everyday speech. It would include signs used to stand directly for simple objects, and no such words are to be found in any natural language. Thus it looks as though Wittgenstein is saying that Tractarian names figure in all propositions including the assertions of ordinary language (because all propositions are produced by the joint denial of elementary propositions) even though signs used to signify simple objects do not figure in unanalysed assertions— including those of ordinary language. We must ask how an unanalysed assertion, 'p₀' is related to its analysed version, 'pₐ', bearing in mind that according to the *Tractatus* every proposition can be fully analysed (*TS* 325, 55563).

Each proposition has a single well-defined sense; each proposition determinately expresses a putative fact (*TS* 323, 325). If 'pₐ' is the analysis of 'p₀', they must have precisely the same sense (*TS* 3343). But in order to have the same sense, they must be expressions of agreement and disagreement with the same truth possibilities of the elementary propositions. Furthermore, a proposition is not the sign (the sentence) used by a speaker to express agreement and disagreement with truth possibilities of elementary propositions. It *is* the *expression* or the *expressing* (*TS* 4431). Thus an ordinary language assertion, 'p₀', and its analysis, 'pₐ', must be instances of one and the same thing (the expression of agreement and disagreement with the same truth possibilities of elementary propositions) accomplished by the employment of different signs. Since the proposition is a symbol and the symbol is what is essential to the expression of a sense, 'p₀' and 'pₐ' must be essentially the same proposition differing only with regard to notational features which are accidental to the expression of their sense (*TS* 334).

This makes it possible to say that simple symbols figure in ordinary language assertions even though the sentences with which we make these assertions do not contain words which we have assigned to simple objects. If 'p₀' has the same sense as 'pₐ' it must register agreement and disagreement with the same truth possibilities of elementary propositions, and hence it must indicate the elementary propositions in question. Part of Wittgenstein's doctrine was that 'p₀' does so by means of a notation employing signs which function as contractions for what would be perspicuously set out by the signs used in 'pₐ'.[34] The upshot of this is that regardless of the way in which it is accomplished in the notation in which 'p₀' is given, the assertion must somehow make reference to the same simple objects as does 'pₐ', and where simples are referred to, we have Tractarian names. The name is a sign only accidentally. In essence, it is or is identified in terms of the use of a sign—a reference to an object.[35] Thus the fact that none of the signs which occur in 'p₀' are explicitly assigned by the conventions of ordinary language to simple objects doesn't show that simple symbols do not figure in 'p₀'.

There is of course another part of the doctrine. In addition to holding that simple symbols must figure in everyday language, Wittgenstein held that signs used to signify complexes are defined and signify *via* their definitions. It follows from this that ordinary names must signify *via* signs which stand for simples, for that is what their definitions would have to contain. This seems indefensible, for no such signs occur in ordinary language. In discussing elliptical sentences in the *Investigations*, Wittgenstein argued that a necessary condition for calling one sentence, S, an elliptical, abbreviated, or shortened form of another sentence, S', is that S' occur in the same language as does S (*PI* 19, 20). This condition is clearly violated by the claim that a bit of ordinary language signifies *via* and abbreviates signs in its Tractarian analysis. I think this objection is conclusive against the thesis that a sign in a natural language is used as an abbreviation for a sign which includes words which stand for simples. But it has no bearing against the doctrine that ordinary language contains the *symbols* exhibited by a Tractarian analysis. It is easy to say that in employing that Tractarian distinction between signs and symbols for this purpose, Wittgenstein fell victim to a philosophical ill he later diagnosed in the *Investigations*. He was predicating of ordinary language assertions what lay in his method of representing them (*PI* 104) and the disparity between what he thought must be found in ordinary language and what he actually found there made him 'dissatisfied with what are ordinarily called "propositions," "words", "signs" ' (*PI* 105). The symbol was to some extent postulated as the 'essential' structure which must underlie the signs and speech acts of ordinary language in order to make up for their apparent logical deficiencies. In this way, the Tractarian account of the symbol is profoundly opposed to the tendencies of Wittgenstein's later work whose aim was to speak of 'propositions and words in exactly the same sense in which we speak of them in ordinary life' (*PI* 108) and to give an account which does not interefere in any way 'with the actual use of language' (*PI* 124). But the theory of symbols also exhibits a tendency which characterized Wittgenstein's later thought. Wittgenstein seized on the symbol/sign distinction because without it, he would have had to maintain, as did many of his followers, that ordinary language is logically defective and therefore radically unsatisfactory in comparison with a logically perfect ideal or artificial language (cp. Russell, *TS* p. x ff.). The far-fetched claim that an ordinary language assertion is essentially the same symbol as its full analysis results from Wittgenstein's insistence that ordinary language is perfectly satisfactory just as it is, without reform. Even the pre-*Tractatus* notebooks insist that 'this is surely clear: The propositions which are the only ones that humanity uses will have a sense just as they are and do not wait upon a future analysis in order to acquire a sense' (*NS* p. 62).

Convinced that ordinary language is perfectly in order and also that it must make reference to simple objects, have a certain multiplicity, produce logically perfect pictures of reality, etc., Wittgenstein had to assume that what is essential is disguised by the outward clothing of the language. The *Tractatus* account of symbols and the theory of analysis is a manifestation of Wittgenstein's belief that the philosophy of language must leave language as it is—without criticizing or reforming it (*PI* 124).

(3.3) What were simple objects supposed to be like? I shall not attempt to give a complete or even a particularly positive answer to this. It is arguable that no coherent theory of simples can be found in the *Tractatus,* and I am inclined to think it a mistake to try to extract one. The unsatisfactoriness of the *Tractatus* on this subject is, I think, due to Wittgenstein's having postulated simples as demanded by the picture theory without trying to arrive at an independent account of them. The features of objects with which we shall be primarily concerned are their unalterability and indestructibility, and their simplicity. The ascription of these virtues to simple objects is the ontological counterpart of the doctrine that names are primitive and undefined and the thesis that genuine names must have referents or bearers. To begin with let us see how these doctrines are connected.

If the meaning of a Tractarian name *is* an object, the possibility that an object could undergo change is the possibility that its name's meaning could alter because of what goes on in the world. The possibility that an object could be destroyed is the possibility that a name could lose its meaning altogether. Because of this, Wittgenstein postulated that the bearers of Tractarian names must be unchangeable and indestructible (*TS* 2027–20271). Otherwise, the *Tractatus* account would have left the meanings of names and thus of propositions in jeopardy.

The thesis that objects are simple goes together with the requirement that genuine names must be undefinable primitives. The connection between indestructibility and immunity to change, simplicity, and the primitiveness of Tractarian names depends upon an assumption of what it is to describe a thing which H. H. Price once characterized as follows:[36]

When we describe something, it is natural to say that we

are analysing it or 'breaking it up'. And the next step is to assimilate this intellectual analysis to chemical analysis or anatomical description.

Whether or not this is a *natural* picture of description, there is at any rate *a* kind of describing which fits it. In order to say what a thing is we sometimes do enumerate its parts and say how they are put together. The ancient view (discussed by Plato in the *Theaetetus*) that knowledge is expressed by naming the elements and describing the composition of the thing known involves the assimilation of *all* description and definition to his model.[37] A related view was prevalent at Cambridge during Wittgenstein's early years there, and the assimilation of description and definition to analysis was incorporated into the *Tractatus* by way of the doctrine that all propositions assert obtainings and non-obtainings of relations among objects (*TS* 2, 44–442).[38] If we must enumerate the parts of a thing in order to describe it or to say what it is, it would make no sense to ask for the description of a simple object. If definition is a Pricean kind of description (as Wittgenstein appears to have believed), the ascription of simplicity to objects secures that names must be primitives.

Saying that an object has changed or perished requires saying *what* (*which* object) has changed or perished. This would require the use of a name or description of the object. But if objects are simple, they have no parts, and cannot be described —given the Cambridge assumption that description is analysis. Thus to say an object has changed or perished, we should have to name it. But the meaning of a name is its bearer, and so the use of a sign to name an object presupposes that its bearer has not perished. It also presupposes that its bearer has not changed. Otherwise, the name would have a new meaning. Thus if objects are simple, an utterance purporting to assert that an object has perished or changed has no chance of being true. At the same time, we cannot *say* of an object that it has *not* changed or perished. To say this we would have to refer to the object, and our very ability to do so would *show* that the object was unchanged and undestroyed before we had a chance to assert it (cp. *TS* 41272). It is in this sense that 'objects are what is unalterable and subsistent' (*TS* 20272): it makes no sense to say of an object either that it has or has not changed or perished. The man who said, 'I want to restrict the term "name" to what cannot occur in the combination "X exists" ' (*PI* 58) was the early Wittgenstein; the quotation explains the sense in which Tractarian objects, because of their simplicity, are exempt from destruction.

(3.4)   What then would be an example of a *Tractatus* object? The *Tractatus* provides two tests to screen candidates. First, there is the doctrine of immutability and indestructibility we have just been considering. If it makes sense to ask whether a thing exists or whether it has changed, it is not a simple object. This rules out the bearers of all or most ordinary proper names including all one-, two-, and three-dimensional spatial objects. Second, there is the doctrine that elementary propositions are logically independent. 'From the obtaining or non-obtaining of one state of affairs it is impossible to infer the obtaining or non-obtaining of another' (*TS* 2062). As Anscombe has argued, this rules out the logical-positivist interpretation of elementary propositions as 'observation statements' which report sense data.[39] Wittgenstein acknowledges that 'the simultaneous presence of two colours at the same place in the visual field is ... logically impossible' (*TS* 63751). He must hold that 'this is a red patch' is not an elementary proposition because its truth allows us to conclude that the patch is not green. Thus the coloured patch is not simple.

These tests rule out all of the examples which Wittgenstein offers in *TS* 20131 to illustrate the doctrine that 'each object is, as it were, in a space of possible states of affairs'. Here he observes that (*TS* 20131):

> A spatial object must be situated in infinite space....
> A speck in the visual field, though it need not be red, must have colour; it is, so to speak, surrounded by colour-space.
> Tones must have *some* pitch, objects of the sense of touch *some* degree of hardness, and so on.

He wants to make the point that what each object is determines the states of affairs in which it can occur (just as the fact that X is a speck determines that there can be true statements of the form 'X is such and such a colour'), and that although there is no single state of affairs in which an object must occur, it cannot occur in the world except as a constituent of *some* state of affairs. The examples in *TS* 20131 are used only as illustrations of the doctrine, and cannot be examples of *bona fide* simples. Wittgenstein would surely say that a speck cannot have two different colours all over at the same time, that a tone cannot be a B flat at the same time that it is a C, and that a spatial object which occupies a certain place cannot simultaneously be somewhere else (*TS* 63751). Thus they could not be named in elementary propositions. Wittgenstein's remark that a speck must have *some* colour even though it need not be red suggests that different colours are possible for the same speck. It would be surprising for him to have allowed this unless he also thought that specks, tones, etc., can change.

Instead of considering and ruling out more candidates, let us ask why in general it should be so difficult to produce satisfactory examples of simple objects. The difficulty lies in the notion of simplicity itself. Wittgenstein's attempts to provide examples of objects in the pre-*Tractatus* notebooks indicate that during his early period he failed to appreciate the force of the point that it makes no sense to say of a thing that it is simple or complex without reference to some standard by which 'simplicity' may be defined (*PI* 47). The objects of the *Tractatus* were supposed to be *absolutely* simple, or simple relative to language *in general*—not just simple relative to a particular language or department of language used to describe things. If the only satisfactory response to the question whether something is simple or complex is 'that all depends upon what you understand by "composite"' (*PI* 47), the search for absolutely simple objects is doomed to failure.

To see how this is so, consider the following from the *Notebooks 1914–1916* which contain, so far as I have been able to tell, Wittgenstein's last attempts to give examples of simple objects during his early period (*NS* p. 50):

Even though we have no acquaintance with simple objects,
We *do* know complex things by acquaintance; we know by
acquaintance that they are complex.—We single out a part
of our visual field for example, and we see that it is
always complex, that any part of it is still complex, but
is already simpler—and so on.

The command 'divide this coloured area into parts' carries the strong suggestion that 'division' should mean division into smaller spatial areas. Suppose we were restricted to a language in which spatial division was carried out by plotting the shape and size of a coloured area on to a matrix of small squares. The language provides for the possibility of calling single squares or combinations of them spatial parts of a two-dimensional area but makes no provision for dividing up a square into smaller squares (cp. *PI* 64). The point of the later criticism of the doctrine of simplicity is that even here we would not have arrived at simple objects for in order to see the 'indivisible' parts as complex, all we would need is a new method for division. This could mean the employment of a new matrix with smaller squares. But it could also mean an entirely new kind of 'division'—for example, the analysis of the coloured areas into the primary colours, into shape and colour, etc. Contrary to the doctrine implied by the *Tractatus* theory of absolutely simple objects, our language provides for alternative schemes for analysis, and for envisaging an unlimited number of schemes appropriate to different practical or theoretical purposes. It is obvious that the elements at which we arrive by one method of division or analysis need not be the same as those to which another method takes us.

'Method of division' does not here mean a method for physically separating a thing into physical parts. It refers to schemes for description in terms of what are treated as elements by a given conceptual scheme. The early doctrine that all description of what a thing is is analysis commits Wittgenstein to the view that *any* ascription or predication of features or properties constitutes an analysis of the thing described. It follows that a thing is simple only if nothing can be predicated of it (except that it does or does not stand in relation to other things). Since the language we use in connection with a thing is what determines what can and cannot be predicated of it we can say that simplicity and complexity are determined by the resources of a language. Thus it is to be expected that anything offered as an example of a simple could be shown to be complex simply by talking about it in a new way. If we were unable to expand our language to ascribe properties or features to the putative simple object, this would show us something about our language and its users, not something necessarily true of the object independent of language.

Surprisingly, the early Wittgenstein appears to have realized that simplicity and complexity are linguistically determined (*NS* pp. 59–60):

> Do not 'complex objects' in the end satisfy just the demands which I apparently make on the simple ones? If I give this book a name 'N' and now talk about N, is not the relation of N to that 'complex object', to those forms and contents, *essentially* the same as I imagined only between name and simple object?

Thus his contention that some things are *absolutely* simple seems here to amount to the contention that language in general is a fixed system whose resources for description are necessarily limited to a description in terms of a fixed set of names. In view of this, I think the most revealing thing Wittgenstein had to say about simples is this from a 1931 notebook (*B* section III, 36, par. 1):

> What I formerly called objects, simples, is just what I can refer to without fear that perhaps they don't exist. That is: that to which existence and non-existence do not apply and that means that which we can speak about no matter what is the case.

What the early Wittgenstein really had in mind when he spoke about objects was *anything* whose existence is presupposed by a use of language. In the *Investigations* Wittgenstein provided examples of things (for example, the standard metre stick once kept in Paris, colour samples used as paradigms, and the coloured squares in the imaginary language described at *PI* 48) whose existence is presupposed by one or a family of linguistic activities and whose descriptions are given and whose existence is questioned only by different employments of language (*PI* 48, 50, 51). These 'objects' are the direct descendants of the simples postulated in the *Tractatus*. They function as 'objects' relative to specific linguistic practices, while the objects of the *Tractatus* were supposed to be simple relative to language in general—and to any possible language, at that.

(3.5) Tractarian objects were supposed to be things which

could be referred to only by name and not by description. Their existence and immunity from change were held by Wittgenstein to be necessary conditions for the possibility of fact-stating discourse. The *Tractatus* contains two arguments intended to show that there must be such things. The first occurs at *TS* 2021–20212: 'Objects comprise the substance of the world. That is why they cannot be composite. If the world had no substance, then whether a proposition had sense would depend upon whether another proposition was true. In that case we could not sketch out any picture of the world (true or false)'. The second consists of a single cryptic line : 'The requirement that simple signs be possible is the requirement that sense be determinate' (*TS* 323). Now it is time to consider these arguments. My purpose in doing so is to show that Wittgenstein's advocacy of the theory of simples can be explained as a result of his advocacy of the picture theory of language. The two arguments for simples in the *Tractatus* rest upon assumptions (that the meaning of a name is its bearer and that sense must be determinate) which arise from the picture theory. The import of the arguments for simple objects is that without objects and simple symbols, propositions could not be representational pictures of reality.

(1) What is wrong with the supposition that the sense of one assertion can depend upon the truth of another? It is tempting to answer by appeal to the unhappy epistemological consequences the supposition could have. In order to determine whether one utterance had a sense we should have to verify another utterance whose sense would be in doubt unless we had already verified another one, etc. This generates a regress from which it could be argued that no one can ever be sure whether any declarative utterance says anything. But this is not Wittgenstein's point.[40] The argument of *TS* 2021–20211 does not contend that without simples we could never *know* whether a declarative utterance had a sense. Wittgenstein argued that if there were no simples and the sense of one utterance depended upon the truth of another, 'we could not sketch out any picture of the world' (*TS* 20212). There could be pictures (propositions) even if we could not know they had senses. The existence of simples could help safeguard the senses of elementary propositions, but that would not be the same thing as guaranteeing

that we can recognize a proposition as a meaningful utterance. Furthermore, the argument makes no explicit appeal to a regress.

Wittgenstein's rejection of the supposition that the sense of a proposition can depend upon the truth of another proposition is in fact a fundamental article of faith of the picture theory. If the sense of a proposition 'p' depended upon the truth of another proposition 'q', then 'p' would be comparable only to (would be a representational picture only of) those realities in which 'q' is true and not to any reality in which 'q' is false. Wittgenstein's thesis was that the proposition is a representational picture of reality no matter what is the case and hence that it represents every possible reality.[41] The facts determine only the truth value of propositions—not whether they *have* senses. Hence if (*per impossibile*) the sense of 'p' depends on the truth of 'q', 'p' is not a proposition.

How does this argue for simple objects? If objects could perish, names could lose their meanings, and elementary propositions their senses. But all propositions are expressions of agreement and disagreement with truth possibilities of a fixed set of elementary propositions and therefore, if objects could perish, even non-elementary propositions could lose their senses. If the bearers of genuine names were complex, they could perish. Or, more accurately, if genuine names were not primitives we could refer to an object by means of its description to assert that the bearer of a name exists or fails to exist. Thus unless the bearers of Tractarian names are simple, there are possible realities in which they do not exist. Then, a proposition could not represent every possible reality but only those in which propositions asserting the existence of the referents of names are true.

If Wittgenstein's insistence that the sense of a proposition must not be affected by the truth or falsity of propositions which assert the existence of perishable things sounds reminiscent of Russell's theory of descriptions and his extension of it to cover propositions involving ordinary proper names, that is as it should be. 'Every statement about complexes can be resolved into a statement about their constituents and into the propositions which describe the complexes completely' (*TS* 20201). As we have seen, a statement about something, X, is about a complex unless 'X does not exist' makes no sense. Where 'X' is an ordinary proper name 'X does not exist' does make sense. Thus, like Russell, Wittgenstein must think that ordinary proper names are not genuine or logically proper names. Statements about complexes must be analysable into propositions which make assertions about the constituents of the complex and a complex can be given 'only by its description which will be right or wrong'. Therefore the non-existence of the complex will render assertions about the complex false but not nonsensical (*TS* 324). This supports the suggestion that Wittgenstein would have espoused something like the Russellian programme for the analysis of declaratives whose grammatical subjects are ordinary proper names or definite descriptions. Further support for this may be gleaned from the parenthetical remark at *TS* 324 which suggests that assertions about complexes are disguised existentials, and from a letter to Russell in which Wittgenstein said he thought the 'theory of descriptions is quite *undoubtedly correct*' (*NS* p. 127).

But despite these points of agreement between Wittgenstein and Russell, there are important differences. For one thing, it is not easy to see how Wittgenstein could have analysed a statement like 'The present King of France is bald' into the form $(\exists x)((Kx \& (y)Ky$ only if $x = y) \& Bx)$ (there is at least and at most one individual who is at present King of France and that individual is bald) without running foul of his own treatment of equations (*TS* 553–5534).[42] Indeed, Wittgenstein's remarks on the analysis of assertions about complexes in the *Tractatus* and the pre-*Tractatus* notebooks are so sketchy that it is doubtful whether he ever tried to work out a Tractarian version of the theory of descriptions in any detail.

A much more important difference between the Russellian and Wittgensteinian accounts of genuine versus apparent proper names is that there is no good reason to think the bearers of Russellian names would have to be either simple or indestructible. When Russell developed the theory that ordinary proper names are not genuine names, he argued that every utterance we can understand must make reference to something with which we are directly acquainted. The chief reason for supposing this, he says, 'is that it is scarcely possible to believe that we can make a judgment or entertain a supposition without knowing what it is that we are judging or supposing about'.[43] Thus assuming that only Bismarck was directly acquainted with Bismarck, it becomes difficult to see how another man could use the name 'Bismarck' and understand it unless he used it as a disguised or abbreviated description of Bismarck mentioning things with which the speaker himself is acquainted.[44] Russell concludes that the bearers of genuine names must be objects of direct acquaintance and suggests sense data as likely candidates. All that this line of argument can hope to show is that bearers of genuine names must be objects of direct acquaintance. It does not support the requirement of simplicity and indestructibility for the bearers of genuine names, for we could be directly acquainted with destructible complexes. Because of this the bearers of Russellian genuine names must not be confused with Tractarian objects and Russell's argument to show that the bearers of genuine names are objects of direct acquaintance must not be confused with Wittgenstein's argument that the bearers of genuine names must be imperishable and, therefore, simple.[45]

(2) The second argument we must consider appears to be that unless signs can be used as primitives to stand for simple objects (that is, unless there can be simple symbols) sense cannot be determinate (*TS* 323). If there must be simple symbols there must be simple objects to serve as their *Bedeutungen*. The difficulty with this argument lies in trying to see why sense could not be determinate unless there are simple symbols.

I argued that when he claimed sense must be determinate, Wittgenstein was saying in effect that there must be no borderline cases. No matter what is the case, a proposition must restrict reality to two alternatives, yes or no (*TS* 4023); the proposition must be *flatly* true or *flatly* false in any possible reality. Thus if sense is determinate, every possible reality must be explicitly included in or excluded from the truth conditions of a proposition. Since a reality is constituted by the situations which do and do not obtain (where by 'situation' I mean what is indicated by any selection of marked squares from any single row of the Ultimate Truth Table), the truth conditions of the proposition must determine for every situation that its obtaining verifies, falsifies, or is indifferent to the truth value of the proposition.

The account of the proposition as the expression of agreement or disagreement with truth possibilities of the elementary propositions and of a possible reality as the obtaining and non-obtaining of states of affairs is what excludes the possibility of border-line cases from the Tractarian universe. One way of glossing the argument of *TS* 323 is to point out that elementary propositions are composed of simple symbols and, therefore, that Wittgenstein's account of the alleged impossibility of border-line cases presupposes the possibility of using signs to refer to simple objects. This is correct, but when so interpreted the argument that determinacy requires simple symbols smacks of triviality. It shows that *one* way of ruling out indeterminacy involves the postulation of simples, and that is sufficient for my purpose of showing that the theory of simples was devised to meet a requirement of the picture theory. But I want to ask whether the postulation of simples was the *only* way open to Wittgenstein to secure the determinacy of sense.

In the *Tractatus* and the *Notebooks,* passages which suggest that symbols signifying complexes are disguised descriptions accompany the claim that determinacy requires simple symbols and discussions of determinacy of sense (see, for example, *NS* pp. 67–9; cp. *TS* 324). The import of *TS* 324 is that a single sign functioning to signify a complex is a contraction for a definite description whose analysis leads to a truth-functional picture asserting the existence of the complex by saying that certain states of affairs do, while others do not, obtain. To say this we need elementary propositions and hence names for simples. Similarly, the *Notebooks* argue that an assertion about a complex must be analysable and that its analysis must lead to simple objects (*NS* pp. 46, 50, 60). In connection with this Wittgenstein says that if a proposition about a complex had a 'final' (I take this to mean a determinate) sense, there must be names for simples (*NS* p. 64). The sense of 'the book is on the table' is not determinate unless 'the book' can be analysed as a description which determines for every possible complex whether or not it is the book in question. I speculate that Wittgenstein thought determinacy of sense would be impossible without simples because a description could not uniquely identify a complex unless it had simple constituents by which the description could identify it, and unless there were primitive symbols by which to mention the simple constituents.

The reader may object that it is outrageous to say that anyone who succeeds in asserting that a certain book is on a table must have given descriptions which uniquely identify the book and the table, let alone descriptions which are mysteriously concealed from view in the utterance. We do not give descriptions to answer the question 'which book?' unless this question arises, and in most contexts it simply does not (cp. *PI* 71, 84–87). This is true, but beside the point, for it simply denies the determinacy thesis. We are not asking whether the determinacy thesis is true. The question is whether it entails the thesis that there are simples by requiring that complexes be uniquely identified by the assertions which mention them.

To answer this let us first ask whether a description which uniquely identified a complex would have to contain names. When the meaning of a term, "X", is explained by a description of the form 'X is the such and such which . . .' we commonly use (ordinary) names to fill in the blanks. If we tried to identify a complex, X, by means of a description of the form 'X is the y such that Fy & Gy & . . .', the phrases 'Fy', 'Gy', etc., would have to ascribe properties which are either accidentally or essentially true of the thing described. But neither accidental nor essential properties will secure the determinacy of assertions about X. Accidental properties are true of a thing in some, but not all possible worlds. If an assertion about a complex is to have a determinate sense, it must determine the identity of the complex for every reality in which the complex could exist. The enumeration of a thing's accidental properties will determine its identity only in the possible realities in which the thing has those properties (*TS* 55302). The predication of essential properties will not determine a thing's identity completely enough to suit Wittgenstein's requirement, for things which are essentially the same (for example, two horses) can be distinct and distinguishable in terms of their accidental properties. Wittgenstein acknowledges this in connection with objects when he allows that objects with the same logical form can differ with regard to their external properties (that is, can be differentiated if they occur in different concatenations) (*TS* 202331). Finally, Wittgenstein maintained that indiscernibles need not be identical

(*TS* 202331, 55302), and so his theory does not even guarantee that a thing could be uniquely identified relative to a given reality by giving its accidental as well as its essential properties. Even if a thing could be so identified this would not determine its identity in all possible realities, for in different realities its accidental properties will be different even if its essential properties remain the same. Thus a description which does no more than ascribe properties to the complex cannot meet the determinacy requirement.

The only sort of description which would have some chance of providing for determinacy is a description which characterizes the complex by enumerating its constituents, and saying how they are combined if the complex exists (*TS* 20201). If the constituents were signified by definite descriptions the descriptions would be inadequate for the reasons given above unless they contained names. It is to be expected that failure to secure the identity of the constituents of a complex must result in failure to secure the identity of the complex. From this we can conclude that the constituents of the complex must be referred to by name in order to give an adequate description of the complex on Wittgenstein's theory. If this is correct, Wittgenstein was justified in saying that sense could not be determinate unless signs can be used to name the constituents of complexes. Since he also assumed that the meaning of a name is its bearer, he could argue further that the constituents named must be simple.

Interestingly, this argument leads to no conclusion about what sorts of things the names name. In particular, it does not allow us to conclude that *Tractatus* objects cannot be properties. The argument purports to show that *predication* of properties cannot secure the identity of a thing for every possible world, and therefore that descriptions of complexes must include names. However, properties can be named (in ordinary language, at least) as well as predicated. It is unlikely that 'green' functions as a name in the assertion 'the sea is green'. But if someone says that green is his favourite colour, or that it is the complement of red, etc., he uses the word 'green' to refer to a colour without predicating it of anything. Thus the argument I have been considering shows (if it succeeds) that determinacy of sense requires that objects be named without showing that what is named cannot be a property.

4 WITTGENSTEIN'S LATER DISCUSSION OF SIMPLES

(4.1) I shall examine here the criticisms levelled by Wittgenstein against his early account of names and objects. My chief concern with this topic is to determine whether Wittgenstein's later views on names and objects account for his abandonment of the picture theory. My discussion is limited to the question how seriously they could be taken by someone who did not have independent objections to bring to bear against the picture theory.

The most extensive commentary on proper names and the theory of simple objects begins at *PI* 39 which initiates a discussion of the idea that 'a name ought really to signify a simple'. This is identified with doctrines discussed in Plato (*Theaetetus* 201d–202c), and espoused by Russell and the author of the *Tractatus* (*PI* 46). Characteristically, Wittgenstein exhibits little concern over differences between these doctrines, has little to say about their finer details, and does not bother to indicate against which doctrine or which philosopher the various stages of his presentation are directed. Nevertheless, we can compare at least some of his more important arguments to the *Tractatus,* and the discussion bears on all of the major considerations which go to make up the *Tractatus* theory. Both of the assumptions from which the *Tractatus* arguments for simple objects proceed are discussed at some length. At *PI* 40–43 Wittgenstein argues that the meaning of a name is not its bearer. The thesis that sense must be determinate is criticized in the course of the discussion of whether concepts must have perfectly sharp boundaries (*PI* 70–107). *PI* 55–59 criticizes the theory that names must signify indestructibles, and the notion of simple elements is taken up at *PI* 47–49 and elsewhere.

(4.2) Let us consider these in turn. (*PI* 40):

First let us consider *this* point in the argument: that a word has no meaning if nothing corresponds to it.—It is important to note that the word 'meaning' is being used illicitly if it is used to signify the thing that 'corresponds' to the word. That is to confound the meaning of a name with the bearer of the name. When Mr. N. N. dies one says that the bearer of the name dies, not that the meaning dies. And it would be nonsensical to say that, for if the name ceased to have meaning it would make no sense to say 'Mr. N. N. is dead.'

It could be objected that the fact that 'Mr. N. N. is dead' has a sense only proves that 'Mr. N. N.' is a disguised description of Mr. N. N. and not a genuine Tractarian name. Wittgenstein attempted to avoid this manoeuvre by introducing names into fictitious languages which contain no resources for description. In sections 2, 8, and 15 of the *Investigations,* he describes an imaginary language whose only utterances are commands. Its vocabulary includes the signs "slab", "block", "pillar", etc., used in connection with kinds of building stone, the letters "a", "b", "c", etc., used in counting, the demonstratives "this" and "there", a number of colour samples, and the sign "N" used to call for a particular tool. The language is used by a builder and his assistants. If the builder wants a stone of a particular colour, he shows an assistant a colour sample, utters the word which indicates what kind of stone he wants, and uses a demonstrative to show where he wants the stone brought. A letter is added to indicate how many stones are to be fetched, and "this" is used in the ostensive teaching of "N" and the general names "slab", "pillar", etc. The sign "N" functions like a proper name used to call for one particular thing. The builders prepare the sign "N" for use as a name by marking a tool with it and teach its use by pointing out the tool which bears the mark (*PI* 15). "N" could never have been used to name the tool unless the tool existed at some time to be marked and pointed to. But it does not follow that the meaningfulness of "N" depends upon the *continued* existence of the tool (*PI* 41):

Now suppose that the tool with the name 'N' is broken. Not knowing this, A gives B the sign 'N'. Has this sign got a meaning or not?—What is B to do when he is given it?—We have not settled anything about this. One might ask: What *will* he do? Well, perhaps he will stand there at a loss or show A the pieces. Here one might say: 'N' has become meaningless; and this expression would mean that the sign 'N' no longer had a use in our language game (unless we give it a new one). . . . But we could also imagine a convention whereby B has to shake his head in reply if A gives him the sign belonging to the tool that is broken.—In this way the command 'N' might be said to be given a place in the language game even when the tool no longer exists, and the sign 'N' to have a meaning even when its bearer fails to exist.

The poverty of the builders' language prevents us from saying what has a meaning without an existing bearer must be a description instead of a name. We could object that if 'Mr. N. N. is dead' has a sense, 'Mr. N. N.' is a disguised description because our language contains the linguistic wherewithal needed to replace 'Mr. N. N.' by a definite description. We cannot think that Wittgenstein's builders use "N" as a description because their language is too poor to allow them to give a description of the tool, disguised, abbreviated, or otherwise. If all that is needed to ensure that "N" should have a meaning after the tool has been destroyed is the addition to the builders' language of the head-shaking convention (which is clearly not a means for describing), then "N" is a name whose meaning does not depend upon the continued existence of the tool and, *a fortiori,* the tool is not the meaning of the name.

Does this argument provide a conclusive objection to the *Tractatus* thesis that the meaning of a name is its bearer? Its cogency depends upon the truth of the assumptions:

(1) the builders' word, "N", is a proper name,

(2) the builders' system of communications is a possible language even though it contains no provisions for describing things.

The question whether "N" is really a proper name would have made no sense for the later Wittgenstein unless it meant: is the builders' use of "N" similar enough to our uses of proper names to allow us to classify it under the same heading? The builders use "N" to call for a tool, and although we seldom give names to such things, this employment of "N" resembles one of the things we do with proper names. However, "N" can never be the grammatical or logical subject of a statement used to describe the tool while our proper names are commonly used to refer to something which we go on to describe. Wittgenstein did not think this a good reason for saying "N" is not a proper name. He did say that naming a thing (giving it a name) is a preparation for description (*PI* 49). But the point he wanted to make was that we do not simply name things. A word is a name only if we use it as such, and to use it as a name means to employ it in calling for, asking about, or saying something about what is named. In saying we never use a name except to do something further (for example, describing or talking about the bearer of the name), he did not intend to maintain that describing is the *only* thing we use names to do and, therefore, that a language without descriptions is a language without names. He would have said "N" functions like a name when the builders use it to call for the tool and, therefore, that the difference between their language and ours is simply that they can do less with a proper name than we. If someone still insisted that what cannot be used in statements about a thing cannot be a name, Wittgenstein might have tried to amend the builders' language to allow the occurrence of "N" in statements about the tool without allowing "N" to be introduced or explained by means of a description. Unless (as seems unlikely) it could be shown that this would be logically impossible, the use of "N" in the fictitious language would closely resemble our uses of proper names, but "N" still could not abbreviate a description of the tool to which it refers.

But all of this assumes that the builders' language is a possible language. If "N" does not belong to a language, it is not a word —and so it is not a name. Someone who thought that the meaning of a name does not depend upon the indestructibility of its bearer might grant that the builders' language is a possible language. But Wittgenstein uses the fictitious language to *show* that the bearer of a name need not be indestructible. To establish this he cannot *assume* the builders' language is a possible language without begging the question. Thus the argument of *PI* 40–42 cannot legitimately be employed against the *Tractatus* or any other theory which offers reasons for saying a name cannot have a meaning when its bearer no longer exists.

(4.3) The Tractarian thesis that the meaning of a genuine

name is its bearer goes with the doctrine that a complex thing must be signified by an explicit or disguised description and, therefore, that ordinary proper names must function as descriptions. This doctrine is taken up at *PI* 79 :

> Consider this example. If one says 'Moses did not exist' this may mean various things. It may mean: The Israelites did not have a *single* leader when they withdrew from Egypt— or: their leader was not called Moses—or etc., etc.— We may say, following Russell: the name 'Moses' can be defined by means of various descriptions. For example, as 'the man who led the Israelites through the wilderness', 'the man who lived at that time and that place and was called "Moses" ', 'the man who as a child was taken out of the Nile by Pharaoh's daughter', and so on. And accordingly as we assume one definition or another, the proposition 'Moses did not exist' acquires a different sense, and so does every other proposition about Moses.—And if we are told 'N did not exist', we do ask 'What do you mean? Do you want to say ... or ... etc.?'
>
> But when I make a statement about Moses, am I always ready to substitute some *one* of these descriptions for 'Moses'? ... Has the name Moses got a fixed and unequivocal use for me in all possible cases?—Is it not the case that I have, so to speak, a whole series of props in readiness, and am ready to lean on one if another should be taken away from me and vice versa?—Consider another case. When I say 'N is dead', then something like the following may hold for the meaning (*Bedeutung*) of the name 'N': I believe that a human being has lived, whom I (1) have seen in such and such places, who (2) looked like this (pictures), (3) has done such and such things, and (4) bore the name 'N' in social life. Asked what I understand by 'N' I should enumerate all or some of these points, and different ones on different occasions. So my definition of 'N' would perhaps be 'the man of whom all of this is true'.—But if some point now proves false? Shall I be prepared to declare the proposition 'N is dead' false? Even if it is only something which strikes me as incidental that has turned out

to be false?—But where are the bounds of the incidental?—
If I had given a definition of the name in such a case,
I should now be ready to alter it.

Someone who said that Moses did not exist might, in explaining what he meant, replace "Moses" by a definite description, retracting the sentence "Moses did not exist" in favour of the sentence "there was no single person who led the Jews out of Egypt". In this case it could be correct to say that " Moses did not exist" and "there was no single person who . . ." were used to make the same assertion. But does this mean that before retracting 'Moses did not exist', the speaker actually used "Moses" to *describe* Moses?

'Moses' could actually be used (and introduced for this purpose) as an abbreviation for a description, although so used it would not function as a proper name. But when names are introduced or explained by means of descriptions, they need not, and usually do not behave like abbreviations of the descriptions. When Wittgenstein said explanations function like props he was thinking of cases in which a name is introduced by a description which functions like a gesture in an ostensive explanation. Suppose I said something and then pointed to N to explain who I was talking about. To understand my utterance, my audience must know to whom "N" refers. The purpose of the gesture is to direct attention to the man in question. We could not say "N" is synonymous with the gesture or the words ("that's N") which accompany it. In order for the explanation to succeed, N would have to be in the place to which I point, but "N" does not become a synonym for "the man standing at such and such a place" or "the man standing at the place to which I point". If N moved I would have to point again, but the fact that I abandon one gesture in favour of another does not change the meaning of my original utterance.

Instead of pointing, I could have said that N is the man standing by the bus stop. My purpose would be to get you to look at the bus stop to see who is standing there; once you see who it is you will understand my use of the proper name "N". The definite description does not define "N" in the Tractarian sense according to which defined signs signify *via* the signs in the definition. It simply provides instructions by which you can find who is meant by "N". If the explanation fails, my substitution of another need no more change the meaning of "N" than would the substitution of one gesture for another. Suppose you know that the man at the bus stop is not named "N"; I had mistaken him for N because they closely resemble one another. Then I would retract the statement 'N is the man by the bus stop' in favour of another one—and keep on until I finally came up with a true description which succeeded in picking out N for you. Wittgenstein would have said the meaning of "N" is its use to refer to a particular person. Although the use is explained and perhaps even made possible by giving definite descriptions, the meanings (or uses) of the definite descriptions are not identical to the meaning (or use) of the name.

This account of the connection between an ordinary proper name and a description used to introduce or explain it is undoubtedly more correct than the Tractarian theory. But its correctness rests on the assumption that 'N' need not describe its bearer and (since N is destructible and complex) therefore that a name can have a complex and perishable thing as its referent. Thus despite its plausibility, the remarks about ordinary proper names at *PI* 79 cannot be brought to bear conclusively against the *Tractatus*. We could not replace the Tractarian with the later account on this point unless we had an independent argument to show that a word can be used as the name of a perishable complex.

(4.4) Let us consider what the *Investigations* has to say about the thesis that the sense of a proposition must be determinate. Wittgenstein commented on this at *PI* 99, introducing it in language reminiscent of *TS* 5156.

> The sense of a proposition—one would like to say—may, of course, leave this or that open, but the proposition must nevertheless have *a* definite sense. An indefinite sense—that would really not be a sense *at all.*—This is like: an indefinite boundary is not really a boundary at all. Here one thinks perhaps: if I say 'I have locked the man up fast in the room—there is only one door left open'—then I simply haven't locked him in at all; his being locked in is a sham. One would be inclined to say here: 'You haven't done

anything at all.' An enclosure with a hole is as good as *none*. But is that true?

An enclosure with a hole is as good as none only if the hole defeats our purposes in constructing the enclosure; it all depends upon what we are trying to enclose. A proposition which fails to meet the determinacy requirement is a sentence so used that border-line cases are possible. But the possibility of a border-line case is nothing more than the possibility of *a* border-line case. A sentence can be used in such a way as to allow an indeterminate truth value in some kinds of case without having an indeterminate truth value in the cases with which the speaker is concerned.

The metaphor of the boundary originated with Frege,[46] whose discussion of this kind of point had great influence over the early Wittgenstein:

> A definition of a concept (of a possible predicate) must . . .
> unambiguously determine, as regards any object, whether or
> not it falls under the concept (whether or not the predicate is
> truly assertible of it). . . . We may express this
> metaphorically as follows: the concept must have a sharp
> boundary. . . . To a concept without a sharp boundary there
> would correspond an area that did not have a sharp
> boundary line all round, but in places, just vaguely faded
> into the background. This would not really be an area at all;
> and likewise, a concept that is not sharply defined is
> wrongly termed a concept. . . . Has the question 'Are we still
> Christians?' really got a sense if it is indeterminate whom the
> predicate 'Christian' can be truly asserted of, and who
> must be refused it?

The early Wittgenstein would have answered Frege's rhetorical question, no. The later Wittgenstein would have said: yes— if we are able to decide who is or is not a Christian for the cases in which we are interested.

But doesn't the rejection of the requirement for sharply-defined concepts lead to the possibility of predicates which violate the law of excluded middle? If the definition of a predicate, 'F', fails to determine its applicability to something, *a*, then 'Fa' would be neither true nor false. A compelling reply to this is the following from Geach,[47] who quotes a fragment from an unpublished draft of the *Investigations.*

> I see no more reason to hold that the logic of vague predicates must be vague than that he who drives fat oxen must be fat. Logic, in Wittgenstein's phrase, must not be bargained out of her rigour; and a valuable remark of his in an unpublished work ... shows how we can certainly ascribe some precise logical properties to vague predicates. To represent a vague predicate, P, we draw two concentric boundary lines, A and B; P will definitely be true of what lies inside the inner boundary, and the negation of P, of what lies outside the outer boundary. 'There would be an indeterminate area left over; the boundaries A and B are inessential to the concept defined. The boundaries A and B are as it were just the walls of the forecourt. They are drawn arbitrarily where it is still possible to draw a firm line.—It is like walling off a bog; the wall is not the boundary of the bog, it merely surrounds it while itself standing on firm ground. It shows that there is a bog inside, not that the bog is just as large as the walled-off area.'

A different application of the bog analogy is suggested by *PI* 87 :

> Suppose I gave this explanation: 'I take "Moses" to mean the man if there was such a man, who led the Israelites out of Egypt, whatever he was then called and whatever else he may or may not have done besides.' But similar doubts to those about 'Moses' are possible about the words of this explanation (what are you calling 'Egypt', whom the 'Israelites', etc.?). Nor would these questions come to an end when we got down to words like 'red', 'dark' and 'sweet'.— 'But then how does an explanation help me to understand, if after all it is not the final explanation? In that case the explanation is never completed; so I still don't understand what he means, and never shall.'—As though an explanation as it were hung in the air unless supported by another one. Whereas an explanation may indeed rest on another explanation that has been given, but none stands in need of another—unless *we* require it to prevent a

misunderstanding—one, that is, that would occur but for the explanation; not every one that I can imagine.

Suppose we mark off a bog to keep people from wandering into it. If people wandered in from only one direction, we would need only to make a boundary on a single side, and would have no need to mark the bog off further unless people began to wander into it from a new direction. Similarly, Wittgenstein suggests, we offer explanations not to avert every possible misunderstanding, but only misunderstandings which actually do or are likely to arise. A partial marking-off of the bog succeeds if it prevents people from wandering into it, and a 'partial' explanation succeeds if it prevents people from making mistakes and misunderstanding what we say.

Let us summarize these considerations:

(1) From the fact that there could be cases in which the truth value of an utterance is indeterminate, it does not follow that its truth value is indeterminate in *all* cases. In so far as the meaningfulness of an utterance depends upon its having a truth value, the possibility of border-line cases is not enough to show that an utterance lacks sense.

(2) If the definition of a concept does not determine whether it applies to a certain thing, it does not follow that its application to other things is indeterminate.

(3) Even though the explanation of an utterance does not make misunderstandings impossible, it does not follow that misunderstandings will or are likely to arise. Thus the use of a bit of language to say something does not require an explanation exhaustive enough to rule out all possible misunderstandings under all possible conditions.

The upshot of these considerations is supposed to be that a proposition which does not meet the Tractarian requirement for determinacy of sense need not lack a sense. Once again, though (1), (2), and (3) are very likely true, the arguments Wittgenstein offers in favour of them do not refute the Tractarian position. If my account of the early Wittgenstein's reason for saying that sense must be determinate was correct, his grounds for holding the determinacy thesis remain unaffected by these considerations. The early Wittgenstein did not hold that sense must be determinate because he thought one border-line case makes all cases border-line. He believed that the sense of a proposition is or corresponds to a possible fact and that facts are individuals which obey the laws of identity. If an indeterminate sense were still a sense, there could be a fact which did not obey the laws of identity, and on the assumption that facts are individuals, this is impossible. (2) and (3) are inconclusive for the same reason. To show that sense need not be determinate, we should have to refute the assumptions from which the determinacy thesis seemed to follow in the context of the *Tractatus*—the assumptions that facts are individuals and that senses are or correspond to possible facts. Because the remarks directed explicitly against the determinacy thesis in the *Investigations* fail to do this, the most to be said for them is that they present highly attractive alternatives which were not available to the early Wittgenstein, and would not be available to anyone who espoused a Tractarian ontology.

(4.5) Finally, we must look at what Wittgenstein had to say about objects and names in sections 46–59 of the *Investigations*. These passages are explicitly devoted to an examination of Socrates' dream (*PI* 46):[48]

'If I make no mistake, I have heard some people say . . . there is no definition of the primary elements—so to speak— out of which we and everything else are composed; for everything that exists in its own right can only be *named,* no other determination is possible, neither that it *is* nor that it *is not.* . . . But what exists in its own right has to be . . . named without any other determination. As a consequence it is impossible to give an account of any primary element; for it, nothing is possible but the bare name; its name is all it has. But just as what consists of these primary elements is itself complex, so the names of the elements become descriptive language by being compounded together. For the essence of speech is the composition of names.'

Both Russell's 'individuals' and my 'objects' (*Tractatus Logico-Philosophicus*) were such primary elements.

The greater part of Wittgenstein's discussion turns upon the consideration of a 'language game', consisting of procedures by which the signs "R", "G", "W", and "B" are used to describe arrangements of coloured squares. Each arrangement contains three rows of three squares each. "R" is used to indicate a red square, "G" a green one, "B" a black one, and "W" a white square. Sentences contain nine signs, the first three for the first row, the second three for the second, and the last three for the third. Thus the sentence 'RRBGGGRWW' describes an arrangement like that in the diagram (*PI* 48).

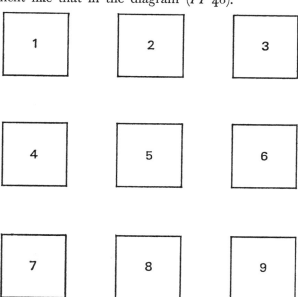

Squares 1 and 2 are red, square 3 is black, squares 4, 5, and 6 are green, square 7 is red, and squares 8 and 9 are white. The doctrines which comprise Socrates' dream are treated as if they had been intended to describe this language game. Wittgenstein attempts to bring out the most natural application of each doctrine to the game. He then compares the game to other (real and imaginary) linguistic practices in order to show how a doctrine which fits the language game of *PI* 48 might fail to fit other linguistic activities. In this way he asks whether the primary elements of the language game of *PI* 48 are simple (*PI* 48), in what sense it would be true to say they cannot be described (*PI* 49), whether they are indestructible (*PI* 50, 55–58) and in what sense the letters can be said to name or correspond to the primary elements (*PI* 51–54). The discussion ends with a puzzling passage in which Wittgenstein compares the theory of simples to mundane cases in which things are made up of parts which can remain the same even though the complex changes or is destroyed (*PI* 59).

(1) Are the coloured squares simple elements?

'I do not know what else you would have me call "the simples", what would be more natural in this game' (*PI* 48). That the squares are simple means that in the language game of *PI* 48, the squares are not describable as composed of elements. The answer to the philosophical question, 'are the elements of the game *absolutely* simple?' is that what functions as a simple element in one language game need not be considered simple in another. 'Under other circumstances I should call a monochrome square "composite" consisting perhaps of two rectangles, or of the elements, colour and shape' (*PI* 48). 'Is such and such simple?' makes sense only with reference to a specific linguistic technique for describing. Therefore, 'is such and such *absolutely* simple?' is meaningless.

In connection with this Wittgenstein considers the question whether a sentence like "RRBGGGRWW" mentions nine elements or only four, that is, whether the elements are individual coloured squares or kinds of square. He replies that it doesn't matter how the question is answered as long as the answer doesn't lead to misunderstandings of the uses of the signs in the actual practice of the game. This rejects the question whether primary elements must be universals or particulars (kinds or instances of kinds). A distinction might have to be made in order to understand some linguistic practices, but in others like the game under consideration, nothing calls for it. No particular ontological classification follows from the fact that a thing is simple. That too is determined (if at all) by the way the thing functions in the practice in which it is simple.[49]

(2) Can the primary elements be described?

Since the squares are mentioned in order to describe combinations of squares, one would expect the answer to be that a single square can be named but never described. But the limiting case of an arrangement of squares would be one in which the schema for an arrangement,

$$1, \quad 2, \quad 3,$$
$$4, \quad 5, \quad 6,$$
$$7, \quad 8, \quad 9$$

is filled in, for example, by placing a single red square in the '1' position without completing the arrangement with squares in the other positions. If the players of the language game agreed to describe this degenerate arrangement, they would use the sign "R". Here a single name is used to describe an arrangement, but since the arrangement is a single square, we might say "R" describes a square (*PI* 49).

But descriptions are sentences and names are only single words; how can 'R' be a description—even of the degenerate arrangement? Wittgenstein holds that a sign 'may be sometimes a word and sometimes a sentence (proposition)' (*PI* 49). When the utterance of "R" does *not* accomplish what the sentences of the language game accomplish (that is, where the utterance of the single sign does not describe an arrangement or degenerate arrangement of squares) it is used as a word. But when, for example, a red square is treated as a degenerate arrangement of squares, "R" gives a description and has the use of a sentence in the language.

Here Wittgenstein departs from the doctrines of the *Tractatus* on a number of points. As in the *Tractatus,* he is prepared to say a description is a sign used in a particular way, and (with reservation) that a sign does not name a thing unless it has a use in or as a sentence. But now he holds that descriptions do not have to be complex. "R" cannot be replaced by a complex sign in the language game of *PI* 48, but its utterance can sometimes be counted as a description and, when so used, the sign is a sentence.

According to the *Tractatus,* the elements cannot be described because description is analysis and the elements of an analysis cannot themselves be analysed. In the *Investigations,* to describe is not necessarily to analyse. It depends upon the linguistic practice, and different methods are possible. That is why "R" can function as a description of the degenerate arrangement.

(3)   Are there elements whose existence or non-existence cannot be meaningfully asserted?

Wittgenstein's explication of this question captures the spirit of the Tractarian doctrine: 'one would ... like to say: existence cannot be attributed to an element, for if it did not *exist,* one could not even name it and so one could say nothing of it at all' (*PI* 50). And if 'X exists' means that its elements are combined and 'X does not exist' means they have been separated, we can't say of an element which is simple that it exists or does not exist (ibid).

Wittgenstein says we can imagine language games in which there are no linguistic resources for saying that a certain thing exists or fails to exist. This would be analogous to imagining a game in which the word 'sepia' is applied only to things whose colour matches that of a standard sample (*PI* 50). In this game it would make no sense to say that the sample is or is not sepia. Therefore, we could not assert the existence or non-existence of the sample under the description 'the sample which is coloured sepia'. Furthermore, if 'sepia' were used to name only things whose colour matches the sample, the name would lose its meaning if the sample were destroyed, and so we could not refer to the sample by using 'sepia' as a name to say that it existed or did not exist (*PI* 55). Thus (*PI* 55):

> What looks as if it *had* to exist, is part of our language. It is a paradigm in our language game; something with which comparison is made. And this may be an important observation; but it is nonetheless an observation concerning our language game—our method of representation.

If I have interpreted *PI* 55 correctly, the argument might be objected to on the grounds that if "sepia" is (by rule or practice) to be applied to something only if it resembles the sample, it functions as a general name or description, and not as a proper name. This seems a difficulty if (as most commentators suppose) Wittgenstein is using this argument against the *Tractatus*. What the *Tractatus* claims we cannot ascribe existence or non-existence to are things which can be referred to with (and only with) proper names. But Wittgenstein's point seems to be simply that what cannot be said of a thing cannot be said relative to a specific linguistic practice. If a game does not allow us to say that X exists or fails to exist, all that shows is that X enters into that game in such a way that we would have to play another one to talk about its existence. The point is that we could construct another game for this purpose if we wanted to. In a game where the variable in the schema 'X exists' can be replaced only by the description of a complex of elements, 'X exists' will mean that such and such elements are combined. We who have a richer language can describe the game and say that 'exists' would have no meaning in it if there were no elements and, therefore, that players of the game cannot say that an element exists. But this is a feature of the game which can be eliminated by changing the game; it is not an eternal ontological truth.

Could a language be changed in the way Wittgenstein imagines? Suppose a sample is used as a paradigm of red to describe the colours of things. The same colour descriptions could be given by people who bore the colour in mind without actually using a sample (cp. *BRB* 33–40). If the same purposes were served by the colour descriptions and, given the intents and purposes of the describers, the descriptions were equally successful, there would be no difference between the two linguistic practices except for a difference in the method of describing. There would be no need to call this difference an essential one (cp. *PI* 562–564).[50] Against the objection that without a paradigm a speaker would be at the mercy of his memory, Wittgenstein observes that users of the physical sample are equally at the mercy of their sample. If memory is fallible, samples are susceptible to change. We may appeal to a sample to correct our memory of the way a colour looks; but sometimes it is necessary to reject a sample because it no longer looks the way it used to. In doing this, we rely on memory. Thus the use of a paradigm is *a* method but not *the only* method for checking colours.

This represents an abandonment of the *Tractatus* notion that the possibility of a conceptual scheme rests upon the existence of primary objects. The later Wittgenstein held that what is and what is not essential to a conceptual scheme or linguistic practice depends upon the point or purpose of the practice— upon its connection with other practices and interests of the speakers (*PI* 562 f.). Within the context of a given culture and the natural environment in which it is set there might be practical activities involving language which would lose their point if a paradigm sample were destroyed. That would be because the purposes served by the language could not be secured by its speakers without the employment of paradigms. Such activities comprise conceptual schemes whose possibilities do rest upon the existence of certain things. If there are such practices, they are as they are because of contingent facts about the speakers and the world. Their existence would not establish the Tractarian thesis that every possible use of language presupposes the existence of a fixed set of objects.

Finally, Wittgenstein observes that if the meaning of a word depended upon the existence of a thing in such a way that it made no sense to say that the thing does or does not exist this would not render the thing in question immune from destruction. If it ceased to exist a word would lose its meaning, and that could happen. Suppose "red" actually did get its meaning from a paradigm and the paradigm was destroyed. We might rely upon our memory of the sample to produce new physical samples or to use "red" without a physical paradigm. But our memory could fail us. 'When we forget which colour this is the name of, it loses its meaning for us; that is, we are no longer able to play a particular language game with it' (*PI* 57). Thus the fact that a use of language depended upon the existence of a thing could not guarantee that the thing must always exist, for there is no *a priori* guarantee against our losing the use of language.

(4)   Do the signs "R", "B", etc., in the language game (*PI* 48) name or refer to the coloured squares? If so, what is the connection between a sign and a square?

By asking this, Wittgenstein hopes to be able to shed light on what it means to say that a sign *refers* or is *used to refer* to a thing. The Tractarian discussion of names says little about this, but it conveys the impression that referring is a special kind of connection set up by rules of projection which correlate a sign with an object. By 'special connection' I mean that whenever a sign functions as a genuine name its connection to its referent is always one and the same specific relation. Had the early Wittgenstein talked about linguistic practices like the language games of the *Investigations* and the *Brown Book,* he would have said that given the correlation of signs with objects, we can use what are essentially the same projection methods to play various kinds of language game. But the possibility of any particular game rests upon the connection between sign and object and this connection would be the same in every game in which the sign could be used as a name for the same thing.

The doctrine of the *Investigations* is that no such distinction is to be drawn between the connection of name and referent and the practice in which the name is used in connection with its referent. Instead, the connection is *constituted* by the practice. To say that "R" refers to or is used in connection with a red square is to give a generalized description of the place of a sign in a language game like that of *PI* 48. To see what the connection consists of we must see 'from close to' exactly what is done with the sign in the game (*PI* 51). Referring is what is done by the speakers. It is not a prior connection presupposed by and independent of their use of the sign. In support of this, Wittgenstein argues that we do not understand what it is for "R" to name or correspond to a red square in the game of *PI* 48 if all that we know is that there is a correlation between the two. That there is a correlation could mean, for example, that the speakers always or usually say "R" where there is a red square, or that when "R" is used, a red square always comes before the mind of a speaker (*PI* 51). But to understand what it is for "R" to *refer* to, *name*, or be *used* in connection with a square requires more than a knowledge of this kind of empirical regularity. We need to know what counts as a *correct* or *incorrect* use of the sign so that we can distinguish between someone's simply saying "R" when he sees a red square and using "R" to refer to the square, between someone's thinking or having a mental image of a red square when he hears 'R' and *understanding* what is said, etc. In other words, we must understand the practice of the language, what the speakers intend to accomplish by means of the language, and how the utterance of "R" functions in its accomplishment in particular cases. A complete explanation of what it is for "R" to refer to a red square would involve all of this.

The 'referring relation' is, therefore, not a single relation. Signs used to refer to things in various language games are at most signs whose roles in the practices to which they belong are roughly comparable. This does not mean that referring in one game is exactly the same or is an instance of exactly the same connection as in another game. Thus Wittgenstein says in connection with the builders' language that someone who did not know the general procedure for using the word "slab" would be unable to understand someone who told him that "slab" refers to this rather than that kind of stone (*PI* 10):

Of course, one can reduce the description of the use of the word 'slab' to the statement that this word signifies this object. This will be done when, for example, it is merely a matter of removing the mistaken idea that the word 'slab' refers to the shape of building-stone we, in fact, call a 'block'. But the kind of *'referring'* this is, that is to say the use of these words for the rest is already known. Equally one can say that the signs 'a', 'b', etc., signify numbers; when for example this removes the mistaken idea that 'a', 'b', 'c' play a part actually played in language by 'block', 'slab', 'pillar'. ... But assimilating the descriptions of the uses of words in this way cannot make the uses themselves any more like one another. For, as we see, they are absolutely unlike.

If this is so, the Tractarian suggestion that reference is a single kind of relation consisting of a correlation between a sign and an object must be rejected. A bare connection between sign and thing is simply a correlation or association. Referring is what is accomplished by *using* the sign. It might be said that unless "R" is associated or correlated with a red square, it cannot refer to it. But even so, the referring is what is done with the sign *after* the correlation has been established. To know what it is for "R" to refer to the square is to know how it is used in connection with the square—how the correlation or association is exploited.

(5) Wittgenstein's discussion of Socrates' dream concludes with the suggestion that the doctrine is a sort of picture—not a picture of anything we can actually find by looking at linguistic practices and the world in which we speak, but a picture of what the philosopher would like to find and thinks he must find if he examines language closely enough (*PI* 59):

This [the doctrine of simples] was the expression of a quite particular image: of a particular picture which we want to use. For certainly experience does not show us these elements. We see *component parts* of something composite (of a chair, for instance). We say that the back is part of the chair, but is in turn itself composed of several bits of wood; while a leg is a simple component part. We also see a whole which changes (is destroyed) while its component parts remain unchanged. These are the materials from which we construct that picture of reality.

'These are the materials from which we construct that picture of reality' suggests that the meaning of the doctrine of simples can somehow be brought out by considering the chair and its parts and the whole which is destroyed while its parts remain unchanged. It is hard to see how this could be so. Even if a philosopher used the case of the chair as an illustration of his doctrine, how could it be *important* that the doctrine should be illustrated in this way? Even though the early Wittgenstein illustrated the picture theory with the picture of two fencers and the description of the Paris court proceedings, little that is *essential* to the theory emerges from the details of these examples. Indeed, in order to understand the picture theory, one must realize how the elements of a Tractarian picture *differ* from the dolls used in the court and the ink marks used to stand for the fencers. Similarly, Tractarian simples are not physical things like the leg of a chair, and they do not combine to form a composite *thing* like a chair; they are indivisible and their combination is a *fact*.

Does Wittgenstein mean that the consideration of mundane composites (like chairs) is what inspires a man like Plato to think of the theory of simples—in the way that the consideration of the accident model is supposed to have suggested the picture theory to the early Wittgenstein? Why should this be of interest to someone who is trying to assess the merits of the theory of simples? What occasioned or inspired a man to hit on a thought should be only biographically or historically interesting.

Neither of these interpretations is terribly convincing, and I think we must suppose that Wittgenstein had something else in mind. A hint is given at *PI* 115–117. Here he says that when a philosopher uses a word like 'knowledge', 'being', or 'object' and tries 'to grasp the *essence* of the thing, one must always ask oneself: is the word ever actually used in this way in the language (*Sprache*) which is its home?' If someone says a certain sentence makes sense to him he should ask himself in what special circumstances this sentence is actually used. 'There it does make sense' (ibid). I take it that this is the kind of exercise Wittgenstein ran through when he compared the theory of simple objects to the enumeration of the parts of a chair. It is in connection with things like chairs that we know how to speak of a thing and its parts, and if someone dismantles a chair without breaking the legs, back, or seat, this is the kind of case in which we know how to apply the sentence 'the whole has been destroyed while its parts remain intact.' The doctrine of *PI* 59 is that the words which the philosopher uses to describe reality as a collection of complexes constructed from simple elements get their meaning from their application to mundane situations like the one in which we enumerate the parts of a chair. These applications are the materials of a philosophical doctrine because they constitute the meanings of the words and sentences the philosopher uses. In order to see what the philosopher is saying when he speaks of complexes and their elements, we must see if his words are used as he uses them when we speak about such things as chairs. The implication of *PI* 59 is that there is such a clear disparity between philosophical and mundane talk about wholes and parts, complexes and elements, that a consideration of ordinary uses of his words will show that the philosophical doctrine is nonsensical (cp. *PI* 119). For example, 'what are the simple elements out of which —— is composed?' makes sense in the context of a situation in which it is clear how a —— is to be divided and where the blank is filled in with a reference to something for which we have a method of division. But we don't know how to use the sentence if the blank is filled in with 'everything' (Z 338, 339).

(4.6) Eventually some of the points I have been outlining will have to be discussed further.[51] But the summary just given of Wittgenstein's discussion of Socrates' dream will serve our present purpose of determining whether it can be treated as a refutation of the Tractarian account of simples. My view is that it cannot. Wittgenstein's announced strategy was to apply the method he used earlier in the *Investigations* in connection with the Augustinian theory that all words are names against the theory of Socrates' dream (*PI* 48). The method is to suppose that the theory of names and simples given in *Theaetetus* and the *Tractatus* is a correct description 'of a language more primitive than ours' (*PI* 2). We then invent such a primitive language (for example, the language game by which complexes of coloured squares are described) and get clear about what the philosophical theory could mean if employed to describe the invented language. When we compare the invented language (the language game) to our own language, we see that although the theory can describe the invented language correctly, 'not everything we call language is this system' (*PI* 3). If someone asks whether the theory of simples is correct, the answer will be, 'Yes, it is appropriate, but only for this narrowly circumscribed region, not for the whole [of language] you were claiming to describe' (*PI* 3).

> It is as if someone were to say: 'A game consists in moving objects about on a surface according to certain rules . . .'— and we replied: You seem to be thinking of board games, but there are others. You can set your account (*Erklärung*) straight by expressly restricting it to those games. (*PI* 3.)

If we bear in mind the arguments Wittgenstein advanced in the *Tractatus* in support of the theory of simple objects and simple symbols, it is extremely difficult to see how this sort of examination could be acceptable as an interpretation or a refutation of the Tractarian theory. If I read him correctly, the early Wittgenstein attempted to solve the Buridanian problem about false assertion by supposing that in essence, every ordinary language assertion is a representational picture of reality. And the assumptions which gave rise to the Tractarian theory of names and simples were postulated to meet the requirements of the supposition that assertions are pictures. None of these assumptions are refuted by the language game method of investigation.

Recall also that in talking about genuine names and simple objects, Wittgenstein claimed to be giving an account of a kind of *symbol* and the objects connected with it; he did not purport to be giving the kind of description of a language that a native speaker or a field linguist might provide. The early Wittgenstein contended that in order to assert, we *must* somehow make reference to simple objects, even though our language does not contain signs explicitly assigned to simples. He believed that ordinary language assertions could be analysed into a notation in which references to simples could be perspicuously achieved through the use of special signs, but he did not claim that the speakers of any natural language produce fully analysed versions of their own assertions. Therefore, ordinary proper and common names are not what Wittgenstein called genuine names, and it would be a distortion of the Tractarian theory to treat words in unanalysed utterances as names and their bearers as examples of simples. Wittgenstein says enough about simple objects in the *Tractatus* to make it clear that when he talks about simples he does not mean coloured squares. If the behaviour of a group of speakers shows that coloured squares are what they think are the simplest elements of the composites they describe, it does not follow that they are the closest we can get to genuinely simply objects. Similarly, if they behave as though the signs "R", "B", "W", and "G" were names, it does not follow that they are genuine names.

Consider the language game method for showing that the notion of simplicity is relative (*PI* 48). It consists of pointing out that what is treated as unanalysable in one language game could be treated as a complex to be analysed in another. The early Wittgenstein could object that we get the conclusion that simplicity is relative by deliberately interpreting 'simple' and 'primary elements' to indicate the sort of thing whose analysis *could* easily be provided for by constructing another language game. The procedure sounds suspiciously similar to a sophistry of the following kind. An atomic physicist claims that certain familiar, everyday phenomena cannot be explained except on the theory that physical objects are collections of atoms, themselves composed of particles called electrons, protons, etc., which cannot be seen by the naked eye or with the aid of the most powerful microscope. I interpret 'atom' as referring to the collection of objects at present to be found on my desk, and 'electron' as referring to its tiniest member. In the present state of my office, I should interpret 'electron' as referring to bits of dust and specks of grime. But now I observe that I could have treated a matchbook as an atom and the heads of the matches as electrons. I conclude that electrons come in different sizes and colours. Relative to a desk atom, an electron is very small, and grey; relative to a matchbook atom, an electron is quite a bit larger, and has a blue colour. I chide the physicist for being so naïve as to suppose that 'electron' actually designates a single kind of particle which goes to make up all of the atoms of which all physical stuff is composed and which has the same properties wherever it occurs. I complain about his proceeding as though all material things were constituted in the same way, and as though their structure lay hidden from the naked eye. I remark that the physicists see in the essence of matter 'not something that already lies open to view ... but something that lies *beneath* the surface' (*PI* 92). The physicist will reply that what I have called atoms and electrons cannot be the particles of which his theory speaks, for they do not have the properties the theory requires of them, and then he will cite whatever evidence he can to show how the explanations of macroscopic physical phenomena turn out on his theory to depend upon the existence of the particles it specifies as the constituents of atoms.

The analogous complaint against the language game method would involve an appeal to *Tractatus* arguments which were supposed to show that unless there are simple elements incapable of analysis by any possible language or conceptual scheme, assertions could not picture reality and, therefore, that there could be no such thing as a false assertion. It would be argued that the simples called for by the picture theory can be nothing like the coloured squares of *PI* 48 and, therefore, that 'simple object' must not be taken to mean whatever the speakers of that or any other language whose assertions are unanalysed may treat as simple. If the user of the language game method replied that he cannot understand the term 'simple object' unless he takes it to refer to something with which he is familiar—a coloured square, for example—why wouldn't that be like saying that we cannot understand what the physicist means by 'electron' unless we interpret it as referring to something we can see with the naked eye?

In saying all of this, I do not claim to have shown that the mistaken accounts of the *Tractatus* are true, that the later Wittgenstein was wrong in saying that what is essential to language is what we can observe by looking at its actual use, or that contrary to all the later Wittgenstein argued, a viable analogy can really be drawn between a philosophical account like that of the *Tractatus* and a scientific theory. The point I have been arguing is simply that the employment of the language game method *presupposes* that the sentences which comprise the theory of simples make no sense unless applied as descriptions of language games or areas of our own language. As long as there is a chance of maintaining (as the early Wittgenstein did) that what is essential to language is hidden beneath the linguistic phenomena with which a field linguist, anthropologist, or native speaker is familiar, we cannot reject the possibility of applying 'simple object' only to the bearers of the signs in fully analysed assertions and, therefore, we cannot legitimize the language game procedure. To rule this out, it must be shown either that the possibility of false assertion *does not* rest upon the correctness of Tractarian thesis that assertions are pictures, or else that the picture theory does not really require that there be simple objects of the kind Wittgenstein thought he was describing in the *Tractatus*. Because none of this is accomplished by the language game method itself, the discussion of *PI* 48–58 cannot stand on its own. Only an independent refutation of the picture theory can clear the language game method of the charge that it caricatures the theory of simples and hence that its results are irrelevant to an assessment of that theory. If this is correct Pitcher's suggestion that Wittgenstein eroded away the picture theory by attacking the Tractarian account of names and objects importantly misrepresents the direction of Wittgenstein's later thoughts about the *Tractatus*.[52]

The same kind of point applies to the rest of Wittgenstein's discussion of Socrates' dream. Consider, for example, his treatment of the thesis that the primary elements must be indestructible. If we take any of the paradigm samples of colour used as examples in the *Investigations* to be examples of simple objects, then we must conclude that they can perish. But if the picture theory is correct nothing follows except that it establishes the necessary existence of objects which are quite unlike the coloured squares and sepia samples Wittgenstein considered at *PI* 50.

Wittgenstein supported his contention that the simple elements of the game of *PI* 48 are describable as well as nameable by pointing out that a single coloured square could be taken as a degenerate instance of the arrangements of squares which the sentences of the game describe. It does not follow from this that Tractarian simples are degenerate instances of complexes and, therefore, that they too can be described. The later Wittgenstein defended himself against the charge that "R" cannot be a description because a description requires the use of a sentence and not just a single sign by arguing that if used to talk about a degenerate arrangement consisting of a single square, "R" accomplishes what can be accomplished by a complex sign and should, therefore, be treated as a sentence. Suppose this is so. The doctrine of the *Tractatus* was that *symbols* which describe must be complex even if—as in the case where *"ambulo"* is used to assert that the speaker walks—the symbol is constituted by the use of a single sign (*TS* 4032). Why not say the use of "R" to describe proves that a fully analysed version of the description would contain more than one word? If the multiplicity of an assertion is perspicuously exhibited only by a fully analysed version of the assertion, what is to be accomplished by counting the signs in an unanalysed assertion? (cp. *TS* 3322, 3323). Doesn't the argument of *PI* 49 confuse symbol with sign, and fully analysed with unanalysed assertions?

Here it is worth elaborating what was said earlier (p. 59) about the *Investigations* discussion of ellipticity. At *PI* 19, 20, Wittgenstein rejects the notion that "slab!" in the builders' language is an elliptical version of the sentence "bring me a slab!" Someone who believed it to be elliptical would hold that the latter sentence says what "slab!" is really used to mean. But if the two expressions mean the same thing, 'why should I not say: "when he says 'Slab!' he means 'Slab!'?"' (*PI* 19). And why say that 'slab!' is a shortened version of "bring me a slab!" when we could have called the latter a lengthened version of the former? (ibid). In a language (L) which contains both sentences and where both are used to accomplish the same thing, there may be grounds for treating "slab!" as an ellipsis. We can make sense out of saying "slab" is elliptical if "bring me a slab!" exhibits a paradigmatic grammatical form in L which the sentence "slab!" falls short of. But in the builders' language, 'slab!' is paradigmatic and "bring me a slab!" does not even occur. Thus there is no room to consider 'slab!' elliptical. The same objection applies to the Tractarian thesis that a sign for a complex is a contraction for its definition if this is taken to means that "R" in the language of *PI* 48 is used as a contraction of a sentence (S) which includes signs used to name simples. But there is another Tractarian doctrine to which this objection does not apply. The doctrine is that in using the sign "R" in connection with a red square a speaker *must* accomplish certain things (for example, making reference to simples) even though his language contains no other signs for their accomplishment. Accordingly, the use of S to analyse what the speaker says by uttering "R" does not require the assumption (combatable by appeal to *PI* 19, 20) that "R" is produced by shortening or abbreviating S. It assumes only that S exhibits more clearly than "R" what the speaker does in saying 'R'. In particular while "R" looks like a name, its analysis would make it clear that red squares are not named (in the Tractarian sense) by the utterance of 'R'. Thus the argument of *PI* 19, 20 refutes the claim that S exhibits the multiplicity of a sentence (a *sign*) in the language of *PI* 48. But it does not refute the more important Tractarian doctrine that it exhibits the multiplicity of a linguistic act performed by uttering the sign "R".

Finally, what about the claim that referring is the use of a sign constituted by a practice like one of the language games rather than a correlation between sign and name established by a projection rule? Let us grant that if we limited ourselves to the data which could be collected by an anthropologist or field linguist concerning the builders' use of "slab" and the coloured square describers' use of "R", it would be very natural to try to explain what it is for a word to refer in terms of what we can see of the behaviour and purposes of the speakers. Grant also that there might be no single thing common to the behaviour and purposes of the speakers who use "slab" and those who use "R". We have still not established that "slab" and "R" are genuine names and we have not discounted the arguments which were supposed to show that the speakers' linguistic activities would be impossible unless a correlation between a genuine name and a simple had been established by a projection rule. If we cannot find examples of the use of such signs and such rules in the speakers' practices, we shall be puzzled by the apparent conflict between their practices and what the arguments for simple symbols purport to establish. But if the arguments for simple symbols cannot be refuted, then they cannot be refuted, and we must learn to live with our puzzlement.

As I have said, the moral of all of this is that the arguments which proceed from the consideration of language games cannot stand alone. Can we find anything short of a direct refutation of the picture theory and its consequences which would be sufficient to support the language game method investigation? All Wittgenstein offers in the discussion under consideration is an enumeration of different methods of analysis and different standards for simplicity and complexity (*PI* 47). If this showed there is no absolute simplicity, we could conclude that simplicity is relative and hence that we must examine specific standards used in specific linguistic activities to see what "simple" can mean. But taken by itself, all the argument of *PI* 47 can show is (as Wittgenstein says) that 'we use the word "composite" (and, therefore, the word "simple") in an enormous number of different and differently related ways' (*PI* 47). This may show that in ordinary language, simplicity and complexity are relative to particular conceptual schemes and methods of description. But the *Tractatus* purports to show that there *must* also be such a thing as *absolute* simplicity, and even though this is doubtless incorrect, I do not see how its incorrectness can be definitively established by means of an enumeration of examples like the ones given at *PI* 47. Wittgenstein's conclusions follow from an examination and a method of philosophizing to which he would not have been entitled had he not already disposed of the picture theory of language.

H

II

THE ABANDONMENT OF THE
PICTURE THEORY

1 THE PROBLEM OF INTENTIONALITY AND THE
SHIPWRECK OF THE PICTURE THEORY

(1.1) My account of the demise of the picture theory is that
Wittgenstein abandoned it because he thought it generated an
insoluble problem which I will call 'the problem of intentionality'. Although this problem is related to issues traditionally
discussed under the rubric of intentionality this is of no particular concern for my discussion which does not purport to represent anything in the tradition outside Wittgenstein's own work.
The label 'problem of intentionality' is only a label and should
not be taken over-seriously.

Let 'p' be the contingent assertion that p is the case. Necessarily

(1) 'p' is true iff it is the case that p, and
(2) 'p' is false iff it is not the case that p.

As already noted, (1) and (2) constitute general conditions for
the adequacy of *any* account of truth. They should not be
treated as special consquences or assumptions which characterize any particular account. The problem is generated when (1)
and (2) are taken together with the assumption that propositions
and the facts which verify them are real individuals. According
to the *Tractatus* propositions are facts, and facts are real individuals which obey the laws of identity. Suppose this is so.
Using "p*" as an abbreviation for "the fact that p is the case" to
signify the individual whose inclusion in reality (the totality of

facts) is asserted by 'p', we may conclude from (1) and (2) that:

(3) No proposition which is not made true by the existence of p* (that is, by the circumstance that reality includes a fact which is identical to p*) can possibly be identical to 'p',

(4) No fact whose existence fails to make 'p' true can possibly be identical to p*,

(5) No proposition which is not falsified by the non-existence of p* (that is, by the circumstance that there is no fact identical to p*) can possibly be identical to 'p',

(6) No fact whose non-existence fails to falsify 'p' can possibly be identical to p*.[1] (3) to (6) characterize internal (essential) features of 'p' and p*.

> A property is internal if it is unthinkable that its object should not possess it. (*TS* 4123).
> An internal property of a fact can also be called a feature of that fact (in the sense in which we speak of facial features, for example). (*TS* 41221.)

Although Wittgenstein appears to have had in mind only the structure of a fact (the way in which its constituents are connected) when he spoke about internal properties (*TS* 4123), (3) to (6) give non-structural properties which must be classified as essential to the facts 'p' and p*. It is unthinkable that the existence of p* should fail to verify 'p' because a fact whose existence does not verify 'p' cannot be p* (4). Whatever is not verified by the existence of p* cannot be 'p' (3). Similar considerations hold with regard to falsification of 'p' by the non-existence of p* (5), (6). Thus it is an internal property essential to the identity of 'p' that it be verified by the existence of p* and falsified by its non-existence, and it is an internal property of p* that its existence verifies and its non-existence falsifies 'p'.[2]

But p* could be the case even if no one ever asserted it and since 'p' is a contingent proposition, there are possible realities in which 'p' is false. So there are possible realities which contain 'p' and not p*, and others which contain p* but do not contain 'p'. Hence

(7) 'p' and p* are existentially independent and, therefore, numerically different individuals.

Notice that we cannot get these results from (1) and (2)

except on the assumption that 'p' and p* are genuine individuals which obey the laws of identity. However, once we make the Tractarian assumption, it follows that although they are numerically different and existentially independent, 'p' and p* are essentially connected in the way specified by (3) to (6). The problem is to explain how it can be an essential property of p* that its existence verifies while its non-existence falsifies 'p' and an essential property of 'p' that it is verified by the existence and falsified by the non-existence of p*, even though 'p' and p* are numerically different and existentially independent individuals (cp. *PI* 94–96; *BB* p. 32). In discussing this I will refer to the kind of connection which is supposed to obtain between the proposition and a possibly non-existent fact as the 'intentionality' of the proposition.[3]

Although the notebooks of 1929–31 and the extracts from them which occur in the *Bemerkungen* (especially *B* section III) show beyond doubt that Wittgenstein was greatly concerned with this problem after his return to Cambridge, it is difficult to determine exactly how much thought he devoted to it while working on the *Tractatus*. However, the *Tractatus* includes everything needed to generate the problem, and some of Wittgenstein's remarks about the picture theory involve the assumption that the intentionality of the proposition is explainable by the theory that a proposition is a picture. The following is an example (*TS* 403):

> A proposition presents a situation to us (*teilt uns eine Sachlage mit*) and so it must be *essentially* connected with that situation.[4]
> And the connection is precisely that it is a logical picture.
> A proposition states something only in so far as it is a picture.

The phrase "logical picture" is redundant; every representational picture is a logical picture according to Wittgenstein (*TS* 218–2181). So Wittgenstein is saying that a proposition could not say anything unless it were essentially connected with the putative fact it presents, and that the connection is essential because the proposition is a picture. His thesis is that the proposition is connected to what it presents as a fact included in reality in the way that a representational picture of X is connected to whatever the picture presents as a feature of X. He assumes that pictures are the kind of thing which can have as essential features their presentation of possibly non-existing features of the subject they represent. Calling a proposition a picture in order to explain its essential connection with a putative fact would seem to represent a possible solution to the problem of intentionality, and if the picture theory was intended to explain what *TS* 403 claims it explains, it would be a serious objection to it to show that it leaves the problem of intentionality unsolved.[5]

In 1929 Wittgenstein wrote that when the element of intention is removed from language 'its whole function is thereby collapsed' (*B* III, 20), and said that 'What is essential to intention . . . is the picture. The picture of what is intended' (*B* III, 21). He illustrated this by comparing what he called 'the picture-view' (*Bild-Auffassung*) to a psychological account of intentionality which he attributed to Russell, Ogden and Richards. The psychological account holds that our calling a thought true is to be explained in terms of three things: the thought, the fact that it is true, and an event which constitutes our recognition of its truth. This last is a psychological occurrence. It is indifferent to Wittgenstein's objection to the theory just what the event is, but he tells us to imagine it as something like the feeling of pleasure or satisfaction which stills hunger (*B* 21). Wittgenstein rejects the theory on the grounds that a fact could produce a psychological feeling of this kind without being the fact that verifies the thought. That is because it is not *essential* to a psychological event of the kind Wittgenstein thought Russell, Ogden and Richards had in mind that it be produced by the fact that the thought is true or the fact which makes it true (*B* 22):[6]

> I believe that Russell's theory leads to the consequence:
> If I give someone a command and what he does makes me happy, then he has executed the command.

The trouble with this is that what makes me happy after I have given a command need not be what was commanded. (I might be forced to give an order which I hoped would not be followed, and then what would satisfy me would be an event which prevents its execution.) To show what is wrong with

Russell's theory, Wittgenstein considers a case in which someone stills my hunger for an apple by hitting me in the stomach
so that I am no longer hungry. If my getting what I desired
consisted in the stilling of my hunger by something, Y, then Y
must be what I desired. That would mean that a thump in the
stomach was the apple I wanted (*B* 22; cp. *PI* 440). Similarly,
if what makes a thought or assertion true is the occurrence of a
psychological event analogous to the stilling of my desire, then
whatever fact produced the psychological event would have to
be said to verify the thought or assertion. If that were true, it
would be an accident if 'p' were verified by p* instead of some
other fact.

The difference between the Russell-Ogden-Richards account
and the 'picture view', says Wittgenstein, is that the latter
treats the verification of a thought as dependent upon an
internal connection between the thought and what verifies it.
The internal connection between thought and verifying fact
is to be explained in terms of the thesis that the thought pictures
the fact. Despite important differences between the Tractarian
exposition of the picture theory and *B* 20–22, these passages
are highly reminiscent of the *Tractatus*. In the *Tractatus* Wittgenstein equated the thought with the proposition (*TS* 3) and
maintained that the essential connection between a thought (or
proposition) and its sense is to be explained by treating thoughts
(propositions) as pictures. In 1929 the picture theory clearly
figured as a putative explanation of intentionality.

(1.2) After Wittgenstein claimed that the picture theory ac-
counted for the internal connection between desire and its
object which Russell and others had failed to explain, he began
to examine the connection between pictures and what they
present. In the course of this investigation (which continued
through the early 1930s up to the completion of the *Blue Book*
and *Zettel*), he developed arguments to show that two existentially independent individuals cannot be internally connected
in the way the picture theory claims they are. My contention
is that his reasons for abandoning the picture theory are to be
found in these arguments. However, before considering them,
we must ask whether they are genuinely relevant to the *Tractatus*. That is because the picture theory which Wittgenstein was
considering as an alternative to the Russell-Ogden-Richards ac-

count differs in important ways from the Tractarian theory. Accordingly, I shall begin by considering these differences in an attempt to show that they do not render the anti-picture theory arguments of the transitional period irrelevant to the *Tractatus*.

(1) The pictures of the Tractarian theory are always assertions or assertive thoughts, while the transitional discussions of intentionality treat pictures as essentially involved in wishes, commands (*B* 20–22), expecting and longing for something (*BB* p. 30), willing (*B* 13), and many other things which are not assertions.[7] The relevance of these to the intentionality of assertions can be established by generalizing the description of the problem of intentionality (see ch. II. 1 (1.1)) to show that Wittgenstein's worries about wishing, commanding, etc., are essentially similar to his worries about the intentionality of assertions. To do this, I use the term 'satisfaction' to take the place of 'truth' in (1) to (6), pp. 102–3, and 'mental act' to take the place of 'proposition'. The rationale for this is as follows. The internal connection which is supposed to hold between a proposition and the fact (if any) which makes it true can be described as a special instance of the connection which is supposed to hold between a mental act and the object whose existence is required for its satisfaction according to all the theories Wittgenstein attacked during his transitional period.

'Mental act' is to be used in connection with such verbs as 'to believe', 'to hope', 'to fear', 'to assert', 'to attempt (try)', 'to think', 'to expect', 'to order', etc., etc., and has to do with *a* use of such words.[8] Such words express 'mental acts' when used in connection with an act, state, or process, ø, such that if X is a ø-er his øing is necessarily the øing *of (that, to, for)* such and such. Asserting is always a mental act because an assertion is always the assertion *of* or *that* such and such. 'Fear' sometimes gives a mental act, and sometimes not. A man can feel anxiety or be afraid without fearing any particular thing, and then his fear is not a mental act. But 'fear' is also used so that X cannot be said to fear unless he fears *something*. In this case, fearing is a mental act. Some mental acts (fear, for example) take different kinds of things as their objects (facts, events, things, etc.). Others (for example, expecting) typically have objects of only one or a few kinds (we generally expect things or events), and others (for example, assertions) are connected with only one kind of object (assertions go with facts). By 'object' here I mean what is given by filling in the blank in the schema 'X øs ——' where øing is a mental act and X is the ø-er. Thus one feature of a mental act is that it always has an object. The other features with which we will be concerned are these:

First, although a mental act always has an object, its object need not actually exist.

Second, something like the law of excluded middle applies to mental acts. A wish must be granted or not granted, come true or fail to come true; a command must either be executed or not executed; an expectation, fulfilled or unfulfilled; an assertion, true or false; a fear or hope, realized or unrealized. This may be expressed by saying that a mental act is always either *satisfied* or *unsatisfied*.[9] The satisfaction of an assertion is its truth; a wish is satisfied if it is granted or comes true; a command if it is executed, etc.

Third, the satisfaction or non-satisfaction of a mental act always depends upon the existence or non-existence of its object. No single account can be given for this dependency. The simplest case is assertion. 'p' is satisfied iff p* exists (that is, iff there is a fact which is identical to p*) and non-satisfied iff p* does not exist. Similarly, if I wish to be given an apple, my wish is satisfied iff an event of the kind : someone giving me an apple occurs, and non-satisfied if no event of that kind occurs. But suppose I order someone to bring it about that p. If it is never the case that p, my command is never satisfied, but its being the case that p does not guarantee its satisfaction. If it is already the case that p, no one will be able to execute my order. Or if the person to whom I give the command brings it about that p even though he did not hear or understand my order, his bringing it about cannot be called an execution of my command.

Fourth, a particular mental act is identified in terms of its object. We do not know a man's wish unless we know what he wishes for; we do not know which assertion he made unless we know what would have to be a fact in order for it to be true, and we do not know what order was given unless we know what was ordered.

Of course, in calling the 'fruitions' or 'fulfilments' of mental acts 'satisfaction', I do not mean to suggest that the satisfaction of a mental act is always satisfying. 'Satisfied' takes the place of 'true', 'executed', 'fulfilled', etc. It is not used to mark any particular psychological state. And I do not mean to suggest that asserting, believing, thinking, fearing, expecting, etc., are all *acts*—things a man does. It is natural to classify asserting as something a man does, but expectation, fear, and hope are more naturally considered states—although Wittgenstein sometimes calls them 'conscious processes' to distinguish them from sensations (*BB* p. 30 f.).

Now let øing be any mental act, and let O be its object. Whenever someone øs—we have an instance of ø. That is to say, when a man wishes, we say he has a wish, when he hopes, that he has a hope, when he orders, that he gives an order, etc. Just as the truth of 'p' depends upon the existence of p* (the proposition is true iff there is a fact which is identical to p*) so, the satisfaction of ø (a wish, expectation, command, or whatever) depends upon the existence of the object of the øing. As noted earlier, it is not true in general that a mental act is satisfied iff its object, O, exists. But we can say that if the non-existence of O does not prevent the satisfaction of a mental act, that act is not the øing of O, and that anything whose existence is not a condition for the satisfaction of the øing of O is not identical to O. If we assume that wishes, expectations, beliefs, attempts, thoughts, fears, etc., and their objects are real individuals which obey the laws of identity (if we assume about mental acts in general what the early Wittgenstein assumed about assertions) then we shall have to say that an instance of ø (a wish, expectation, or whatever) and its object, are existentially independent and numerically different individuals which are internally connected to one another. Thus we can easily generate analogues to the problem about the connection between 'p' and p* from the case of any mental act which is not an assertion.[10]

(2) The second difficulty in applying Wittgenstein's transitional discussions of pictures to the *Tractatus* is that the things the 'picture view' (criticized in *B, BB,* and *UPN*) treats as pictures are not always things of the same kind as Tractarian propositions. For example the pictures (or shadows) discussed in the *Blue Book* are sometimes sentences (signs) and some-

times senses, while Tractarian pictures are signs in use (or uses of signs) which *have* senses (*BB* pp. 31 ff.). But Wittgenstein thought he could show that *no matter what* we think of as a picture there can be no such thing as an internal connection between it and a possibly non-existing object. If Wittgenstein's argument was so general as to apply to *any* picture theory which treats a mental act and its object as real individuals which are existentially independent and numerically different, then it is understandable that he should have little concern over what kind of thing he chose as an example of what a picture theory treats as a picture. If his argument succeeds, it refutes the Tractarian as well as all the other picture theories he considered during the thirties.

(1.3) Here is a characteristic account of what Wittgenstein thought the picture theory could not explain (UPN; cp. *TS* 4023; *B* 16, 29, 30; *PI* 461):

> What is remarkable . . . is that the event is *completely* anticipated in the expectation, so that if it occurs, we need only say *yes* to the expectation—that one can say *'that's* what I expected' and not be take by surprise by reality.

As noted earlier, we identify a mental act by a specification of its object. Thus I do not know what wish a man has until I know what he wishes for, what order a man gave until I know what was ordered, or what assertion a man made until I know what he asserted (what he asserts to be a fact). As a result, as soon as I know what expectation X has, I know what event must occur if his expectation is to be satisfied. If X tells me he expects Ludwig to come into his room and later that what he expected happened, I know what occurred: Ludwig came into X's room. This is what Wittgenstein has in mind when he says the event is completely anticipated.

The reason it is remarkable that the expectation should completely anticipate the event is that there can be so many things about the event which X did not expect. He could be completely surprised by Ludwig's entrance (suppose he flies or crawls in instead of walking), by Ludwig himself (he is oddly dressed, says and does unexpected things), by the room (X expected Ludwig to come to his office and when he got there to wait for him, he was amazed to discover that someone had painted the walls bright green). And even the event itself can be surprising if, for example, Ludwig arrives much sooner or later than X would have thought likely. But no matter how the event transpires, it still satisfies the expectation that Ludwig would come. At the same time, there are any number of events which would be very similar to Ludwig coming into X's room (for example, the arrival of Ludwig's identical twin brother), whose occurrence would not satisfy the expectation. Yet no matter how much like the expected event the non-satisfying event may be, X is entitled to say, 'No, that's not what I expected.' And so, no matter how surprising the satisfying or non-satisfying event may be, it does not take the expectation by surprise (cp. *PI* 461, par. 3).

How are we to explain the ability of a mental act to anticipate completely its object on the assumption that the mental act is one individual thing and its object (if there is one—if the act is satisfied) is another? We cannot say that intentionality is a *relation* which connected the øing of *O* with *O,* for the øing of *O* may be non-satisfied, and then we should have a two-term relation which obtains when there is only one *relatum* for it to connect.

One possibility is that the properties of the mental act determine which properties a thing must have in order to qualify as its object. This kind of explanation sounds like 'because it has such and such shape, size, etc., nothing can fit into this hollow unless *it* has such and such a shape and size and anything of the requisite shape, size, etc., must fit into the hollow' (*B* 33, 34; *Z* 54; *PI* 439). Consider, for example, 'this vase goes with that table because the vase is squat and blue and the table is yellow and very wide', and 'since the trousers are of such and such colour and design, the jacket which goes with them must have the colour . . .' (cp. *Z* 54). And, of course, it is also reminiscent of someone pointing out features of a picture (or a man in a picture) and saying, 'if this is a real man he must look like . . .' and going on to describe his appearance on the basis of the picture (*BB* pp. 31–8; *B* 21, etc.).

We can point to the features of the hollow which determine the shape and size of the solid which fits it and we can explain why a given solid fits it by appeal to its shape and size. But if we try to do the same thing with a mental act and its object, we encounter difficulties. If a mental act is an individual, a specification of the kind of mental act it is (wish, command, assertion, etc.), the person whose mental act it is, the time at which the person asserts, expects, etc., and the object of the act should serve to identify it uniquely. If intentionality is an *essential* property its explanation should lie in what is given by a description of the form 'the øing of O by X at time t', for it is difficult to see how anything else which might be said about the mental act could be essential to it. But even the description 'the øing of O by X at t' mentions things which appear not to bear on the internal connection between O and the øing of O. It should make no difference if the expectation had been someone else's and it could just as well have occurred at a different time. Ludwig's arrival should satisfy Y's expectation that he will arrive just as well as X's, and the event he expects should be no different from the event he would have expected had he begun to expect a bit earlier or later. (Assume that X and Y identify the same man as Ludwig.) If we subtract from the expectation all of the non-essential features (without which it could still have been the same expectation) and all of the essential features (for example, its being X's expectation at time t) which have nothing to do with the identity of the event its satisfaction requires, we are left with the fact that it is the expectation that Ludwig will arrive.

From the fact that a hollow has such and such shape and size, we can infer some things (for example, shape and size) that must be true of the solid that fits it. What must be true of an event if it is to satisfy X's expectation that Ludwig will arrive? We have already seen that it is indifferent how Ludwig arrives, when he arrives, what the room is like when he arrives, etc., etc. And it is equally indifferent whether the event delights or depresses X, what consequences it has or fails to have, what reason Ludwig has for coming, etc. Subtracting all of these, the only thing to require of the event would seem to be that it can be truly described as Ludwig's arrival (Z 54):

> It seems as though the expectation and the fact satisfying the expectation fitted together somehow. Now one would like to describe an expectation and a fact which fit together to see what their agreement consists in. Here one thinks at once of

the fitting of a solid into a hollow. But when one wants to describe these two, he sees that to the extent that they fit, a single description holds for both.

'A single description holds for both' sounds like an absurdity of the following kind. A murder is committed. A detective says the butler did it. When asked what proves this he says that since the murder was committed by the murderer, and since the butler is the murderer, the butler must have done it; all other facts about the crime and the butler are irrelevant. But the apparent absurdity was put forth in all seriousness by G. E. Moore immediately before Wittgenstein's arrival at Cambridge. In the 1910 lectures which comprise *Some Main Problems of Philosophy* Moore says that if someone asserts or believes lions exist, the universe contains at least one fact, the proposition or belief, 'lions exist'. If it is true, says Moore, there must be another fact in the universe—the fact that makes the proposition or belief true. And what fact is that?

> Every true belief has to one fact and one fact only, this peculiar relation namely that we do use and have to use the *name* of the fact in *naming* the belief. So that we might say: *The* fact to which a belief refers is always *the* fact which has the *same name* as that which we have to use in naming the belief. (*Some Main Problems of Philosophy*, p. 279.)

This would be an absurdity if it were supposed to *explain* what it is about the fact that lions exist which makes it satisfy the proposition 'lions exist'. But we might ask what it is about the fact and the proposition which makes possible their characterization by a single description. Wittgenstein devoted considerable attention to two accounts of intentionality which purport to answer this.

(1.4) One explanation would be that p* is the sense of the proposition 'p' with something (for example, truth or reality) added to it. Meinong, Moore, and Johnson offer accounts of this kind.[11] Surprisingly the *Tractatus,* though generally anti-Meinongian, includes one (atypical) passage which carries a suggestion of this kind. *TS* 313 says the sense of a proposition (and hence a possible fact) is something which lies outside the proposition. What a proposition projects is its sense, and in the proposition, 'what is projected is not ... included, its possibility is'. On the basis of this, a sense could be taken to be a fact made possible but not brought into reality by asserting. This conjures up the picture of a sense as a shadowy being capable of becoming a full-fledged fact but subsisting somehow even if the proposition remains unsatisfied.[12]

Although this occult account is not required by the *Tractatus* theory, Wittgenstein criticized it at length in unpublished notebooks of 1930–1, the *Blue Book,* and *Zettel,* and also discussed it briefly in the *Investigations.* Consider the related theory that the description which fills in the schemas 'X expected ——' and 'What fulfilled X's expectation was ——' signifies one and the same event which is unreal while it is being expected but takes on reality when the expectation is satisfied (*BB* p. 37). Wittgenstein urges us to

> shake off this comparison: a man makes his appearance—
> an event makes its appearance. As if an event even now stood in
> readiness before the door of reality waiting to make its
> appearance in reality—like coming into a room (Z 59).
> Reality is not a property still missing in what is expected
> which accedes to it when one's expectation comes about—
> Nor is reality like the daylight that things need in order to
> acquire colour, when they are already there, as it were,
> colourless in the dark. (Z 60; cp. *BB* pp. 37 ff.)

Even though we do say of an event that *it* is what we expected (*PI* 428, 455, 94–96), the comparison between a man who appears and an event which occurs is surely incorrect. The man who comes into the room was a man before he came in, but an event which does not occur and a putative fact which is not a fact are nothing at all. Suppose I see someone pointing a gun and expect a report (*PI* 442). If the report I expect exists or subsists in my expectation before the gun goes off does it include the noise produced when the gun is actually fired? If so, the noise was there in my expectation and, therefore, the report I expected made a noise—was a real report. If not, the event which occurs when the gun goes off cannot be what I expected for it is noisy while the report that subsisted in my expectation was not. Thus either an unsatisfied expectation is impossible because the object of an expectation is always a real event, or else a satisfied expectation is impossible because what occurs is always different from what was expected (*PI* 442).

(1.5) The second and most important account of intentionality which Wittgenstein considered is the 'picture view'. It is necessarily the case that if something, X, is a representational picture of something, Y, then it is Y's picture. Similarly, it is necessarily the case that what pictures Y as having a certain feature is a correct picture only if Y has the feature in question, and is incorrect if Y does not have the feature. Furthermore, X (the picture of Y) and Y are existentially independent and numerically different individuals, both of which may be identified by using the same locution. X is called 'the picture of Y' and Y is called 'Y'. We wanted to know why the same phrase ('Ludwig coming into the room') could be used to identify the expectation and the event, and to explain the connection between the two. The answer suggested by the facts just noted about Y and Y's picture is that the expectation is a picture of the event—or a picture which represents reality as containing the event (in the way that the picture which represents Y can show Y as containing something which Y in fact may not have). This is the essence of the Tractarian picture theory as well as the somewhat different picture theories Wittgenstein considered during the transitional period.

Wittgenstein's longest published criticism of this is in the *Blue Book* (*BB* p. 31):

> How can one think what is not the case? If I think that King's College is on fire when it is not on fire, the fact of its being on fire does not exist. Then how can I think it? How can we hang a thief who doesn't exist?

When the college is not on fire the fact that it is on fire does not exist at all—it need not even 'exist' in the form of unconnected constituents of a fact, because (contrary to the *Tractatus*) a fact is not a complex of elements (see ch. II.2).

> We may now be inclined to say: 'As the fact which would make our thought true if it existed does not always exist, it is not the *fact* which we think.' (*BB* p. 31.)
> The next step we are inclined to take is to think that as the object of our thought isn't the fact it is the shadow of the fact.

There are different names for this shadow, e.g., 'proposition',
'sense of the sentence'. (*BB* p. 32)

As noted earlier, a *Tractatus* picture is not the sense of a sentence; it is a thought or proposition which *has* a sense. However,
the argument Wittgenstein directs against the shadow theory is
intended to establish that pictures in general are not internally
connected to their subjects or to features they show their subjects as having. If this argument succeeds it is as fatal to the
Tractarian picture theory as the shadow theory because both
assume that a picture is internally connected to what it shows
(*BB* p. 32):

> The question now is: 'How can something be the shadow of a
> fact which doesn't exist?' I can express our trouble in a
> different way by asking: 'How can we know what the
> shadow is a shadow of?'—The shadow would be some sort of
> portrait; and, therefore, I can restate our problem by
> asking: What makes a portrait a portrait of Mr. N?

The switch from shadow to portrait is probably due to the
consideration that there cannot be a shadow without an existing thing to cast it. Since what a man believes need not be a
fact, we could not treat a belief as a shadow unless we thought
there could be shadows with nothing to cast them. But a
portrait can include non-existent putative features of its subject,
and we can have portraits of non-existent subjects (for example,
a portrait painted from another picture of a man who perishes
before the portrait is completed).

'An obvious and correct answer to the question, "What makes
a portrait of so-and-so?" is that it is the *intention*' (*BB* p. 32).
The correctness of this answer shows what is wrong with the
picture theory. It is necessarily and trivially true that under the
description 'portrait of Y', X is a portrait of Y. That is, a man
who thinks of X as a portrait of Y thinks of X as a portrait of
Y. But if the truth of the description 'X is a portrait of Y'
depends upon whether or not X is so intended or used, then
even if X is intended as a picture of Y, its being a picture of Y
is a contingent, not a necessary or essential fact about X. What
is used and intended as a picture of Y could also have been
used as a picture of someone else, or as a genre picture (hence

as a picture which does not represent any particular person), as part of a code by which the features are interpreted as parts of a map or a message, etc., etc. (*BB* pp. 32–7). Thus if the belief that King's College is on fire were really a picture, it would not be *internally* connected with the fact (it there is one) that King's College is on fire.[13]

But couldn't there be something whose features were such that it *had* to be a picture of something—which could not fail to be a picture, and a picture of that very thing? If so, it would be a picture of such and such no matter whether it was so used or intended. The only even vaguely plausible candidate for such a picture would be one thing which resembled another so closely that they could easily be mistaken for one another (*BB* p. 32):

> It is quite clear, however, that similarity does not
> constitute our idea of a portrait; for it is in the essence of
> this idea that it should make sense to talk of a good or a bad
> portrait, it is essential that the shadow should be capable of
> representing things as in fact they are not.

On the other hand, if X does not resemble Y (if they have different features), our characterization of X as the picture of Y would require the application of a method of comparison which would make sense of our characterization by determining the grounds on which X will be called an accurate or inaccurate picture of Y. But then it is only contingently true that X pictures Y; if we can apply a method of comparison to X we can also refrain from applying it.

> Here my thought is: if someone could see the expectation
> itself—he would have to see *what* is being expected. (But in
> such a way that it doesn't require ... a method of projection,
> a method of comparison in order to pass from what he sees
> to the fact that is expected.) (*Z* 56.)

The upshot of the *Blue Book* discussion is that no picture can be so connected with the expected fact, and therefore that nothing is to be accomplished by calling the expectation a picture.

The early Wittgenstein realized it would not serve his purposes to treat sentences as pictures because the connection between a sentence and its sense depends upon contingent facts about how the sentence is used. Because of this, he treated the proposition (symbol) as a picture interposed, as it were, between the sentence and reality. But this (as well as the interposition of the sense of the sentence between sentence and fact which is characteristic of the 'shadow theory' criticized in the *Blue Book*) only pushed 'the question one step farther back' (*BB* p. 36). If the proposition or the sense were a real picture, its connection with the expected or asserted fact would still be contingent upon a use or intended use which does not reside within the picture. Thus (*BB* p. 37; cp. Moore, *Philosophical Papers*, p. 260; *PI* 389):

> the interpolation of a shadow between the sentence and
> reality loses all point. For now the sentence itself can serve as
> such a shadow. The sentence is . . . a picture which hasn't
> the slightest similarity with what it represents.

(1.6)   To recapitulate: Let us use dot quotation marks to indicate a mental act. For example, ˙p˙ is any mental act (for example, an assertion, or a wish, etc.) whose satisfaction depends upon its being the case that p. The *Tractatus* holds that propositions are facts and that facts are numerically different real individuals. Thus if 'p' is true, 'p' and p* are two facts, either of which could occur in a reality which does not contain the other. After his return to Cambridge, Wittgenstein generalized this account to include other mental acts besides assertion. It is essentially and not just accidentally the case that p* is the fact which figures in the satisfaction of ˙p˙. On the assumption that ˙p˙ and p* are real individuals, Wittgenstein had to find the features of ˙p˙ and p* in virtue of which they are internally connected. The only relevant feature appeared to be that the same locution is used to identify the mental act and the fact. For example, if Ludwig's arrival satisfies someone's expectation we use the locution 'Ludwig's arrival' to say what he expected and also to say what happened to fulfil his expectation.

One putative explanation for this was the Meinong-Moore-Johnson sort of account. It held that the expectation is or includes an unreal fact which has the same name or identifying description as the fact (if it exists) which satisfies the expectation. Thus 'p*' refers to something identical to the shadowy fact referred to by "p" except that p* has one property which the shadowy fact lacks—reality.[14] Wittgenstein rejected this account on the grounds that an unreal fact is no fact at all.

In view of this, the only explanation left which seemed feasible involved the notion that 'p' is a picture of a putative fact, or a representation of reality which shows it as including a putative fact. But if 'p' were a picture, its connection with p* would be accidental and not essential.

Wittgenstein believed that philosophers (including his early self) were inclined to postulate such entities as Tractarian propositions and Moore-Johnsonian propositions (senses of sentences) as pictures which are *essentially* connected to what they represent or present. But since no picture is internally connected with its subject, he suggested that if we wish to imagine that mental acts include pictures, we might just as well call the sentence with which an assertion is made, an expectation expressed, etc., a picture, even though the sentence used to say that such and such is the case need not have been so used and cannot be thought to be internally connected with what is a fact in case it is true.

2 THE INTENTIONALITY OF ASSERTIONS

(2.1) In late 1930 or early 1931 Wittgenstein developed the germ of an account of intentionality much like that of his later period.

> What is remarkable is that the event is *completely* anticipated in the expectation, so that if it occurs, we need only say *yes* to the expectation. (UPN *circa* 1930)
> ... the explanation for this appears always to be that the language cannot grasp (*fassen*) any more of reality than it could express ahead of time in the expectation. That is: that the language sees no more of reality than what it itself comprehends (*versteht*), and that is what has already been expressed in the expectation. For the language has not described an expectation and then a fact which somehow fits it. (As one can describe a table and then a vase that suits it.)

Rather, it *was* the expectation (for the expression of the thought is the thought; the thought is the expression of the thought) and now it is fulfilled. In the expectation, the language has already said all it could say. (UPN *circa* 1930, cp. *B* III, 30, 33.)

The idea that language grasps no more of reality than it could have expressed ahead of time in the expectation amounts to this: we use the same words to explain what we expect as we use to describe an event if the event is what we expected. 'The expectation completely anticipates the event' is really a misleading way of registering the commonplace that if I expect what is called 'an explosion' and what happens is truly described as an explosion, then what happens is what I expected: whatever is called an explosion is called an explosion. There is a necessary connection, but it is not a connection between a mental entity (a thing, state, or process called 'the expectation of an explosion') and an event. 'It is in language that an expectation and its fulfilment make contact' (*PI* 445; cp. *PI* 429). The internal connection holds between the statements 'I expect an explosion' and 'That was an explosion'—it holds in virtue of the speaker's use of the word "explosion".

But what about the connection between the event (what we describe as an explosion) and the expectation (what is expressed by the words "I expect an explosion")? Wittgenstein provides for the following answer:

(1) Although certain feelings, memories, mental images, states, etc., as well as certain behaviour may and generally do occur when a man expects something, these are not *essentially* connected with the event (if there is one) which occurs later on, and

(2) When I am expecting an explosion which has not yet occurred, there is no event yet for anything to be connected with, internally or externally.

What is it for a man to expect an explosion? It could be his using the sentence "I expect an explosion", and in the unpublished passage I cited, Wittgenstein appears to equate the expectation with the expression. But it could also be equated with his pacing up and down, thinking of loud noises, feeling anxious, tying down his breakables to prevent damage, etc.

Such things are characteristic of an expectation but a man could do exactly the same things without expecting an explosion (he expects something else which makes loud noises and breaks breakables) or without expecting anything at all (the man goes through a daily routine of tying things down and thinks of loud noises, feels uneasy, etc., even though he doesn't expect anything to happen). And a man who expected an explosion would not have to exhibit this behaviour or have these thoughts and feelings; I now expect that there will be an election in 1980, but spend no time thinking about it or preparing for it.[15] In addition to the expression "I expect that . . .", there is nothing more, Wittgenstein held, except behaviour, feelings, thoughts, etc. These include genuine mental states and events, but since any one of them could occur in the absence of the expectation, their connection (if any) with the event which is later said to satisfy the expectation cannot explain the intentionality of the expectation (*BB* pp. 22, 29 f. *PI* 444, 582–586).

On the other hand, if we call the speaker's expression (e.g. his use of the words "I expect such and such to happen") his expectation, as Wittgenstein did up to some time during the completion of part I of the *Investigations,* then an explanation of intentionality calls for nothing more than an account of the use of the words by which the expectation is expressed and the satisfying event described. That is to say that we require an account of how the man who expected the explosion uses the word "explosion" in connection with a certain kind of event. But here again, we have only contingent facts to account for and not necessary connections. It is necessarily true that when used in connection with explosions, the sign "explosion" is used in connection with explosions. That is the only 'internal connection' we need to deal with and it is a trivial one. The genuine questions we need to answer are questions about how a man identifies an event as an explosion, how he learned to use and understand the sign, etc., and the answers to these questions are contingent. It is not a necessary truth that English speakers use particular signs in the way they do. Difficult though a procedure for using signs may be to understand, the problems involved in this kind of study are quite different from the problem of intentionality, for intentionality seemed to call for a necessary connection between a mental act and a possibly non-existing object, not a contingent connection between a sign and what it is used to talk about.

Finally, notice what happens on this kind of account to the idea that a mental act anticipates an event or a fact. Although there can be no question as to whether what is truly called an explosion satisfies the expectation of an explosion, there can be serious question over whether what happens really is an explosion. A man who thought his expectation had been satisfied could be wrong if, for example, what he took to be an explosion was really a thunderclap which sounded like an explosion. What sort of anticipation is there if this kind of mistake is possible?

A man who knows how to use the word "explosion" should know something about what an explosion is like, how it differs from other kinds of events, and how to tell if what happened was an explosion or something else. The anticipating is, therefore, done by the man and not by his expectation; it is the man who knows what he thinks will happen and knows what to look for to find out if it did happen. But this does not constitute an ironclad connection between the expecting and the event, for the man may make mistakes. If we want to talk about any sort of anticipation in addition to this, all that is left is the fact that before the event occurs (that is, before anything happens), the word "explosion" is ready to be used (rightly or wrongly) to describe what finally does happen.

In the *Blue Book,* Wittgenstein offered the same kind of account of the connection between a belief or assertion and a putative fact (*BB* p. 37):

If we keep in mind the possibility of a picture which, though correct, has no similarity with its object, the interpolation of a shadow between the sentence and reality loses all point. For now the sentence itself can serve as such a shadow. The sentence is just such a picture which hasn't the slightest resemblance with what it represents. If we were doubtful about how the sentence 'King's College is on fire' can be a picture of King's College on fire, we need only ask ourselves: 'how should we explain what the sentence means?' Such an explanation might consist of ostensive definitions. We should

say, e.g., 'this is King's College' and 'this is a fire' (pointing to
a fire). This shows you the way in which words and things
may be connected.

The belief or assertion is treated here as a use of the sentence
"King's College is on fire" to say something about a college.
The question 'how can a mental act be internally connected to
an existentially independent and numerically different fact?'
gives way to the question 'how can this sentence be used to say
of a college that it is on fire?' The connection between the
sentence and the college is to be explained in terms of the
use of "King's College", and the connection between this sign
and that college is contingent. Similarly, it is a contingent and
not a necessary truth that the sign "fire" is available for use to
describe colleges as on fire. To explain the connection could be,
for example, to explain how ostensive training enables a man
to employ the words in the way he does, and to explain the
practice or practices which he engages in when he employs
them.

(2.2) So far, we have seen that Wittgenstein's account involves replacing the question 'how can an assertion be internally
connected with a possibly non-existent fact?' with the question
'how does a speaker use such and such a sign to say so and so?'
But what about the fact (for example, that King's College is on
fire) which he uses the sentence to assert? If the assertion is
true, then according to the *Tractatus*, the fact that King's
College is on fire is a real individual, a member of the collection
of facts which constitutes reality. After his return to Cambridge,
Wittgenstein gave up this doctrine in favour of the kind of
account of facts now associated with Strawson.[16]

> A complex is not a fact. For I can say of a complex, e.g.,
> that it moves from this place to another, but not of a fact.
> Instead, that this complex is now to be found here is a fact.
> Thus in English one can say 'The three vases form an
> ornament in this room' or . . . 'it is a fact that in this room
> . . .' and that means the same as 'The arrangement (the
> complex) of the three vases is to be found in this room.'
>   I call the flower, the house, the constellation, complexes—
> of petals, of bricks, of stars. That this constellation is here
> can, of course, be expressed by a proposition in which only its

stars are mentioned, and the word 'constellation' or the name of the constellation do not occur. But that is all that one can say of the relation between complex and fact. (UPN 1931, cp. *B* pp. 301–3).

The relation between complex and fact, Wittgenstein holds, is, for example, that "it is a fact that there is a . . . in such and such a place" (where the dots are filled in by the name or description of a complex) can be used in place of "there is a . . . in such and such a place". What is said to exist and to occupy the place is not the fact, but the complex. The substitutability of "it is a fact that . . ." for "there is a . . ." does not mean that facts *are* complexes. What can be said of a complex (for example, that it is a collection of parts, that it moves from place to place, that it was put together at such and such a time, and destroyed at such and such another time) cannot be said of a fact. The reason we can substitute the fact locution for the locution "there is a . . ." is simply that its being a fact (the case) that a complex is in a certain place amounts to nothing more than the occupation of that place by the complex.

This raises doubts about the significance of Wittgenstein's early dictum that the world is a collection of facts and not of things (*TS* 11, 12). It would make sense to say that the world consists of complexes and not simple things. That would mean that simples occur only in combination and never singly. That this marks a distinction is shown by considering that a world which contains chairs (complexes made of backs, legs, and seats) is different from a world which contains only disconnected parts. But a complex is not a fact, and so if the dictum of *TS* 11, 12 means anything, it cannot just mean that the world contains complex things. Since 'it is a fact that X is to be found at place P' means that X (and not the fact that X is at P) is to be found at P, it is difficult to see what it could mean to say that facts and not things are to be found in the world.

> One can . . . point to a constellation and say: 'This constellation consists entirely of parts with which I'm already familiar'; but one cannot 'point to a fact' and say this. I cannot say, pointing to something with my finger: 'Look at this fact.' For then the other person can ask 'which fact?' and the answer must be a proposition which

expresses the fact. It cannot be something like the response 'this one, here' which can be given in answer to the question 'which flower do you mean?' The expression 'to describe a fact' or 'the description of a fact' is misleading if applied to the statement (*Aussage*) which asserts the obtaining of the fact, for it sounds too much like 'to describe an animal that I have seen'.

Of course, one does also talk of 'pointing out a fact' but that always means 'point out the fact that . . .'. Whereas 'to point out a flower' does not mean pointing out that this blossom sits on this stalk. . . . Nor can it mean pointing to the fact that this flower stands there. To point out a fact means to maintain, to assert something. To point out a flower does not mean that. (UPN 1931, cp. *B* pp. 301–3.)

This assumes that facts are always expressed by assertions or by phrases (for example, of the form 'that such and such is the case') used to report an assertion in indirect discourse.[17] If pointing to, pointing out, mentioning, or describing a fact *always* means asserting that such and such is the case or reporting what someone has asserted or could assert, we can give an account of 'fact-giving' locutions without assuming that facts are real entities. First of all, the word 'fact' can be eliminated from the locutions in which it occurs. For example, 'I believe the fact that King's College is on fire' 'is just a clumsy expression for saying I believe that the college is on fire' (*BB* p. 32). 'The fact is (it is a fact) that such and such is the case' can be replaced with 'such and such is the case'; 'if it were a fact that such and such . . .' with 'if such and such . . .', etc. This would show that 'fact' need not refer to any entity above and beyond those referred to by a sentence used to assert that such and such is the case without the word 'fact'. What about fact-giving locutions which do not contain the word 'fact'? If expressions of facts are always assertions or indirect discourse reports of assertions, then to express a fact is to make or report an assertion about entities which are not facts. If an assertion (for example, 'King's College is on fire') is true, there must be a thing called King's College, and there must be flames, heat, smoke, etc., but none of these are facts. A fire at the college requires no additional entity called a fact. Nor can we say that the complex constituted by the parts of the college or the college and the flames is a fact. This complex is a college on fire, not the fact that a college is on fire.

Austin points out that there are a great many fact locutions in addition to assertions and 'that . . .' clauses used in indirect discourse. Among them are such locutions as 'the collapse of the Germans' which Austin says expresses what was and is a fact.[18] If so, Wittgenstein's assumption that *all* fact-giving locutions make or report assertions is false. However, this wouldn't itself show that fact-expressing locutions cannot in general be eliminated in favour of locutions which mention only persons, places, things, events, etc., etc. If they can, we can give a full inventory of the contents of the universe without mentioning facts. Our inventory must, of course, state the facts. But that only means that the descriptions in our inventory must be true. Fortunately, my present purpose of introducing Wittgenstein's later account of intentionality does not require a resolution of this issue between Wittgenstein and Austin.

I introduced the problem of intentionality by noting that (1) 'p' is true iff it is the case that p, and (2) 'p' is false iff it is not the case that p. On the assumption that 'p' is one fact and p* another and that facts are real individuals, we had to explain how 'p' could be necessarily connected with a possibly non-existent fact, p*. On Wittgenstein's later account, this problem quite literally dissolves. Let 'p' be the assertion 'King's College is on fire'. 'It is the case that King's College is on fire' is equivalent to 'King's College is on fire' and so (1) is equivalent to the truism (1′) ('King's College is on fire' is true) iff King's College is on fire. Similarly, (2) is equivalent to the truism that (2′) ('King's College is on fire' is false) iff King's College is not on fire. These are truths whose explanation requires no postulation of essentially connected but existentially independent entities.

It might be objected that 'p' and p* must be distinguishable individuals because the one can exist without the other. But " 'p' exists' simply means that someone has used a sentence to assert that p is the case, and "p* exists" simply means that things are as the speaker who makes the assertion says they are. Thus " 'p' could exist even if p* did not" means only that a man who says that p is the case could be wrong and "p* could exist even if 'p' did not" means that things could be as no one asserts them to be.

(2.3) The later account of intentionality makes it impossible to present a correspondence theory which amounts to more than the trivial thesis that 'p' is true iff p. For example, if we say that 'King's College is on fire' is true because reality contains the fact that King's College is on fire, the most this could mean is that 'King's College is on fire' is true because King's College is on fire. We cannot say that to verify the assertion is to discover the fact that King's College is on fire unless we mean by this that the assertion that the college is burning is verified by the discovery that the college is burning. The existence of a burning college makes the assertion true, but a burning college is not a fact. Thus the appeal to facts loses the explanatory value it was intended to have in traditional correspondence theories like the Tractarian theory.

What then does "true" mean if " 'p' is true" cannot be informatively analysed in terms of correspondence? The later Wittgenstein has very little to say about this—even in *On Certainty*, to whose subject a discussion of truth would surely seem relevant—and little of what he does say applies specifically to common or garden assertions of the kind we are used to classifying as contingent. He appears to be suggesting an answer to the question 'what does "true" mean?' in the following passages:

> For what does a proposition's *'being true'* mean?
> 'p' is true = p. (That is the answer.)
> (*RFM* p. 50, cp. *PI* 136.)
> 'p' is false = not-p. (*PI* 136.)

Notice that Wittgenstein sets up an equation and not merely an equivalence between 'p' and ' 'p' true', 'not-p' and ' 'p' is false'. I take it that this is intended to make it emphatic that ' "p" is true' says no more than 'p', and ' 'p' is false', no more than '-p'. The doctrine that 'is true' adds nothing to the meaning of an assertion to which it is added provides a suitably unmysterious explanation of why 'p' is true iff p. If 'it is the case that p' says the same thing as 'p', it also provides a suitably trivial doctrine to replace the idea that the truth value of 'p' depends upon the existence or non-existence of the fact to which 'p' is essentially connected.

But isn't the truth of a proposition a *reason* for affirming it? Suppose I want to convince someone of something. Mightn't I decide to use 'p' instead of 'q' as a premise on the grounds that 'p' is true, while 'q' is false and I'd be caught up on that if I used 'q'? Surely the truth of 'p' couldn't be a reason for asserting it if 'p' and ' 'p' is true' mean the same thing. This objection is spurious. The reason I would do better using 'snow is cold' as a premise than 'snow is hot' is that snow *is* cold, and that is what someone would find out if he checked my premise. The assertion ' 'snow is cold' is true' gives no further reason for asserting that snow is cold.

But all the same, we do want an account of the difference between true and false propositions, and the Tractarian version of the correspondence theory did give us one. I do not think the later Wittgenstein did, and it is far from clear that he intended to do so.

The equation of 'p' and ' 'p' is true' occurs in *PI* in a discussion of the definition 'a proposition is whatever can be true or false' (*PI* 136). Setting aside the characterization of propositions (here I think Wittgenstein has in mind a class of sentences collected on the basis of what is done with them) by appeal to rules for sentence formation in a given language, Wittgenstein observes that the notions 'true' and 'false' are relevant to the characterization of propositions in terms of the use of signs in a language game. 'The use of the words "true" and "false" may be among the constituent parts of this game' (ibid). He compares explaining what a proposition is in this way to characterizing the king as what can be checked in chess. Although Wittgenstein does not extend the analogy in this direction, it is worth noting how the notion of checking depends upon the game of chess. If the word "check" were also used in connection with games which differed from chess as much as formal logic differs from various ordinary linguistic activities which involve the words "true" and "false", the word should not mean exactly the same thing in connection with one game as in connection with another. An explanation of checking in a given game would involve an explanation of that game. Whether we could usefully give a general characterization of checking would depend upon how the games resembled one another, and what bearing their resemblances had on the purposes to be served by the general account. I think the position with regard to 'true' and 'false' in Wittgenstein's later theorizing is roughly analogous to this, and that disanalogies between distinct games like chess and distinguishable areas of linguistic activity prevented Wittgenstein from offering a general theory of truth.

The claim that 'p' is true = p is given in the *Remarks* in answer to the question 'what is called a true proposition in Russell's system?' (*RFM* p. 50).[19] Wittgenstein suggests that since 'p' is true = p, and since this tells us 'what a proposition's *"being true"* means',

> we want to ask something like: under what circumstances do we assert a proposition? Or: how is the assertion of the proposition used in the language game? And 'the assertion of the proposition' is here contrasted with the utterance of the sentence, e.g., as practice in elocution,—or as *part* of another proposition, and so on.
>
> If, then, we ask in this sense: 'Under what circumstances is a proposition asserted in Russell's game?' the answer is: at the end of one of his proofs, or as a 'fundamental law'. ... There is no other way in this system of employing asserted propositions in Russell's symbolism (*RFM* 1/Appendix 6).

This provides a way of answering the question about what sets a true assertion off from a false assertion in Russell's system: a sentence which is true is one we are entitled to mark with an assertion sign, one which the system allows us to maintain and use in arguments to deduce further assertions. The system itself tells us what credentials a sentence must have in order to be maintained and used in this way: the sentence must be one of the axioms Russell provides at the outset, or it must be obtainable by means of the transformations which Russell's rules allow for. And so a true proposition in Russell's system is a sentence which can be certified by means of the procedures which count as certification within the system; a false proposition is one whose denial can be so certified (*RFM* p. 50).

An application of this account to assertions which fall out-side Russell's system is suggested by the following (*RFM* p. 50):

> 'But may there not be true propositions which are written
> in this symbolism but are not provable in Russell's system?'
> —'True propositions' hence propositions which are true in
> another system, i.e., can rightly be asserted in another game.
> Certainly, why should there not be such propositions, or
> rather: why should not propositions—of physics, e.g.,—be
> written in Russell's symbolism? The question is quite analogous
> to: Can there be true propositions in the language of Euclid,
> which are not provable in his system, but are true?—Why,
> there are even propositions which are provable in Euclid's
> system, but are *false* in another system.—May not triangles be
> —in another system—similar (*very* similar) which do not
> have equal angles?—'But that's just a joke! For in that case
> they are not "similar" to one another in the same sense!'—
> Of course not, and a proposition which cannot be proved in
> Russell's system is 'true' or 'false' in a different sense from a
> proposition in *Principia Mathematica*.

It would seem that a generalization of Wittgenstein's re-marks about truth in a formal system would involve the notion of more or less discrete areas of linguistic activity in which a speaker can be said to assert, state, believe, etc. If we are to explain what it is for an utterance to be true in Russell's system in terms of the conditions a user of the system must meet to put forth and maintain an utterance as an assertion, an account of the truth of an ordinary language assertion should require our locating areas of linguistic activity in which the appropriate utterances can occur, and finding features of these activities which play the kind of role in justifying the assertion played by the features of *PM* to which we appeal to explain when a proposition is to be certified or rejected for assertion. An answer to the question when a proposition can be asserted and maintained in a particular department of ordinary langu-age would constitute an account of what it is for a proposition to be true in that department of language. (In speaking of 'maintaining' I have in mind the contrast between those pro-positions which can stand in the face of tests, questions, objec-tions, etc., and those which must be rejected on testing. For example, a visitor who saw Claremont, California, only during the winter might be entitled to assert that it has little smog, but he could not maintain his claim against the evidence which summer brings.)

I think the above, together with the assumption that there are importantly different departments of language use, underlies a very late criticism of the Tractarian view that truth is the agreement of a proposition with reality (*OC* 203):

> If everything speaks *for* an hypothesis and nothing against
> it, is it objectively *certain*? One can *call* it that. But does
> it *necessarily* agree with the world of facts? At the very best
> it shows us what 'agreement' means. . . . What does this
> agreement consist in if not in the fact that what is evidence
> in these language games speaks for our proposition?
> (*Tractatus Logico-Philosophicus*)

In the *Tractatus*, 'agreement with reality' is treated as a single notion to explain what makes each true utterance true regardless of what kind of utterance it is and how (if at all) it is actually confirmed. If a Tractarian concerned himself with actual methods of verification (for example, in the various sciences, in history, etc.) he would hold that what makes a procedure a sound method of verification or confirmation is that its correct application reliably indicates whether the tested propositions agree with reality. In *On Certainty,* Wittgenstein no longer thinks 'agreement' can be a single, independent notion whose meaning can be fixed apart from a consideration of methods of confirmation or verification. If the phrase 'agreement with reality' meant anything, its meaning would be constituted in different ways by the verification and confirmation procedures which figure in various linguistic activities involving assertions. Thus there is no room for a single notion which can have the explanatory use that 'agreement' was supposed to have in the *Tractatus*.

Wittgenstein's remark that a proposition which cannot be proved in Russell's system is 'true' or 'false' in a different sense from a proposition which belongs to the *PM* system is to be interpreted in connection with the remark that such propositions belong to different 'games'. Compare the notion of making a true assertion or showing that an assertion is true to the notion of making a winning move or winning in a game.[20] We can say what it is to make a winning move in a particular game (chess, for example), but not for games in general. For example, an explanation of what it is to checkmate an opponent's king explains what it is to win in chess, but not in draughts or baseball. The explanation of winning as scoring the highest number of points applies to a great many (though by no means to all) games, but what it is to score a point is determined by each game in which points are scored. We've seen that the analogy appears to be that what is to be true in *PM* is different from what it is to be true in another system. But at the same time, a man who wins at chess has won a game just as surely as a man who wins at draughts or at tennis. Thus we can say of a man who won one game of draughts, one chess game, and one tennis game, that he won three games. It would not do to object that in view of the differences between winning at chess, draughts, and tennis, it is misleading to call all of the man's accomplishments 'wins'. Consider the scoring of the decathlon in the Olympic Games. It is crucial that we be able to say the same kind of thing about truth. If 'true' meant something *completely* different in connection, for example, with empirical and legal assertions, it would be impossible to have a valid argument showing that a man should pay damages by premises stating what he did together with statements of common law precedent. An argument is valid only if its conclusion can't fail to be true if its premises are true. How should we explain any such connection between the truth values of premises and conclusion unless there is a close connection between the senses in which they can be called true?

One supposes there might be some general notion of defeating an opponent, securing the object of a game, or something of the kind, in terms of which we could justify our saying that wins in various games are *wins*—even though what it is to win in each game is determined by rules and practices which need not be shared by the others. It is not clear how a similar justification could be given for saying that the various senses of 'true' constituted by different linguistic activities are still close enough to secure the applicability of the notions of validity and soundness to arguments involving different kinds of assertion. If competition and the aim of defeating an opponent are common to competitive games, what is common to all of the activities which involve assertion? (cp. *Z* 320). I do not believe Wittgenstein provides any answer to this question.

A second difficulty arises from Wittgenstein's tendency to equate the assertability and maintainability of an assertion with truth. The equation gains some plausibility from the consideration that one ought not to assert what one does not have grounds for believing is true and that a man who mistakenly thinks that p is the case will therefore be mistaken in asserting 'p'.

But Wittgenstein says little about conditions under which we are entitled to maintain an assertion outside a special system like *PM*. He does discuss cases where there are 'criteria' for what is asserted, and his discussion suggests that the fulfilment of the criteria entitles a speaker to make the assertion. For example, part of what he tries to establish in his discussion of private languages is that when the criteria for pain are present, we have every reason to say that another man is in pain (*PI* 243–303). And he also suggests that where criteria for something are absent, it may be meaningless to say it is present (*PI* 344, 349). Thus, it may seem that in cases which involve criteria, the criteria constitute conditions for asserting the presence of that whose criteria they are.[21] But, did Wittgenstein think the presence of criteria for such and such (and hence the obtaining of conditions which entitle us to assert that such and such is the case) satisfies or guarantees the satisfaction of the truth conditions of the assertion 'such and such is the case'? Many commentators (e.g. Malcolm, Albritton, and Rollins) hold that he did.[22] This interpretation appears to depend primarily upon passages in the *Blue Book* and *Investigations* in which Wittgenstein distinguishes what he called criteria from 'symptoms' and evidence (*BB* pp. 24–5, *PI* 354). Symptoms for something, X, are signs which experience has taught us are reliable indications of the presence of X. The connection between X and its symptoms is a matter of empirically established correlation, and it is possible for the symptoms to be present when X is not. What is meant by 'criteria for X' is less clear. Wittgenstein maintains that they are 'logically', 'conceptually', or 'grammatically' connected with the name or description of X (ibid). There is at least one passage which can be read as supporting the view that if C is a criterion for X, the presence of C logically guarantees the presence of X (*BB* p. 25):

> I call 'symptom' a phenomenon of which experience has taught us that it coincided, in some way or other, with the phenomenon which is our defining criterion. Then to say 'A man has angina if this bacillus is found in him' is a tautology or it is a loose way of stating the definition of 'angina'. But to say 'A man has angina whenever he has an inflamed throat' is to make a hypothesis

It is tempting to say that if 'has such and such a bacillus' *defines* angina, then it is necessarily the case that if Y has the bacillus, he has the disease. Even if this is the doctrine of the *Blue Book* concerning criteria, it is not the doctrine of the *Investigations*.[23]

> The fluctuation in grammar between criteria and symptoms makes it look as if there were nothing but symptoms. We say, for example: 'Experience teaches that there is rain when the barometer falls, but it also teaches that there is rain when we have certain sensations of wet and cold, or such and such visual impressions.' In defence of this one says that these sense impressions can deceive us. But here one fails to reflect that the fact that the false appearance is precisely one of rain is founded on a definition. (*PI* 354.)

> The point here is not that our sense impressions might lie, but that we understand their language. (And this language like any other is founded on convention.) (*PI* 355.)

The criteria of rain are experiences of the kind one has when standing in the rain, while symptoms of rain are, like a falling barometer, things one could experience without actually seeing or feeling the rain. In the passages just quoted, the difference between symptoms and criteria is *not* that the presence of symptoms fails to guarantee the truth of 'It is raining' while the characteristic experiences (the criteria) of rain do. If wet and cold (etc.) are criteria for rain, their presence guarantees that it *appears* to be *raining* (and not, e.g., snowing, hailing, etc.). But it does not guarantee the truth of 'it is raining' for our impressions can lie and appearances can be false (*PI* 354, 355).

Thus it would seem (assuming that the presence of C entitles me to assert the presence of X) that in the case of contingent assertions, Wittgenstein distinguished (in *PI* if not in *BB*) between conditions for asserting and truth conditions for what is asserted. The later works do not tell us, even for specific linguistic areas, what conditions must be met in addition to assertability to secure the truth of an assertion. Thus Wittgenstein did not provide for the generalization of his account of truth in a formal system to ordinary empirical truths. In particular, he did not characterize anything which functions analogously to the conditions for certification of a sentence for assertion in *PM*.

It is tempting to think that Wittgenstein saw various departments of ordinary language as too interestingly disparate to allow for any general account of conditions for asserting and maintaining an assertion in terms of which the notion of truth can be given a general explication. This is very likely so, but it is not a suggestion to be taken with unqualified enthusiasm. In discussing the difficulty of explaining the validity and soundness of arguments which include different kinds of proposition, we saw that it won't do to treat 'truth' as having entirely disconnected senses in connection with propositions from different linguistic areas. If Wittgenstein believed no general account of truth should be given, his position would have been more attractive if we knew what connections might hold between different senses of 'true' if the linguistic activities which determine these senses are too different to allow a general account.

In addition to these unanswered questions, there are difficulties which arise in connection with the notions 'language game', 'department of language', 'linguistic activity', etc. Discussion of these is postponed to chapter III. 3 of this book.

3 CONSEQUENCES OF WITTGENSTEIN'S POST-TRACTARIAN ACCOUNT OF INTENTIONALITY FOR DOCTRINES OF THE *TRACTATUS* AND FOR THE COURSE OF WITTGENSTEIN'S LATER WORK

(3.1) If we look back on the theses which comprise the picture theory of language, we can see how importantly the account of intentionality Wittgenstein developed in the early 1930s could have figured in his abandonment of doctrines and approaches which were central to the *Tractatus*. The picture theory maintained that:

(PT1) Reality is a collection of facts.

(PT2) Propositions are representational pictures of reality.

(PT3) A proposition represents reality as including what it presents as a fact.

(PT4) The truth value of a proposition is determined by comparing it to reality.

(PT5) A proposition is true if and only if reality includes what it presents as a fact and is false if and only if reality does not contain what it presents as a fact.

(PT6) Propositions present putative facts by either elementary or truth-functional methods of projection. Elementary propositions are concatenations of names whose arrangement shows how the named objects would be concatenated if they were true. Truth-functional projections (non-elementary propositions) present the obtaining and non-obtaining of states of affairs by expressing agreement and disagreement with truth possibilities of elementary propositions.

(PT1) treats facts as numerically distinct individuals of which reality is a collection. It gives rise to the questions about the makeup of facts which Wittgenstein attempted to answer by means of the ontological account of *TS* 1 to 2063. That the *Investigations* contains no positive account of the ontology of the fact is due to the way in which Wittgenstein's later account of intentionality precludes the possibility of thinking that facts are individuals (real, structured entities). In explaining why it is true that King's College is on fire we might speak about the structure and constituents of the college buildings (for example, to explain how a fire could have started there) but not about the structure and constituents of the fact that King's College is on fire.

Wittgenstein's abandonment of the Tractarian thesis that facts are individuals helps to explain his rejection of the thesis that sense must be determinate. If the sense of a proposition is a possible fact and if facts are real individuals, the possibility of indeterminate senses would be the possibility of indeterminate individuals—single things which violate the laws of identity (ch. I. 2 (2.5)). Once Wittgenstein had given up the view that facts are numerically different individuals which obey the laws of identity, he was able to take seriously the examples of indeterminate concepts which he offered as objections to the determinacy thesis in the *Investigations* (*PI* 68–71, 76, 77, 79, 99, etc.). On the Tractarian theory, border-line cases could not be allowed because a fact which figured in a border-line case would violate the laws of identity. On the later theory, border-line cases held no such terrors.

During the transitional period, determinacy reared its head again, but for different reasons. In 1929 and the early 1930s Wittgenstein sometimes held that uses of words which are not strictly determined by rules are meaningless. To show that there were cases in which the sentence's application was not secured by the rules under which it was used would throw its meaningfulness into question. The reasons for Wittgenstein's abandonment of this kind of determinacy requirement will be considered in chapter III.2 of this book.

(PT4) and (PT5) represent the verification of the proposition as a matter of looking through a collection of facts to find the one which the proposition presents. Even in the *Tractatus,* it sounds superfluous to mention facts in an account of verification when we consider that looking for the fact, for example, that aRb would be explainable on the *Tractatus* account in terms of looking to see how the objects a and b are deployed. However, it was not until after 1929 that Wittgenstein realized that the description of verification in terms of comparing a proposition to the totality of facts covers up some of the more interesting and important problems connected with the ways in which we ascertain the truth value of an assertion (UPN 1929; cp. *PI* 80):

> Events seem not to verify or falsify propositions in my
> original sense but instead it is as if they always leave a door
> open. Verification and its opposite are not definitive. . . .
> If I say 'there is a chair', this proposition gives rise to a
> series of expectations. I believe that if I went up to it I
> could feel it, and that I could sit on the chair. I believe it is
> made out of wood, and expect it to have a certain hardness,
> inertia, etc. When certain of these expectations turn out

to be mistaken, I take this as proof that there is no chair there. Here one sees what leads to the pragmatic account of truth and falsity. The proposition is true so long as it proves useful to me.

Wittgenstein did not become a pragmatist, but the passage marks a pronounced and lasting shift in his approach to the notions of verification and falsification. From this point on he was less and less inclined to try to offer a general account, and especially to try to explain verification and falsification in terms of facts. He was beginning to concern himself with the epistemological aspects of verification and was becoming impressed with the need to explain how the things we see, hear, taste, and touch bear upon the truth value of assertions. In this way, the fact began to drop out of Wittgenstein's consideration of verification as it finally had to when Wittgenstein decided to treat facts in such a way as to render trivial the dictum that the assertion is true iff what it presents as a fact is a fact. And as we saw earlier, Wittgenstein finally came to believe that the picture of verification as a procedure aimed at finding out whether a proposition agrees with reality is misleading. In *On Certainty,* he holds that what makes a contingent proposition true is the evidence for it—not something *further* (agreement with reality or reality's including what it presents as a fact) which the evidence for it establishes.

(PT2), (PT3), and (PT6) gave rise to the Tractarian discussions of the mechanics of asserting and picturing. In the later works, discussions of the structure and form of the proposition gave way to examinations of the ways in which words and sentences are used by speakers. The explanation for this is that the Tractarian account of the mechanics of picturing was intended to secure the intentional connection between a proposition and a putative fact. The later account of intentionality reduces the doctrine of a necessary connection between an assertion and what it claims is a fact to a truism for which no such explanation is required. Because of the complexity of the Tractarian account of the proposition this point must be considered with some care. The early theory of the proposition contains the germ of Wittgenstein's later account in addition to the theory of an internal connection between propositions and facts whose rejection is characteristic of Wittgenstein's later work. As a result, we shall now have to look at a question I have avoided so far; we shall have to ask what sort of thing the proposition was supposed to be. This will make it possible to assess the effects of the later account of intentionality on the theory of the proposition and to separate the forward-looking elements of the theory from those which Wittgenstein abandoned during the 1930s.

(3.2) In order to determine what sort of thing a Tractarian proposition could have been, I will describe the most plausible candidates and then compare them to what the early Wittgenstein has to say about the proposition. Towards this end let us ask what a speaker does or produces when he asserts. Although one can assert by gesturing (or by moving one's hands, for example, in using a deaf and dumb alphabet) we may limit our consideration to cases in which written or spoken words or sentences are used.

Suppose a speaker, X, asserts (to himself or to someone else) that a particular cat is on a particular mat. He may then be said to have done at least the following things:

(1) X produces or exhibits a mark or sound whose component parts are marks or sounds. *Qua* mark or sound, what X produces or exhibits is neither true nor false, meaningful nor nonsensical, grammatical nor ungrammatical, informative nor uninformative, pointless nor appropriate, etc. It is something which could have been produced for non-linguistic purposes (for example, as a design or ornament) by someone who did not know that the marks belonged to a language. Let us call this a sign. Signs are physical marks or sounds which may or may not also be words or sentences in a language.

(2) X produces an English sentence whose component parts are words in the English language. Let us suppose the sentence is "the cat is on the mat", bearing in mind that other sentences could have been used. (If asked whether the cat is on the mat, the speaker could have used the word "yes". In so doing he would have told us the same thing he could have told us by using the words "the cat is on the mat".)[24]

Although we can say of a sentence or word what would be false or nonsensical if said of a sign, a sentence is not a second separate item in addition to a sign. Sentences and words are signs used in or belonging to some language. Thus a sentence is a sign whose consideration as a bit of language subjects it to morphological, lexical, and grammatical standards which make it possible to say what we couldn't say of it *qua* sign. This is why a word or sentence can be said to be misspelled or ungrammatical (respectively) while a sign considered merely as a mark or sound cannot. There is a great deal to be said about the difference between a sign *qua* sign and a sign *qua* sentence, but for our purposes, only the following need be mentioned.

Grammatical sentences may be called meaningful or meaningless; signs *qua* marks or sounds are neither.[25] Thus under some grammars, "Quadruplicity drinks procrastination" is grammatical though meaningless, while "the cat is on the mat" is grammatical and meaningful, but these assessments apply to signs only when considered sentences.

It is tempting to conclude from this that sentences, unlike signs, have truth values. This means not just that meaningful sentences can be used to say what is true or false (of course, they can), but that *qua* sentence and apart from its use on a particular occasion, a sentence or sentence token is true or false. I believe this is incorrect. Sentences are produced or exhibited mainly for the purpose of making a truth claim, but we can also produce or exhibit a sentence as an example in a grammar lesson or in elocution practice without saying anything true or false. On the blackboard as a grammatical example, the sentence token "the cat is on the mat" says nothing true or false because reference has not been made to any particular cat or mat. The sentence is meaningful because it can be used to say something and we can explain its meaning by indicating what (sorts of things) can be said with it. But what is true or false is what we say in or by producing the sentence, not the sentence itself.

My discussion of what a proposition is will require me to emphasize here that a sentence token is a thing. *Inter alia* a sentence is a sign whose parts are *inter alia* signs. Like a sign, it is something we make, and the discrepancies between what we can say of a sign and what we can say of a sentence (for example, that is grammatical elliptical, elegant, or economical meaningful, etc.) should not be allowed to obscure this fact.

(3) Whatever else X accomplished in saying that the cat

is on the mat (for example, giving a piece of information to someone, making a listener worry about what will happen to his mat), we can say that he said something about the cat (and the mat) which is either true or false. Since ordinary language provides no standard label for this accomplishment, and philosophical terminology and theory is far from settled here, I shall have to choose a term for use in this connection somewhat arbitrarily. Considered simply as having used a sentence to say what is either true or false and abstracting from everything else he might have accomplished in or by so doing, let us say that X *asserted* that the cat is on the mat.[26]

It is a nice question whether speakers can or do *just* assert. When a speaker soliloquizes, informs, warns, reminisces, etc., he asserts. It is not clear (a) whether a speaker ever asserts except in doing something further like soliloquizing, etc., and if not, (b) whether it is possible in principle to assert without doing something else (like informing, etc.) as well. It is highly unlikely that the early Wittgenstein would have worried about this, but the later Wittgenstein held that the linguistic significance of an utterance is bound up with the place of the utterance in a broader activity and, as a consequence, he seems to have held that there can be no such act as asserting *simpliciter*. This accounts for his failure to include 'asserting' or any equivalent in lists of linguistic performances like the one at *PI* 23. Although I am inclined to agree with the later Wittgenstein on this, the correctness of his position is irrelevant to the present discussion. Even if a man cannot assert without doing something further, it is clear, for example, that a man who tells someone that the cat is on the mat asserts what is true or false of the cat and the mat. Thus we may include 'X asserted that . . .' in our list of what it would be true to say X did even if one can only assert in doing something further and X must, therefore, have done more than simply asserting.

Unlike sentence production which can issue in a sign with no truth value, asserting must issue in what is either true or false. Because a man asserts only if he succeeds in saying what is true or false, we cannot straightforwardly claim that what is asserted is meaningless unless by this we mean it is pointless, inconsequential, irrelevant, silly, or odd. Grammaticality has to do with lexical and syntactical features of a sentence. Thus a man should not straightforwardly be said to have asserted grammatically or ungrammatically unless this means that in asserting he produced a grammatically correct or defective sentence.

In asserting, a speaker produces or exhibits a sentence and, since every sentence must belong to some language, he can be said to have asserted in a given language. But when a man asserts (says what is true or false) we may also speak of what he asserted (what he said that is true or false). The same thing may be asserted using sentences in different languages. Thus while a man cannot assert without asserting in some particular language, what he asserts cannot be said to belong specifically to any particular language (even though, of course, there could be languages in which what he asserted could not be said because of impoverished vocabulary, etc.). We can point to sentences used by an English speaker in order to give examples of assertions in English. But these would be assertions which *happen* to have been made with English sentences and could have been made with the sentences of other languages. It is, therefore, not essential to the assertion of 'the cat is on the mat' that it be done in English even though it is essential to the sentence 'the cat is on the mat' that it belong to the English language.

For our purposes, the most important contrasts between assertion and mark- or sentence-production have to do with an ancient distinction drawn by Aristotle between kinds of action. On the one hand we have activities which terminate in the production of something (for example, building and shipmaking) and on the other, activities which, says Aristotle, have no aim beyond their performance (for example, flute playing).[27] Similarly, we can distinguish the act of producing something from actions in which something is done but nothing is made. The production of a sentence or sign is the making of something (a mark or sound or token of a sentence type). Asserting cannot be so classified. In this respect, it is closer to scoring a goal than to making a goal post. 'X made a goal post' mentions a person and a thing which he manufactured. 'X scored a goal' mentions a person, and tells us that he succeeded in doing something. In X's performance and its success (scoring) we do not have two separate individuals as we do in the case of X and his goal post. The same thing can be said of X and his assertion. In saying that X made an assertion, we report the upshot of his use of a sentence; 'assertion' does not refer to something which his asserting manufactured. Typically, we produce sentences in asserting, but we can assert just as well by exhibiting a sentence which has already been produced—by ourselves or by someone else. Thus a man who has asserted is more properly described as having done rather than as having produced something.

Part of the importance of this distinction lies in the fact that because making an assertion is more like doing than like producing something, we cannot talk about assertions and their elements in the same way in which we can talk about sentences or signs and their elements. A sentence token (sign) is a complex thing which we produce by forming and combining word tokens (signs). Hence its parts are individual things—words (signs). We cannot speak *in this sense* of *things* combined making up an assertion, and we cannot speak of the parts or elements of an assertion in the same way as the parts or elements of a sentence or sign. If an assertion has 'parts' or 'elements' they are things *done*—not made—in asserting. We can say the assertion of 'the cat is on the mat' involves a reference to the cat, a reference to the mat, and a predication. This means that someone who makes the assertion refers and predicates. But the references and the predication are not things like the words or signs. They are what the speaker may be said to have done with the words he used. They are not elements which can be put together into an assertion in the sense in which words or signs can be put together to make up a sentence. The reason for this is that the 'parts' of an assertion do not exist on their own independently of the assertion or other assertions in which they occur. When we use the words in the sentence "the cat is on the mat" to refer to the cat and say that it is on the mat, we accomplish references and a predication. But we cannot first refer and then predicate and then combine the two to make up an assertion. The mere utterance of "the cat" does not make reference to the cat, and taken alone (without the utterance of "the cat") the utterance of "is on the mat" does not predicate or refer to the mat (cp. *TS* 33, *PI* 49). Thus asserting is different from sentence-construction, for we can produce each word (token) in a sentence, combine them, and then break up the resulting sentence into its component parts. Asserting also differs from a complex activity like shaving. Usually a shaver lathers his face and then shaves. But it is possible to shave first and then lather, or to lather without shaving and shave without lathering, even though the activity usually involves both acts. Asserting cannot be broken up analogously into acts performable independently under the descriptions 'referring', 'predicating', etc.

Finally, it is of great importance that while the elements of a sentence may be used, to refer, ascribe, etc., (that is, may be produced or exhibited in such a way as to accomplish these linguistic feats) the elements of an assertion are not used to do any such things. Instead, they are what a speaker who has succeeded in making an assertion can *also* be said to have done by producing or exhibiting the words in the sentence he used to assert. It would be as much a mistake to think that an assertion contains an element which is used to refer as to think that the drinking of a bottle of wine contains an element which drinks or is used to drink, or that the act of shooting a clay pigeon contains an element which puts shot into the target.

Someone might object that asserting is making something and an assertion is what is made on the grounds that if I assert by writing the sentence "the cat is on the mat", someone can point to it and say things about it, for example, 'that is the last thing he said' or 'what that says is true'. If he can say this about what he points to, mustn't the assertion be what he points to? If so, isn't the assertion identical to the sentence and, therefore, a thing produced in asserting? Compare pointing to the horseshoe someone just threw round the post and saying 'that's a ringer'. The piece of iron the player picked up and tossed was a horseshoe; he did not pick up and throw a ringer. If we point to the horseshoe and say that it's a ringer, we are showing someone how a shoe must land if the throw is to score a certain number of points, or else we are scoring a toss on the basis of the position of the shoe. The shoe we point to is what the player used to score; it is not his score. For analogous reasons, we can say 'that's true' pointing to a sentence to indicate what we think is true without conflating the sentence used to assert with the assertion it is used to make or what it is used to assert. In writing down the sentence, a speaker may assert what is true and that is why we can point to the sentence to indicate what we think is true. The fact that asserting is (*inter alia*) writing down the sentence does not justify calling the sentence the assertion or what is asserted any more than the fact that one scores a ringer in throwing a horseshoe round the pole justifies saying that the shoe is the ringer that was tossed, or the toss. What is true or false is what a speaker says. The sentence he uses to say it is not what he says.[28]

(4) Depending upon the circumstances in which the sentence "the cat is on the mat" is used, the speaker may, in using the sentence, give information, assure someone that the cat is on the mat, warn someone that the cat is on the mat, etc. That is to say, he may perform one of the acts which Austin classifies as illocutionary.[29] Since I am inclined to think the notion of asserting is an abstraction from an act of this kind, I am also inclined to say that where there is assertion there must be illocution as well. However, it is indifferent to the question I eventually want to ask—what a Tractarian proposition should be said to be—whether this is necessarily the case. Even if there are exceptions, we can at least say that in most of the cases in which someone asserts (says what is true or false), he makes an assertion in performing an illocutionary act.

(5) X may also be said to have performed an action of the kind which Austin called 'perlocutionary'—his saying that the cat is on the mat may have as a consequence the effect of boring, surprising or irritating someone, opening a conversation, getting someone to move the cat, etc.[30] While it is doubtful whether assertion is possible without the performance of an illocutionary act, it is clear that we can say something and hence assert without intending or securing a perlocutionary effect.

(6) According to Frege, X should be said to have *asserted the proposition* 'the cat is on the mat'. The Fregean proposition differs from the sentence and the sign because it has a truth value. It differs from the assertion in two respects. First, an assertion is a speech act (or its upshot) while a Fregean proposition is not. On Frege's account, the proposition 'the cat is on the mat' gives the content of the assertion 'the cat is on the mat', the question 'is the cat on the mat?', the supposition that

the cat is on the mat, etc. The speaker's act is the asserting, questioning, etc., of the proposition; it is not the proposition itself. For Frege the act of judgment corresponds roughly to what I have been calling 'asserting'. It is the act by which a speaker commits himself to the truth of a proposition which is itself true or false regardless of whether it has been asserted.[31] Secondly, because the Fregean proposition is not a speech act or its upshot, but the content which a number of different kinds of speech act may have in common, it is not to be ascribed to any particular speaker or speakers. It makes sense to ask who made an assertion, or who judged a proposition true, but 'Whose (Fregean) proposition?' makes no sense.

Before we go on to ask which if any of these six items corresponds to a Tractarian proposition, notice again that descriptions (1) to (5) above are descriptions of one and the same performance, and not descriptions of six different events. One does not make marks, then a sentence, then a statement, etc., as one might make a clay ball and then make it into a cylinder, and then turn it into a pot. In the case I have been describing, a single performance occurs: X bores, irritates, etc., Y in or by informing him that the cat is on the mat, and in accomplishing all of this he uses a sentence (hence a sign) to make an assertion.

(3.3) What then is a Tractarian proposition?[32] Because a proposition is 'a *Satzzeichen* (sentence) in its projective relation to the world' (*TS* 311), it looks as though whatever else it may be, a proposition is at least supposed to be *inter alia* a sentence and hence a sign. But if it is a sentence, it is not *just* a sign or sentence. A proposition is always true or false, and it has a sense. *Qua* sign (mark or sound) this cannot be said of a sentence, and we have observed that sentences need not be used to assert and therefore need not have senses or truth values. We said that a sentence has a meaning, but *qua* sentence, it has a meaning only in the sense that we can say how (in the cases of some sentences at least) it could be used— we can indicate what assertions it would be used normally to make.

Could there be a proposition which did not involve a sentence or sign? For instance, could a man assert something to himself—in thought—without producing or exhibiting a sentence or sign? I am inclined to think Wittgenstein would have allowed covert assertions and would have treated them as projective uses of words or images a man thinks tacitly, but there is no explicit indication in the *Tractatus* of whether or not this is so.[33] The exemplary propositions in the *Tractatus* seem always to involve written or spoken sentences.

But even if it is essential to (and not just always true of) a proposition that it is *some* sentence, a proposition involving a particular sentence is not essentially that very sentence. What is essential to the proposition is what all propositions with the same sense have in common (*TS* 331). Suppose I say that Wittgenstein is clever by writing the sentence 'Wittgenstein is clever'. I could have expressed the same sense by writing the sentence '*Wittgenstein ist klug*'. Propositions with the same sense are identical but the German and English sentences are not. Hence, even if a proposition is always some sentence or other, the proposition which says that Wittgenstein is clever is not essentially any one of the various sentences or signs which could be used to assert that Wittgenstein is clever. Furthermore, the proposition is a symbol and one and the same sign 'can be common to two different symbols' (*TS* 3321). If the proposition were identical to a particular sentence the same sentence would have to be common to two different sentences. If anything in the *Tractatus* should be called a mere sentence, it is the *Satzzeichen* which we use to express a sense. If the proposition is a sentence, it is not *just* a sentence.

There is no plausibility in identifying the proposition with a perlocutionary act, and little in calling it an illocutionary act. Wittgenstein holds that we have a proposition when and only when we have said what is true or false. Thus we can have a proposition whether or not perlocutionary effects have been secured. Furthermore, the proposition is supposed to be nothing more than the expression of a sense. This strongly suggests that it involves much less than an Austinian illocution or any of the speech activities (describing, story-telling, etc.) listed at *PI* 23, even though it would not be inconsistent with the *Tractatus* to imagine that propositions are involved in such speech acts and activities as these.

Can we identify the proposition with the Fregean proposition? This is ruled out by the circumstance that Tractarian propositions are not assertible contents. The proposition 'shows how things stand *if* it is true. And it *says that* they do so stand' (*TS* 4022). The Fregean proposition does not *assert* that things stand in a certain way; it is the content asserted by someone who says they so stand. What is asserted in the *Tractatus* is a sense, not a Tractarian proposition.

It may be objected that Tractarian propositions have truth values. If this means that 'true' and 'false' apply primarily to them, then the propositions of the *Tractatus* would seem to be more like Fregean propositions than assertions or sentences. An assertion is the saying of what is true or false, and a sentence is what is produced or exhibited to say it, while what *is* true or false is what is asserted (what a sentence is used to say). Since what is said is true or false, it is more like a Fregean proposition than any of the other six items I considered. But even if we ignore Frege's characterization of a proposition as a complex name and Wittgenstein's flat rejection of that characterization, it is still implausible to identify Tractarian with Fregean propositions. What is asserted is as much like a Tractarian sense as a Fregean proposition, and it surely won't do to identify Tractarian propositions with their senses. We (philosophers and speakers of stilted ordinary language) may call assertions true or false even if we think that 'true' and 'false' apply most properly to what is asserted. When we call an assertion true, we mean that it asserts something that is true. Similarly, Wittgenstein says that what agrees or disagrees with reality is a sense and that the truth or falsity of a proposition consists in this agreement or disagreement (*TS* 2222). Thus a Tractarian proposition can be true or false because it says what agrees or disagrees with reality and not because it is (like a Fregean proposition or a Tractarian sense) what is asserted.

Is the proposition an assertion? We have seen that Wittgenstein talks as though a proposition is a sentence used to assert instead of the assertion accomplished by its use (for example, *TS* 311). But he also talks about the proposition in ways more appropriate to the characterization of the assertion than the sentence. These two conceptions are incompatible, and I will suggest that their conflation in the *Tractatus* marks a confusion in Wittgenstein's theory.

Like the assertion, the proposition says what is true or false.

Like the assertion, it is the expression of truth conditions, not something used by a speaker to express truth conditions or something the speaker expresses (*TS* 4413, 403). Like the assertion, the proposition says (asserts, states, etc.) that things are as it presents them (*TS* 4022).

The referring elements of the proposition, like those of an assertion, are essentially, and not just accidentally, connected with their referents: 'a picture ... includes the pictorial relationship, *which makes it into a picture*' (*TS* 21513, my italics). Thus, nothing is an elementary picture unless it has the pictorial relationship, and this is included in the picture (hence proposition) itself: 'The pictorial relationship consists of the correlations of the picture's elements with things' (*TS* 21514).[34] It follows that nothing is an elementary picture element unless it is correlated with something. An element which was not so correlated would not be part of a picture, because the correlations are what makes something into a picture. Although the 'parts' of an assertion are not things correlated with other things, they are essentially connected to what they signify. We said that one element of the assertion of 'the cat is on the mat' is a reference to a particular cat. It is essential to a reference to the cat that it be a reference to the cat, and so the connections between assertion and proposition elements and what they refer to are not accidental.[35] It would seem to follow from all of this that a proposition, like an assertion, is what is accomplished by the use of a sentence to say something. Furthermore, the essential proposition is what is common to the uses of all of the sentences which could be used to express the same sense. Thus in essence, the proposition is the assertion that such and such is the case and it 'consists' of the referrings, etc., which must be achieved by anyone who uses a sentence to say just that.[36] That this rather than that particular sign is used to make the assertion is accidental to the assertion; the same holds for the proposition. That is why Wittgenstein tells us that we recognize symbols (including propositions) by attending to the uses to which signs are put (*TS* 3326).

If propositions are assertions, why is there no talk in the *Tractatus* of the speakers who make them, and why aren't propositions ascribed to particular speakers in the way assertions can be? The answer to this is that the theory of the proposition

L

is a theory of judgment. Wittgenstein believed that any one speaker's asserting that such and such is the case must be essentially the same as any other's asserting of the same thing (*TS* 334, 331). If two speakers make the assertion 'p' their propositions can differ only with regard to accidental features—including the identities of the speakers; otherwise they must be the same. Each proposition is what a speaker must accomplish in order to express a particular set of truth conditions. Thus we can talk about the proposition which says that such and such without considering the speaker who does the asserting for the same reason that we can explain the Sicilian Defence in chess without concerning ourselves over which players actually played the Defence—even though its actual play requires a player. As Schwyzer says:[37]

> On this theory of language, any mention of the speaker is simply redundant. Had Wittgenstein chosen 'sentence' or (Fregean) 'proposition' as the basic linguistic unit, he could not have avoided referring to those who use sentences, express propositions. But a proposition is not the kind of a thing that can be used or expressed. For it is itself a use, for Wittgenstein, the use of a sentence, the expressing of a sense. . . . It is the act of making a statement. And if language consists of acts, then there is no cause to look beyond its 'internal features' for whatever it is (the speaker) who makes it mean 'something other than itself'. That is why *Bild, Gedanke, Satz, Name,* appear to have lives of their own. The remarks 'the name names the object', 'the thought thinks the object', 'the thought thinks the state of affairs', 'the picture presents a sense', are . . . disguised explanations of these terms.

This fits a great deal of what Wittgenstein has to say about propositions in the *Tractatus*. The proposition 'reaches right out' to reality (*TS* 21511), includes the correlations between its elements and the things it makes reference to (*TS* 21513–21514), pictures reality (instead of being something used to picture) (*TS* 2173, 219, 2201, 222), and presents its sense (*TS* 2221, 3142). It is not something we use to say something; it shows how things stand if it is true and says that they so stand (*TS* 4022). It uses expressions to communicate (*TS* 403).

It states (*TS* 403). And so forth. We can say such things of an assertion, but not of a sentence, a sign, or a Fregean proposition.

But there are serious difficulties with this interpretation of "proposition". We have been saying an assertion is something a speaker accomplishes; it is the upshot of what he does when he asserts. Now it is time to recall that *inter alia* a Tractarian proposition was said to be a sentence and hence a sign. How can something done *also* be a thing—a string of signs which are words? It is easy to see how sentences are *involved* in assertions. The assertion that such and such is the case is a use of some sentence, and whenever a particular person makes the assertion, he uses some sentence to assert. However, Wittgenstein identified the proposition and the sentence more closely than this. He says that the sentence in use (the sentence in its projective relation to the world) *is* the proposition and this does not jibe with the characterization of the proposition as an assertion. The passages we have been considering made it look as though the proposition 'p' is what is accomplished in saying that it is the case that p (where its being the case that p is the possible fact, the sense expressed by the proposition). If so, the proposition could not also *be* a sentence. In general we do not consider the fact that something is used to do or accomplish something grounds for identifying it with the accomplishment. We do not identify an arrival with the car one arrives in, a knockout with the fist used to knock someone out, a win in the pole vault with the pole used to vault, etc. Why then should Wittgenstein have identified the proposition with the sentence if the proposition is the assertion of something and the sentence is what is used to assert?

Perhaps by "proposition" Wittgenstein meant the sentence used to say that such and such is the case *qua* in use to say that such and such is the case. This fits some of the remarks which made it plausible to identify the proposition with the assertion. For example, Wittgenstein said that the proposition shows, presents, says, etc., that such and such is the case, and that the proposition represents reality. When a map is in use to represent Northern Ohio as including the towns Oberlin, Kipton, and Elyria in a certain geographical relationship to one another, we do say of the *map* that it represents Northern Ohio, shows the towns (and shows their locations) and says, for example, that

Kipton is west of Oberlin. Wittgenstein thought propositions were like maps and other representational pictures in use, and he apparently thought of sentences (*Satzzeichen*) as what we use to assert. Even though it sounds unnatural for us to say that a sentence represents, shows, etc., (except in locutions like 'this sentence represents a deterioration in Dylan Thomas's use of rhyme', 'this sentence shows little concern for the niceties of English grammar', etc.) we can imagine Wittgenstein talking about sentences in this way.

Nevertheless, some of the things Wittgenstein said about the proposition are incompatible with the notion that a proposition is a sentence in use. Here are some of them.

(1) Wittgenstein said the proposition is a fact (*TS* 2141). If the proposition is an assertion, it is what someone succeeds in doing when he uses a sentence—the saying of something. If a fact is what makes a true assertion true, we might perhaps call the saying of something a fact, for someone's having said that such and such is what makes it true to say 'He said that such and such'. We cannot say this of a sentence. Even the sentence in use to say that such and such is the case is not what makes it true to say 'he said . . .' and so it has no claims to classification as a fact. 'He said . . .' is made true by the sentence's *being* used to say . . . or by the fact *that* the sentence is used to say . . . , but not by the *sentence*, the sentence used, or the sentence in use.[38] The early Wittgenstein says that the sentence is a fact (*TS* 3143) and part of his reason for saying this was his belief that *all* complexes are facts. But this isn't (can't be) true, even if by "sentence" he means: sentence in use. We saw that during the 1930s Wittgenstein decided he had once been guilty of confusing facts with complexes, and I believe *TS* 3143 is a case in point.

(2) According to the *Tractatus* what is essential to a proposition is what all propositions with the same sense have in common. If the proposition is an assertion, then there is something which all propositions with the same sense clearly have in common: they are all uses of words with the same upshot —the expression of the same sense. Furthermore, it is plausible to say (ignoring possible counter examples in which sentences like 'yes' are used to say that such and such is the case) that the same references, predications, etc., are common to assertions with the same sense. On the other hand, it is not easy to think of

things which *sentences* in use to say the same thing have in common which are also essential to those sentences. In use to say Wittgenstein died, the sentence "Wittgenstein died" has two elements while "Wittgenstein passed away" has three. In use to say something about Munich, the sentence, "Munich is . . ." includes one word ("Munich") used to stand for Munich, while the sentence "*München ist* . . ." includes a different word used to refer to Munich. If the essential proposition is what these propositions have in common, the proposition is not essentially any particular sentence, sentence element, or feature, and so it is difficult to see how the proposition could in essence by any particular sentence or sentence element, or future in use. Wittgenstein might reply that every sentence in use to say the same thing consists of the same symbols and the same number of symbols. But this seems implausible. While it is natural to think of assertions as consisting of the kinds of thing Wittgenstein called symbols (if symbols are, for example, references or referrings), we can't very well say this of sentences. The most obvious difficulty is that a sentence in use should have the same number of parts as a sentence neat, and even when used to say the same thing, "Wittgenstein was a bachelor" does not have the same number of parts as "Wittgenstein was an unmarried man". This indicates that the parts of sentences in use are not symbols; if they were, "Wittgenstein was a bachelor" and "Wittgenstein was an unmarried man" would have the same number of parts when used to say the same thing.

(3) According to Wittgenstein, it is an essential feature of a picture element which refers to an object that it refers to that object. It is easy to say this kind of thing about the elements of an assertion, but not of a word which belongs to a sentence in use unless we are prepared to trivialize the doctrine. Consider the sentence 'Wittgenstein was Viennese' in use to say that Ludwig Wittgenstein was Viennese. When the sentence is used in this way, 'Wittgenstein' refers to Ludwig Wittgenstein, but it is only trivially true that 'Wittgenstein' refers to Ludwig Wittgenstein when used to refer to Ludwig Wittgenstein. The later Wittgenstein could have admitted that Tractarian symbols are only trivially connected to what they signify, but I do not think the early Wittgenstein wanted to hold that what he took to be essential connections were merely the consequences of trivial

truths. It seems more natural to call the elements of a sentence in use (a sentence of which it is true that someone is using it to say that . . .) *words*, than to call them words-in-use, and it is not essential to the *word* "Wittgenstein" that it be used to refer to Ludwig instead of some other Wittgenstein. Furthermore, it is worth observing that the referring is done by the speaker who uses the word, not by the word in use. If we take seriously the fact that the speaker refers, it becomes clearer that because a word in use is still only a word, it is misleading to say that in use to make a reference it is *essential* to a word that it refers. One might just as well say that being placed next to a square in a design is an essential feature of a triangle which someone has placed next to a square in a design. Someone who wanted to give us an essential feature would do better to mention the number of sides or angles of the triangle. On the other hand, its connection with Ludwig *is* essential to the assertion element, the reference to Ludwig. The word "Wittgenstein" used to refer to Ludwig is identical to "Wittgenstein" used to refer to Paul, but what is not a reference to Ludwig cannot be identical to a reference to Ludwig.

To summarize: I have been asking what the proposition would have to be in order to fit the early Wittgenstein's characterizations of it. My contention is that some characterizations would best fit the proposition if it were an assertion (the saying that such and such is the case which a man accomplishes by using a sentence) while others would have been true of the proposition only if it were the sentence or a sentence in use to make an assertion. I think these are fundamentally different conceptions, and that the early Wittgenstein conflated them.

(3.4) Now we can go on to see what was living and what was dead in the Tractarian theory of proposition after Wittgenstein attempted to reduce the intentionality of the proposition to the truism that a sentence used to assert that such and such is the case is true if and only if such and such is the case. The reason I went on at such length to distinguish what I take to be conflicting accounts of the proposition in the *Tractatus* is that I believe (1) that taken separately, they can be accommodated to what Wittgenstein said about intentionality during the early 1930s and (2) that the elements of the Tractarian account which Wittgenstein abandoned before he wrote the

Brown Book were largely the results of his early conflation of the notions of assertion and sentence in use.

If the true proposition 'Thelonius is tall' is the *assertion* that Thelonius is tall, the later Wittgenstein can hold that it is necessarily connected with the fact that Thelonius is tall. The proper statement of the connection is the truism 'The successful use of a sentence to say that Thelonius is tall is the assertion that Thelonius is tall'. What needs explaining is *how* a sentence is used to assert this—how we succeed in referring to Thelonius by uttering his name and how we predicate tallness of him by saying "is tall". On the other hand, if the proposition is a sentence in use to say something, an examination of the proposition should reveal just that; it should tell us what it is to use a sentence, how this is accomplished, etc., etc.

When the early Wittgenstein thought of the proposition as a sentence in use (a *Satzzeichen* in its projective relation to the world) (*TS* 311) his remarks about it often agreed in rough direction, though not in detail, with his later theories. He tended to think of the proposition as a sentence employed according to rules of projection, and that to say or assert is to apply projection rules to a sentence and to employ it according to them (*TS* 311, 40141). Up to a point, we can read his remarks about the elementary and truth-functional methods of projection as an account of how in general signs are used according to rules of projection, and (again, up to a point) his remarks about 'logical syntax' can be interpreted as remarks about allegedly general features of the projection schemes by which signs can be used to assert (*TS* 3325-3334). Furthermore, he takes the fact that a certain sign has a certain use in a notation to be a contingent and not a necessary fact about the sign. This fits some of the things Wittgenstein had to say about intentionality later on. In particular, it fits the idea that since an account of intentionality should be an account of the ways in which we do things with words, an explanation of intentionality should tell us what brings about the contingent connections between signs and the things they are used to talk about. The *Tractarian* theory of use is strikingly similar to Wittgenstein's transitional discussions of use. The idea that using a sentence was like using a drawing as a projection guided much of Wittgenstein's work up to the period which ended with the *Blue*

Book. From the *Brown Book* on, we find a very different conception of use, but it still accords with the Tractarian idea that the proper study of meaning is the study of use. Even if the *Tractatus* gave a distorted account of what it is to use words, it still maintained (what Wittgenstein always believed) that the use of a sign is what makes it meaningful.

But at the same time, the early Wittgenstein's belief that the proposition and its satisfying fact (if there is one) are essentially connected but numerically different real individuals led him to try to explain intentionality in terms of a mechanism by which the proposition connects itself with reality and with the putative fact which it presents. The discussion of the details of picturing in the 2s, 3s, and 4s constitutes this account. Here we find the elements of the Tractarian doctrine which Wittgenstein flatly rejected after his return to Cambridge. It should be clear by now why this aspect of Wittgenstein's early theory was incompatible with his later account of intentionality. When Wittgenstein discussed the mechanics of picturing in the *Tractatus* he was not trying to explain the contingent connections between signs and things which make assertion possible. Nor was he drawing our attention to the truism that the assertion of 'p' asserts that it is the case that p. Instead, he was trying to expose features of the proposition which explain its necessary connection with a possibly non-existent individual called a fact. On the later account of intentionality, it makes no sense to ask for such an account.

In this connection, consider Wittgenstein's account of elementary projection:

> The fact that the elements of the picture are related to one another in a determinate way presents that the objects are related to one another in a certain way. (*TS* 215.)
> One name stands for one object, another for another, and they are combined with one another. In this way the whole group—like a *tableau vivant*—presents the state of affairs. (*TS* 40311.)

What is the 'whole group' which does the presenting? If it is the sentence in use to present, then it is not essentially connected with what is being presented. While it is necessarily (though trivially) true that a sentence used to say 'p' says 'p', it is not essential to the *sentence* in use that it be used or that it be used to say 'p'. Nevertheless, Wittgenstein is trying in this passage to explain how a proposition is *essentially* connected with what it presents (*TS* 403). Thus the 'whole group' would have to be the assertion and not the sentence used to assert.

But if the proposition is an assertion, Wittgenstein's remarks about the proposition functioning like a *tableau vivant* turn out to be very hard sayings. While the *sentence* "a b" consists of elements (the words "a" and "b") which could be *used* to stand for objects (*a* and *b*) and arranged to show *a* standing in a certain relation to *b*, the assertion does not consist of such elements. The elements of the assertion are a reference (a referring) to *a* and a reference to *b*. A *reference* or referring does not *stand for* or *represent* a referent (cp. *TS* 213, 21414, 3203, 40311, 40312, etc.). It is what is accomplished by using a *sign* to stand for, refer to, or represent (be the representative of) a thing.

Although it makes perfectly good sense to talk about the words in a sentence standing in determinate relations which show certain things standing to one another in a certain way (*TS* 314), this does not seem true of the elements of an assertion. To see why this is so, let us ask what kinds of relations can obtain between assertion elements, things which can be said to have been done in making an assertion. Such things as referrings cannot be spatially related in any significant way. The sign "a" could be placed to the left of "b" in order to show a certain relation between *a* and *b,* but a speaker's *use* of "a" to refer to *a* cannot be said to be to the left or to the right of his *use* of "b" unless this means, for example, that the speaker did his referring to *a* in one place and his referring to *b* in another. One relation which can pretty straightforwardly be ascribed to uses is logical priority; a certain use of one word may logically presuppose a certain use of another. But no relation of this kind could show how objects would stand if an elementary proposition were true. We might say that a speaker presents *a* as related to *b* instead of the reverse by referring to *a* 'before' referring to *b*. But what could 'before' mean? Suppose the speaker accomplished his references by writing "a b" with two pencils, producing the signs simultaneously. Or suppose he wrote "b" on the right before he wrote "a" on the left.

In what relevant sense could we then say that the reference to *a* comes 'before' the reference to *b*?

I suppose someone could invent a catalogue of relations suitable for ascription to uses of languages for the purpose of explaining how an elementary proposition presents putative facts, but this would be neither natural nor helpful. It would be unnatural because we do not speak of assertion elements standing in signifying relations. It would be unhelpful because even if references to *a* and *b* could be so related as to present the possible fact that *aRb*, the connection between the assertion and the putative fact should then by Wittgenstein's own later arguments be no less contingent than the connection between signs and the fact they could be used to signify when arranged in suitable ways.

In this way we can see that Wittgenstein's attempts to expose a mechanism by which picture and fact are essentially connected were doomed to failure. The Tractarian conflation of the concept of the proposition as an assertion and the concept of the proposition as sentence in use looks like a by-product (or partial cause) of this unsuccessful enterprise. What is essentially (though trivially) connected to the putative fact is the assertion of 'p'. What has elements which stand for things and are arranged to say something is the sentence used to make the assertion. I believe that when he spoke of the necessary connection between proposition and putative fact, Wittgenstein was muddling the two: he spoke as though the sentence (which has arranged parts but is only accidentally connected with things and facts) were the assertion (which is essentially connected with what is said but has no parts arranged to say something) and as though the elements of the assertion were like the elements of the sentence.

(3.5) In the Introduction I suggested that the 'fixed point' round which Wittgenstein said he had rotated the axis of his investigations was the need to understand the 'paradox' of *PI* 94–96. Wittgenstein offered two formulations of the paradox: 'When we say and *mean* that such and such is the case, we—and our meaning—do not stop anywhere short of the fact; but we mean: *this-is-so*' and '*Thought* can be of what is *not* the case' (*PI* 95). If these statements are heard as paradoxical they can lead us to think that 'a proposition is a queer thing' (*PI* 93, 94, 96, etc.). In particular, says Wittgenstein, we may be led 'to assume a pure intermediary between the propositional signs and the facts. Or even to try to purify, to sublime, the signs themselves' (*PI* 94). Wittgenstein's account of the mechanics of picturing in the *Tractatus* is, I submit, a cardinal example of this. It is here that he speaks as though the proposition were a miraculous sign composed of elements something like the elements of a sentence, but which manages somehow to connect itself to a putative fact in the way that an assertion does and no sentence can. At other times, he speaks of the proposition as if it were an intermediary between signs and facts instead of a remarkable kind of sign. Propositions are symbols, and a symbol is sometimes described as a sort of invisible intermediary whose presence is indicated by the sentence (*TS* 332).

How do we take the statements 'When I say and mean ———, I say and mean ———' and 'Thought can be of what is not the case' as paradoxes? In the early writings of Wittgenstein, the paradox is generated by thinking that the phrase which tells us what a man says, means or refers to an individual thing (fact or putative fact); that the verb "to assert" ("to believe", "to say", "to think", etc.) expresses an essential connection (act or relation) between what is asserted and the assertion; and that the phrase "an assertion" ("belief", etc.) refers to a second individual to which the fact or putative fact is internally connected. On this view, propositions *must* do something queer (*PI* 93); they must connect themselves internally to what may not even exist. And by the same token, they must *be* something queer and unique (*PI* 94, 95), for *nothing else* can be internally connected to what is numerically different and existentially independent from it. Thus 'thought must be something unique' can be understood as an expression of the Buridanian problem: how can a man think that such and such is the case if a man who thinks always thinks something and if his assertion may be false and there may be nothing which is the such and such he thinks? And 'when we say and mean that such and such is the case ... we mean: *this is so*' becomes an expression of the problem of intentionality—the problem of explaining how one thing can be internally connected with another if they are distinct individuals. When these expressions are taken to be paradoxical, we must imagine that the proposition is a pure intermediary between signs and facts—or a sublime sign—for it is painfully obvious that *real sentences* are only contingently connected with the things they are used to talk about. In this we have the germ of those aspects of the Tractarian theory of the proposition which Wittgenstein later abandoned—the conflation of sentence with assertion, and the related account of the mechanics of picturing.

Wittgenstein suggests that the only solution to the problem he expresses at *PI* 94–96 is a dissolution; nothing short of realizing that the allegedly paradoxical expressions are really truisms will help. In fact, all that it means to say that thought can be of what is not the case is that thoughts (assertions) can be false, and to say that when we say ——, we mean ——, is simply to say that what a man who says that ——says, is that ——. We take these remarks ('thought can be of what is not the case', etc.) to be paradoxical because of a grammatical misunderstanding (*PI* 110 and elsewhere). If my interpretation is correct, the misunderstanding is construable as genuinely grammatical (in the ordinary sense in which grammar has to do with the classification and function of parts of speech). The mistake is to take "this" in "we say and mean that *this-is-so*" and "fact" in "we and our meaning do not stop anywhere short of the fact" as functioning to indicate individuals or entities. That is, we take them to give what Anscombe calls 'material objects'.[39] As a result we misunderstand the phrase "there is" and "something" in the expressions "if a man thinks (asserts) he thinks (asserts) something" and "If a man thinks (asserts), there is something which he thinks (asserts)". Because we think that "something" means an entity, we think that "there is" means something like "there exists" as used in connection with things like tables, chairs, situations, and events. And we misunderstand 'when an assertion is true there is something which makes it true' as saying that the fact which makes an assertion true is an existing entity to which it is connected. Wittgenstein's later account of intentionality serves to clear up grammatical mistakes of this kind, and in so doing, it renders the Tractarian account of the mechanics of picturing and the symbol otiose.

In the same vein, we can now say something about what it was for Wittgenstein to rotate the axis of his investigation. Part of the shift in his investigations was from an examination of the properties which allegedly connected the proposition to reality (whose representation was supposed to be an essential feature of the proposition) and to a sense—a putative fact. Wittgenstein's post-Tractarian enterprise (which as we have seen is not wholly uncongenial to other aspects of the *Tractatus* theory) was to examine what it is to use a sentence or word. In the later works, Wittgenstein gives up the postulation of the symbol and the deduction of its features in favour of an examination in which we 'speak of sentences and words in exactly the sense in which we speak of them in ordinary life' (*PI* 108) and try to determine what our ordinary use of them actually consists in.

This goes along with one of the more mysterious methodological remarks in the *Investigations* (*PI* 109):

> We may not advance any kind of theory. There must not be anything hypothetical in our considerations. We must do away with all *explanation,* and description alone must take its place.

'Description' is opposed to explanation in terms of processes and entities supposed to underlie the described phenomena. In the *Tractatus* Wittgenstein believed that (*TS* 4002):

> It is not humanly possible to gather immediately from [everyday language] what the logic of language is [because] language disguises thought. So much so that from the outward clothing it is impossible to infer the form of the thought beneath it.

If this were true, no mere *description* of ordinary linguistic practice could solve problems like the problem of intentionality and the problem of falsehood. That is why the early Wittgenstein found it necessary to postulate the symbol and ascribe to it whatever features he thought he could show *a priori* that it must have to convey a sense. As he remarked in the *Investigations,* he was not describing what we do with signs. He believed that what must be true of the symbol (for example, that it is a picture with a certain multiplicity, that it is a truth function of the elementary propositions, etc.) could not possibly be detected in the mundane uses of language which we can observe and in which we engage (*PI* 104, 105, 92–98, etc.). His later view of many of the Tractarian doctrines was that they comprised parts of a theory analogous to a scientific hypothesis which explains familiar phenomena in terms of mechanisms which are unfamiliar and hidden in normal situations. This theory was devised to solve problems which Wittgenstein later thought arose merely from a misdescription of language. A proper description solves the problems and refutes the Tractarian theory by showing that there was no need for it in the first place.

(3.6) Wittgenstein's later treatment of the possibility of false assertion and his rejection of the early ontology of the fact also account for his abandonment of the Tractarian account of the general form of all possible propositions (*PI* 65). Commentators often explain this abandonment as a consequence of the 'family resemblance' account of classification. The text of the *Investigations* lends some support to this interpretation:

> Someone might object against me: ... you let yourself off from the very part of the investigation that once gave you the greatest headache, the part about the *general form of* propositions and of language.
>
> And this is true.—Instead of producing something common to all that we call language, I am saying that these phenomena have no one thing in common which makes us use the same word for all,—but that they are *related* to one another in many different ways. And it is because of this relationship, or these relationships, that we call them all 'language'. (*PI* 65.)
> I can think of no better expression to characterize these similarities than 'family resemblances'; for the various resemblances between members of a family: build, features, colour of eyes, gait, temperament, etc., etc., overlap and crisscross in the same way. (*PI* 67.)

Wittgenstein is rejecting the notion that individuals A, B, C, and D, etc., can be classified as individuals of the same kind, K, only if they share the same property or properties. His own view is that A, B, C, and D can be classed as instances of the same kind on the basis of some properties shared by A and B, others shared by B and C, etc., even if there is no single property or set of properties which each one of them has. On this account, there is no fixed set of properties which *every* instance of K must have (although we can enumerate properties typical of things of kind K). Wittgenstein's introduction of the 'family resemblance' theory in connection with his remarks about giving up the quest for the general form together with the familiar story of Sraffa's objection to the *Tractatus* is probably what prompted commentators to say Wittgenstein stopped looking for the general form of the proposition because he realized the classification of a number of different things as propositions did not require that they all share the same properties (cp. Z 444).[40] This could be biographically correct, but it is philosophically unsatisfying. The Tractarian grounds for thinking there must be a general form for the proposition are entirely independent of the theory of classification which the 'family resemblance' account replaced. The arguments Wittgenstein offered for the existence of a general form presuppose the correctness of the Tractarian account of facts in such a way that the later discussion of facts and language use renders them highly implausible. Whether or not this reveals Wittgenstein's own train of thought, it provides an argument against the *Tractatus* which is far more to the point than the argument that classification does not require uniform shared properties.

What was the general form supposed to be? Wittgenstein claimed in the *Tractatus* to be able to set it out in the form of a variable, $[\bar{P}, \bar{\xi}, N (\bar{\xi})]$ which takes all possible propositions as its values (*TS* 6, 52522). As Wittgenstein observed much later, the presentation of a variable which takes all propositions as its values need not be wildly interesting. As used in the sentential calculus "p" is such a variable but all that shows is that we may replace it by any proposition we choose. It would be extraordinary if someone thought this use of "p" showed anything important about the nature of the proposition (*PI* 134).

The early Wittgenstein's use of the variable $[\bar{P}, \bar{\xi}, N (\bar{\xi})]$ (let us call it 'the truth-operational variable') depends upon a more interesting principle. The truth-operational variable takes all propositions as its values, says Wittgenstein, because it gives:

the most general propositional form: that is ... a description of the propositions of any sign language whatsoever. It describes them in ... such a way that every possible sense can be expressed by a symbol satisfying the description, and every symbol satisfying the description can express a sense, provided that the meanings of the names are suitably chosen. (*TS* 45.)
The general propositional form is the essence of the proposition. (*TS* 5471.)

Wittgenstein held that by appropriate replacements of its component variables the truth-operational variable may be used to present every proposition as a truth function of the elementary propositions. The sign "$\bar{\xi}$" is a replaceable by the specification of any set of propositions (*TS* 5501) The sign "N ($\bar{\xi}$)" symbolizes the joint negation of the members of "$\bar{\xi}$" (*TS* 5502). The propositions which are jointly negated are the 'bases' of the joint denial operation (*TS* 521). 'Successive applications of the joint denial operation' means the joint denial first of a selection of propositions, then of a selection of propositions resulting from the denial of the original bases, and so on (*TS* 52521). The sign "$\bar{P}$" stands for the set of all of the elementary propositions (*TS* 6001). Thus each proposition is represented by [$\bar{P}$, $\bar{\xi}$, N ($\bar{\xi}$)] as the last term of a series which begins with the elementary propositions and whose members are generated by successive applications of the joint denial operation. In the presentation of any given proposition, 'q', $\bar{\xi}$ is replaced by a selection of propositions generable from the elementary propositions by successive joint denial such that *their* joint denial will express the truth conditions of 'q'.

The claim that the truth-operational variable gives the essence of the proposition involves two contentions:

(1) The variable describes the propositions of all possible sign languages—all of the propositions of every language in which facts could possibly be stated (*TS* 45).

(2) Every possible sense can be expressed by a proposition which fits the general description (*TS* 45).

(1) is difficult to interpret. It could mean either that every assertion could be described *as if* it were produced by successive joint denials of elementary propositions, or that whenever a

speaker asserts, he *actually does* express a sense *by* jointly deny-ing the elementary propositions. On the first interpretation (which is suggested by *TS* 521), the truth-operational variable is simply a schema for the description of propositions, a stand-ardized form by which assertions can be represented. On the second interpretation the variable tells us what it is to assert. This, I think, was Wittgenstein's view. Despite the suggestion of *TS* 521, he holds that the variable gives us the *essence* of the proposition (*TS* 5471) and that truth functions of elementary propositions (hence propositions in general—*TS* 5) *are* results of operations performed upon elementary propositions (*TS* 5234). I take it that the 'tacit conventions on which the under-standing of everyday language depends' (*TS* 4002) are 'enor-mously complicated' conventions by which the joint denial operation is performed upon elementary propositions.

(2) is easier to interpret. It denies that there is anything to be said which cannot be expressed by a value of the truth-operational variable. Wittgenstein supported his contention that every sense can be expressed by a proposition of the truth-operational form by presenting a theory under which the pos-sible realities and the values of the truth-operational variable comprise closed systems whose members stand in a one-to-one relation. His attempt to secure this involved the following prin-ciples:

(2a)   The sense of a proposition is a possible fact (or else, the such and such whose being the case would constitute a fact). Hence the totality of senses (of things to be said) is (or corresponds to) the totality of possible facts (cp. *TS* 4031).

(2b)   The totality of possible facts (hence senses) is the totality of possibilities for the obtaining and the non-obtaining of states of affairs (*TS* 205, 206).

(2c)   What states of affairs (hence what facts and hence what senses) are possible is determined by which simple objects subsist (*TS* 20124).

(2d)   Every simple object can be named.[41]

(2e)   The simple symbols (names of simples) determine what elementary propositions are possible (*TS* 421).

(2f)   The number and grammar of names is such that there can be one and only one elementary proposition for each pos-sible state of affairs (*TS* 425–426).

M

(2g) If an elementary proposition is true a state of affairs obtains; if it is false, that state of affairs does not obtain (*TS* 425). Therefore, the truth possibilities for the elementary propositions correspond to the possibilities for the obtaining and non-obtaining of states of affairs, and hence to the totality of possible facts (*TS* 43).

(2h) Therefore, every possible fact (hence every possible sense) can be presented by an expression of agreement and disagreement with truth possibilities of elementary propositions (*TS* 4421).

It follows that there is nothing to be said which cannot be expressed by a truth function of the elementary propositions. Had Wittgenstein been able to show in addition that every truth function of the elementary propositions can be produced by their successive joint denial, this would have established that every possible sense can be expressed by a proposition which fits the general form (*TS* 52–532, 5474–551, 6, 6001).[42] It also follows that what fails to express agreement and disagreement with the truth possibilities of the elementary propositions cannot express a possible fact, and thus has no sense. This does not establish the strong thesis (1) that the assertions of every possible sign language must actually be produced by successive applications of the joint denial operation to elementary propositions. But it does entail the weaker thesis that the assertions of every possible language must be equivalent to truth functions of the elementary propositions and must, therefore, be representable by means of the truth-operational variable.

This shows how the Tractarian ontology and theory of language support the claim that the truth-operational variable represents the general form of all possible assertion. A fixed set of objects determines what facts are possible while a fixed set of names determines what assertions are possible. The correspondence between names and objects guarantees that the limits of language coincide with the limits of reality. This secures that there is no sense which cannot be expressed by a truth function of the elementary propositions and (excepting tautologies and contradictions) no truth function of the elementary propositions which fails to express a possible fact. Since the truth-operational variable is a general descripion of the truth functions of the elementary propositions, it gives a general description of all assertions.

Wittgenstein's later account of facts turns the correspondence between possible assertions and possible facts into a truistic equation from which it does not follow that either language or reality must be closed systems bounded by limits which can be established *a priori*. On the later theory there is a possible fact for every assertion only in the sense that we do not call an utterance an assertion unless we are prepared to say that it is true or false. Saying that such and such is a possible fact is a way of saying that an assertion of it could be true. The thesis that there is an assertion for every possible fact thus becomes trivial. We cannot say that such and such could be the case (is a possible fact) unless there is a way of asserting that such and such is the case. Fact locutions on the later theory are either assertions or reports of what has been or could be asserted. A possible fact is nothing more than what a speaker can assert, and so the coincidence between assertions and possible facts is guaranteed. All we can conclude from it is that phrases of the form ". . . is the case", ". . . is a fact", "that . . . is the case (is a fact)" are available in our language for use in making and reporting assertions. We cannot conclude that language is a closed system with *a priori* limits. The only limits on the fact-stating resources of a language are those imposed by contingent facts about human needs and linguistic ingenuity. These are limits, but they are not fixed *a priori* (*PI* 23):[43]

> How many kinds of sentence are there? . . . There are
> countless kinds: countless different kinds of use of what we
> call 'symbols', 'words', 'sentences'. And this multiplicity is
> not something fixed, given once and for all; new types of
> language, new language games as we might say, come
> into existence, and others become obsolete and forgotten.

Because we can invent new kinds of use, and new expressions, no fixed set of assertions can ever be shown capable of saying all there ever will be to say. Even if we could enumerate all of the assertions possible in a given language, this would not prove the language incapable of further development, and we could never prove that there could not some day be new things to say, hence new assertions, and hence new facts—even though it is truistically true that at any given stage in the development of a language there will always be an assertion for every possible fact and vice versa. This shows that no putative general description of the assertion can be proved adequate *a priori*. To prove that a description which applies to any fixed set of assertions will also apply to every possible assertion would be to prove *a priori* that a language cannot develop further.

More importantly, it shows that we do not need to assume a general form in order to explain the correspondence between possible assertions and possible facts. The explanation lies in a trivial correlation of possible facts and assertions which has nothing to do with a uniform form for either.

III

USE

---

1 THE 'CALCULUS THEORY' AND ANTI-PSYCHOLOGISM

(1.1) Stripped of the Tractarian ontology and the account of picturing made otiose by the later account of intentionality, what remains of the Tractarian picture theory is the doctrine that we assert by employing a sentence according to the rules of a projection system.

During Wittgenstein's early period, to project meant to construct logically independent elementary propositions and their truth functions. The first significant departure from this emerged in 1929 in 'Remarks on Logical Form'. Wittgenstein's rethinking of his earlier account of colour incompatibilities led him to reject the doctrine that elementary propositions are logically independent. He argued that it is impossible to explain why 'one shade of colour cannot simultaneously have different degrees of brightness or redness, a tone two different strengths, etc.' if ascriptions of degrees of quality are treated as truth functions of logically independent elementary propositions (or 'atomic propositions' as he was then calling them), (RLF p. 34).[1] He sketched a theory according to which ascriptions of quality or degree of quality are to be treated as unanalysable and mutually exclusive atomic propositions (RLF p. 35). The notion of 'contradiction' is reserved for application to truth functions of atomic propositions representable by marking a 'T' in the right-hand column of a truth table against rows of the truth table which contain only Fs. The *exclusiveness* of two atomic propositions is registered by eliminating from a truth table the 'T-T' row. Thus if 'p' and 'q' are exclusive atomic propositions, their truth table would look like (i) instead of (ii).

(i)

p	q
T	F
F	T
F	F

(ii)

p	q
T	T
T	F
F	T
F	F

In RLF Wittgenstein continued to speak as though ordinary language assertions could be analysed as truth functions of a set of elementary propositions, but he did not say much about how a programme for carrying out such an analysis might look. Important changes in the notion of truth functions and their construction and enumeration would result from the decision not to treat elementary propositions as logically independent, and considerable adjustments in the Tractarian theory of the general form and the early programme for analysis in terms of joint negation would be required to accommodate it to such a view.

There is little in the unpublished works which followed RLF to indicate that Wittgenstein continued to devote much attention to the development of a truth-functional account of ordinary language. It is difficult to decide whether this was because of the difficulties raised by the doctrine that atomic propositions are not logically independent (which Wittgenstein did continue to make remarks about from time to time with regard to colour language) or because his developing concern over intentionality and his disenchantment with his original treatment of it diverted his interests until he had abandoned so much of the Tractarian theory that there was no point in returning to the programme of trying to explain ordinary assertions as truth functions of elementary propositions.

However, he did continue to maintain that sentences are used as projections (RLF p. 36) and that the projective use of a sentence is strictly bound by syntactical and semantical rules (RLF p. 37). Early in 1930 he began to call systems of projection rules (syntactical and semantical rules) 'grammatical systems', and maintained that the meaning of an utterance is constituted by its 'place' in a language. The 'place' of an utterance, he said, is completely determined by the rules of a grammatical system.[2] Wittgenstein's remark that he once thought 'if anyone utters a sentence and means or understands it he is operating a calculus according to definite rules' (*PI* 81) applies to many of his transitional writings up to and perhaps including the *Blue Book*. It also applies, of course, to the *Tractatus* (*TS* 5514):

> Once a notation has been established, there will be in it a rule governing the construction of all propositions that negate *p*, a rule governing the construction of all propositions that affirm *p*, and a rule governing the construction of all propositions that affirm *p* and *q*; and so on. These rules are equivalent to the symbols; in them their sense is mirrored.

This refers to artificial notations like *PM*, but since Wittgenstein held that ordinary language is logically in order and that its assertions share the general form of the proposition, he must also have thought that its assertions are governed by rules for the construction of truth functions of elementary propositions. Thus it is characteristic of the early and transitional accounts to treat the use of words and sentences as governed strictly by projection rules. I shall refer to this view as the 'calculus theory' of use (following *PI* 81) in order to emphasize the extent to which it assimilates all uses of language to the manipulation of signs according to fixed rules.

(1.2) Wittgenstein's reasons for thinking the uses of words in ordinary language are strictly determined by fixed rules are not explicitly stated in the *Tractatus* or the pre-Tractarian notebooks. The most likely explanation is that the theory that language is rule-bound supported the stipulations that every assertion must share the general form of the proposition and of reality, and that the sense of every assertion must be perfectly determinate. After 1929, further reasons emerged for treating language as a calculus. It is difficult to say whether or to what extent they influenced the early Wittgenstein, but they accord with the *Tractatus* and especially with its position regarding psychological accounts of meaning. They are of particular interest because of the way in which they anticipate doctrines and arguments in the *Investigations*.[3]

When Wittgenstein said in 1931 that the meaning of any single word in a language is ' "defined," "constituted," "determined," or "fixed" (he used all four expressions in different places) by the "grammatical rules ... in that language" ', one of his chief concerns was to combat a conception of meaning and understanding which he called 'the causal theory' and ascribed to Russell.[4] This theory treats the meaning of a sign in terms of its causal efficacy, and understanding in terms of response to stimulus.[5] It goes together with the theory that the object of a 'mental act' or intentional mental state is whatever allays a feeling of discomfort with which the mental act is associated. A 'causal theory' of commands would go as follows. A desires something (that is, feels a certain dissatisfaction or restlessness) and believes (from past experience perhaps) that his feeling of discomfort will be quieted if B does something. This leads him to give B an order by producing signs. If A's production of signs causes B to do something and if what B does quiets A's feeling of discomfort, B will be said to have executed A's order.[6] Wittgenstein believed that on this kind of theory, 'B understood A's words' would have to mean that B did what satisfied A and did so because his hearing the words caused him to. The meanings of the words would have to be explained in terms of what they caused B to do.[7] The question whether this is fair to Russell is of no interest here. It is what Wittgenstein thought Russell's behaviouristic treatment of mind had to lead to, and our interests lie with Wittgenstein's response rather than Russell's texts.

Wittgenstein did not deny that certain feelings, mental states, and processes may accompany the use of a sentence to command, or that the use of language depends upon causal mechanisms; a suspension of causal mechanisms having to do with the production and perception of signs, the working of the brain, etc., would make it impossible for us to use language as we do. And he realizes a man could experience all sorts of discomfort which the execution of a command might alleviate. ('Cure my headache!') What Wittgenstein objected to was the equation of meaning with causal efficacy, and understanding with being affected by a cause—even though there are cases in which saying and meaning something is *inter alia* the cause of someone else's behaviour or thoughts, and understanding an utterance is *inter alia* to be affected by the words (*PI* 492–496). The question of what the command meant is only accidentally connected with the question of what performance on B's part would have relieved A's discomfort, and the mere fact that A's words caused B to do something is neither a necessary nor a sufficient condition for B's having understood the command. We can be affected by meaningless as well as meaningful utterances, and we can fail to respond to meaningful utterances which we understand perfectly well.

In the early 1930s Wittgenstein argued that the causal theorist's mistake was analogous to the mistake of thinking that the significance of the marks which constitute a plan used in building a machine is their ability to produce physical and mental effects in the users of the plan: 'If you consider that every proposition ... projects a plan, then you will see clearly where the causal theory *overlooks* what is essential' (UPN *circa* 1931). He thought the correction of the causal theorist's mistake would involve pointing out that the drawing is not a plan of anything apart from the system of projection under which it is to be used. When drawings are used as work diagrams, the distinction between significant and meaningless drawings is quite different from the distinction between drawings which do and drawings which do not causally elicit certain responses from those who see them. Similarly, the notions of understanding and failing to understand a diagram are quite different from the notions of reacting and failing to react to it in a given way. These are analogous to the dimension of language which the causal theory of language fails to do justice to. The appeal of the theory that language is rule-bound and depends for its significance upon the accordance of its use with strict rules was partly due to the means it provides for drawing these distinctions which the causal theory obliterates (UPN 1930):

The way in which I follow an order shows quite well how I understand it. But the connection between execution and command is the invisible body of symbols which is made visible in the rules of language. . . . The sign works only dynamically, not statically. . . . That means that the sign operates as a sign only when I direct myself according to it. (Money operates as money only if I receive and pay it for something.)

To show how the meaning of an order is different from effects the words may produce, Wittgenstein postulated that what counts as the order's execution is strictly delimited from all other possible responses to it by the application of a system of rules to the sentence used to give the order. To distinguish between following an order and reacting to a stimulus, Wittgenstein supposed that to follow an order is to guide one's actions by a sentence. At this point he thought guiding oneself by a sentence is distinguished from reacting to a stimulus in that guiding oneself means following the sentence in the way in which the grammatical rules call for its being followed. The distinction between correctly and incorrectly understanding an utterance was thus conceptualized in terms of accord and lack of accord with rules and set off from the model of stimulus-response on the grounds that the application of rules plays no part in merely responding to a stimulus.

Wittgenstein continued to attach great importance to the distinction between meaning and causal efficacy long after he gave up the calculus model of language. Thus in the *Investigations* he argued that when we say the form of words "Milk me sugar" makes no sense (*PI* 498),

> that does not mean the utterance of this combination of words has no effect. And if its effect is that the other person stares at me and gapes, I don't on that account call it the order to stare and gape, even if that was precisely the effect I wanted to produce.

However, the later Wittgenstein opposed the causal theory of language on importantly different grounds. If the only difference between uttering words and using them to say something, between responding to the words as stimuli and understanding them, turns upon whether or not the employment of the words is rule-bound, it follows that every meaningful use of language must be strictly determined by rules. The calculus theory cannot distinguish between speaking and uttering nonsense, understanding and failing to understand, except in terms of the distinction between what does and does not accord with linguistic rules. The theory that someone who is using a language must be following fixed rules (*PI* 81) is as foreign to Wittgenstein's later philosophy as the causal theory he once used it to oppose.

(1.3) The causal theory of meaning was only one of the psychologistic accounts of meaning Wittgenstein opposed during the transitional period by treating the use of language as the construction of projections according to strict rules. The same model was pressed into service against a variety of theories which explain meaning and understanding in terms of the occurrence of purely internal mental processes.

One such theory is that the occurrence of a mental image of something, X, turns a form of words into an expression which means or conveys X. Against this Wittgenstein objects that the interpolation of an image in the mind's eye between a word or sentence and what it signifies can be of no more explanatory value than the interpolation of a shadow or picture between a sentence and what it is used to talk about. A speaker could treat a mental image as the image of X, but abstracted from the use to which he puts it, it is not essential to the image that it be an image of X—or of anything at all. Even if someone formed a detailed mental image of King's College, it could resemble any one of a dozen other buildings just as well as King's College (*BB* p. 39). Thus the supposition that the image always occurs when we understand the words "King's College" does not help to explain what makes "King's College" the name which refers to King's College because the question what makes X a picture or image of Y applies in essentially the same way to a mental picture as to a physical picture or sentence. To emphasize this Wittgenstein suggests that 'we could ... replace every process of imagining by a process of looking at an object or by painting, drawing, or modelling' (*BB* p. 4). If a mental image does figure in a use of language, its role will be similar to that of a real picture used, for example, as a sample or a diagram, and its use will need just as much explanation as the use of any sign used in speaking. If we had an account of how diagrams, etc., are used as projections, we could apply it directly to spoken or written signs without needing to consider any mental images which might accompany the signs.

A second kind of internal process theory holds that what gives our words meaning is an internal act we perform as we say, write, or listen to words (*PI* 34, p. 18 n., 332, 339, 508, 547, etc.). In opposing this conception, Wittgenstein was not quarrelling with the characterization of saying, meaning, and understanding as mental acts. From the early period to some time before the completion of *Investigations* part I he was prepared to equate saying with thinking (*TS* 3, 31, 35, 4, 5542, 55421; *PI* 32), and he must have considered thinking a mental act. What he was objecting to was a particular theory of mental acts, the theory that they are special conscious processes which accompany and supplement publicly observable uses of words. The picture he opposes is that the meaningful use of language 'consists of two parts, an inorganic part, the handling of the signs, and an organic part which we may call understanding them, interpreting them, thinking' (*BB* p. 3).

The calculus model was employed by Wittgenstein during the transitional period to ward off both of these psychologistic theories. On the assumption that to say and mean something is to apply projection rules to a sentence, there is no need to think the occurrence of mental images is essential to the meaningfulness of a form of words. Even a mental image would have to be used according to projection rules if it were to have any linguistic significance. And if thinking and understanding, etc., are uses of signs as projections, there is no need to think of them as special, essentially interior acts performed by a curious organ called the mind which must occur alongside the publicly observable employment of signs as projections (*BB* p. 3).

I am inclined to think the calculus conception of language served much the same purpose in the *Tractatus*. It might be objected that the early Wittgenstein sometimes wrote as though he favoured a psychologistic account of language use. For example, he says '*Wir benützen das sinnlich wahrnemhbare Zeichen (Laut- oder Schriftzeichen usw.) des Satzes als Projektion der möglichen Sachlage. Die Projektionsmethode ist das Denken des Satz-Sinnes*' (*TS* 311).

That may sound as though we use a proposition sign as a projection by thinking a sense into it—by performing a special sort of mental act of the kind which the *Blue Book* disallows.

This impression is heightened unduly by the Pears-McGuinness translation of '*Die Projektionsmethode ist das Denken des Satz-Sinnes*' as 'The method of projection is to think out the sense of the proposition.' According to this translation the passage says that the way to turn a sentence into a projection is to think out its sense. The German does not carry this suggestion as strongly. *'Das Denken'* is more literally translated as 'the thinking', and the text allows us to interpret Wittgenstein as explaining what it is to think in terms of 'projection method' instead of explaining 'projection method' in terms of 'thinking'. A related textual point arises in connection with *TS* 35 where Wittgenstein says, *'Das angewandte, gedachte Satzzeichen ist der Gedanke.'* Pears and McGuinness read this as 'a propositional sign, applied and thought out is a thought'—as if applying the sign and 'thinking it out' were two different things. The German sentence contains no conjunction. *'Gedachte'* is used appositively. (And again, *'gedachte'* should be translated by 'thought' instead of 'thought out'.)

In *TS* 35, then, 'to think' is equated with 'to apply', and in *TS* 311 'thinking' is correlated with 'method of projection'. Which is being explained in terms of which? While Wittgenstein said nothing in the *Tractatus* about what sort of activity thinking is apart from the passages just cited, he did say something about projection and application. In *TS* 40141 he spoke of

> a general rule by means of which the musician can obtain
> the symphony from the score, and which makes it possible
> to derive the symphony from the groove on the gramophone
> record, and, using the first rule, to derive the score again.

This rule is

> the law of projection which projects the symphony into
> the language of musical notation. It is the rule for
> translating this language into the language of
> gramophone records.

Ignoring the question what the symphony really is, and the many difficulties involved in the notion of a language of gramophone records, it is apparent that Wittgenstein wanted to treat the score and the record as things used as projections of the symphony. They are analogous to different proposition signs which can be used to project the same possible fact. Just as the record and the score used according to the appropriate rule(s) of projection are both projections of the same symphony, two proposition signs, for example, 'the book deals with problems of philosophy', and *'Das Buch behandelt die philosophischen*

Probleme', project the same possible fact when used according to the appropriate rules of projection.

The definitions and syntactical rules governing the application of signs correspond to the rule(s) by which the score and the record are used to project the symphony and so should be considered to be the rules of projection. Accordingly, the projecting may be characterized as using signs according to definitional and syntactical rules. Hints about and explanations of the nature of such rules are to be found scattered about the *Tractatus*.

The *Tractatus* provides some explanation of projection and application apart from their equation with thinking while there is no characterization of thinking apart from *TS* 311 and *TS* 35. This is a reason for reading *TS* 311 as an explanation of what it is to think the sense of a proposition rather than an explanation of 'method of projection' in terms of 'thinking'. As an explanation of 'method of projection' *TS* 311 would be hopelessly inadequate, for on this interpretation we are left entirely in the dark about the meaning of the purported explanatory term. But as an explanation of what it is to think, this passage taken together with the rest of the *Tractatus* provides the beginnings of a more fully worked out theory.

According to the *Tractatus* to assert just is to think, and vice versa (cp. *NS* p. 82). To think (assert) is to apply signs according to the rules of a projection system.[8] If signs are put together and used according to the rules of a projection no further act, physical or mental, is required here. It it were, it would presumably also be required to obtain the symphony as it is being conducted and played, or as it is being produced by a gramophone record. But a conductor and an orchestra who were following a score could not fail to produce a symphony simply because they neglected to perform a special internal mental act of thinking the music while they were playing it, and once the needle has been placed upon the record, nothing further need be done to obtain the music.[9]

If thinking and understanding are the manipulation of signs according to a projection system, a distinction can be drawn between the psychological and the philosophical studies of thought and assertion. Wittgenstein's adoption in the *Tractatus* of a position (essentially similar to that of the *Blue Book*) that to think and assert is to manipulate signs according to rules made it possible for him to pursue philosophical questions about meaning, truth and logic without considering the kinds of information about thinking and speaking which psychologists are supposed to be able to provide (*TS* 41121):[10]

> Psychology is no more closely related to philosophy than any other natural science. . . . Does not my study of sign language correspond to the study of thought processes which philosophers used to consider so essential to the philosophy of logic? Only in most cases they got entangled in unessential psychological investigations, and with my method there is an analogous risk.

The way in which the treatment of language as a calculus avoids the risk is illustrated by a remark from a notebook written in 1930 (UPN):

> in a certain sense I conceive of the understanding of a language behaviouristically. By 'language' I mean only that for which a grammar can be written, and by 'calculus', only that for which a list of rules can be laid out. . . . The behaviourism of my conception consists in this: that I make no distinction between 'inner' and 'outer' because psychology is none of my business.

As is well known, Wittgenstein later argued that in some senses of "private", private uses of language and applications of rules are inconceivable (*PI* 258, 259, 380). This is *not* the point Wittgenstein is making in the passage just cited, and it is doubtful whether his picture of language use at the time he wrote the passage contained the conceptual wherewithal required for the later arguments against private languages. Here he is saying that *even if* a speaker's use of language did involve 'inner' mental processes which are not publicly expressed, and even if it were impossible for them to be made public, the 'internal' or 'private' aspect of the speaker's mental transactions would be of no interest to the philosopher. If the rules of a grammatical system define and strictly determine the meaningful use of signs, then they do so for covert just as much as for publicly expressed assertions and thoughts. Thus what is essential to the explanation of the linguistic significance of a tacit or spoken sign is given by the grammar of the language and by that alone. The distinction between 'internal' and 'external', 'private' and 'public' is indifferent and irrelevant to the philosophical account of the meaning or truth of an utterance or thought if the grammatical system is defined by rules which remain the same whether they are applied externally or covertly.

As a means for avoiding the psychologistic conflation of meaning and causal efficacy and the treatment of meaning as an internal act or process, the theory that language is a calculus anticpated doctrines involved in the later Wittgenstein's contention that the philosophy of language is a grammatical rather than a psychological study. But if following grammatical rules distinguishes between meaningful speech and linguistically non-significant utterances, and if language use is exhausted by procedures guided by a body of rules, every meaningful utterance must be a manipulation of signs which can be justified by appeal to the rules which define language. This is a conception of language use which the later Wittgenstein repudiated (*PI* 289, etc.).

2 WITTGENSTEIN'S REJECTION OF THE CALCULUS THEORY

(2.1) The nerve of the theory that to speak a language is to manipulate a calculus is the contention that the rules of a grammatical system make marks and sounds into projections of reality: 'the co-ordination of the sentence to reality ceases to be arbitrary only as the sentence belongs to a system of language' (UPN *c.* 1932). A sentence whose co-ordination with reality is only arbitrary would be like a map abstracted from the practices, conventions, rules, and accompanying legends or scales which make it into a correct or incorrect map of a specific geographical region. So abstracted, the map would be nothing more than a collection of marks on a paper. There would be no more reason to call it a map of one area than of another, and no more reason to call it correct than to call it incorrect; so considered, it should not be called a map. The linguistic analogue of this would be a sentence which could be called an incorrect or correct assertion about anything we chose. According to the calculus theory, the sentence becomes the assertion that such and such (and nothing else) is the case once its place in the language is fixed by the rules which attach to it and its constituent signs.

The later Wittgenstein's objections to this view stem from his examination of the question of what it is to follow a rule. This question becomes relevant if we ask how—even on the assumption that we could produce fixed rules to which the uses of words and sentences accord—the rules of a grammatical system can transform a collection of signs into a sentence with a non-arbitrary, determinate correlation with reality. Let L be a body of utterances—the productions of marks and sounds by a certain group of people during a given period of time. Suppose we could produce a set of rules to which all of the utterances in L accorded. This by itself would not even establish that the utterances in L were uses of language—let alone the meanings they would have if they were. The regularities which made it possible to bring the utterances of L under a set of rules could be non-linguistic. Suppose an investigator observed men who regularly produced certain sounds in identifiable patterns and set up a one-to-one correspondence between the individual sounds and certain words in the English language. We might even suppose he can produce 'translations' which make sense 'semantically' to an investigator of Quinean persuasion.[11] It is compatible with all this that what he took to be words in a language belonged to an elaborate non-linguistic system, for example, of vocal music. Then the natives would have produced the sounds according to rules that were neither syntactical nor semantical. What looked like the results of following syntactical rules could have been productions of sounds according to the rules of a native composition theory. Perhaps what appeared to be 'semantical' regularities between words and things were due to customs according to which certain combinations of sounds are produced only on certain occasions; the natives think that each pattern is aesthetically suited to a specific background situation. It could even happen that the natives produce sounds at random (perhaps they are deaf and are not even aware of them). Then their accordance with the investigator's rules would be a fantastic non-linguistic coincidence. All of this is highly unlikely, and these are not possibilities about which any field linguist would be likely to worry. However, they are logically compatible with the fact that the utterances accord perfectly with a set of linguistic rules, for rule *accord* requires nothing more than regularity.[12]

Suppose that for some reason an investigator could be sure that the body of utterances he has observed consists of uses of words and sentences; but was somehow able to make sure of this without knowing what any of the utterances meant. (The improbability of this supposition does not affect the argument.) We could in principle find or invent a number of different systems of rules to which any given utterance accorded (*BB* p. 13). If the investigator assumed that the meaning of an utterance is fixed by its accord with a rule, he should assign entirely different meanings to the same utterance—one for each new rule which the utterance could be described as fitting.

The moral of all of this is that the mere fact that an utterance happens to accord with the rules of a system cannot ensure that or explain why it has a non-arbitrary 'correlation with reality'. If a system of rules were capable of fixing the meanings of words or sentences, it could do so only in so far as the rules were used and followed by the speakers who utter the words. That is why the later Wittgenstein attached great importance to the distinction between 'what one might call "a process being *in accordance with* a rule" and "a process involving a rule" ' (*BB* p. 13; see also *PI* 54, 82).

An activity *accords* with a rule if it exhibits regularities expressed by the rule. But it *involves* a rule only if agents actually use the rule to guide and assess their actions. Wittgenstein does not attempt to set out necessary and sufficient conditions for saying that an activity involves a rule. But he does sketch a necessary condition for calling something a rule: 'Roughly speaking, it characterizes what we call a rule to be applied repeatedly in an indefinite number of instances' (*BRB* section 34). We cannot say a linguistic practice is governed by rules unless the speakers can apply the relevant rules to cases which fall under them, can determine which cases do fall under them, and know what it is to apply the rules to the cases correctly. The difficulty Wittgenstein believed to be fatal to the calculus theory is that no rule taken by itself can determine what is and what is not its correct application (*PI* 85):

A rule stands like a signpost. . . But where is it said which way I am to follow it; whether in the direction of its finger or (e.g.), in the opposite direction?—and if there were not a single signpost, but a chain of adjacent ones or of chalk marks on the ground, is there only *one* way of interpreting them?

Even if a rule referred to particular cases, specifying, for example, that on the nth application by a particular person, X, in a particular situation, S, we are to understand the rule as calling for X to do something, Ø, this rule would still have to be applied. What it is to apply it correctly depends upon whether a given case is to be called the nth case, whether a particular person is to be called X for the purpose of applying the rule, and what is to count as øing. What is to tell us all of that?

There can be cases in which the application of one rule is governed by another rule. Examples are judicial principles which specify the circumstances which determine the application of precedents or rules extracted from them. And there is no limit to the number of rules whose addition might become necessary (*PI* 86, 87). But even so, the last rule we appeal to in a given case must itself be applied, and there must be a last rule; it would be impossible to apply an *infinite* number of rules in order to determine the application of a rule in a given case. In short, the application of rules is itself a linguistic practice whose regularities cannot in principle be explained as being due solely to the guidance of rules.

Now the calculus theory assumes (C) that the *only* distinction between arbitrary (hence meaningless) and non-arbitrary uses of signs is the distinction between uses which are and uses which are not strictly governed by rules. Since rules do not determine their own application it follows from (C) that all applications of rules and hence all uses of signs governed by them are arbitrary. This reduces the calculus theory to an absurdity. What the theory holds to be non-arbitrary turns out to be arbitrary if the use of rules is not strictly determined by rules. And it cannot be.

(2.2) It could be objected that in comparing rules to signposts and chalk marks, Wittgenstein confuses a rule with the sign used to express it. It might very well be true (the objection goes) that a signpost or other expression can be interpreted in different ways, and that it would be incomprehensible to someone who could not understand the rule it expresses. But this shows us nothing about the rule itself.

Wittgenstein did not attach great importance to the consideration of rules apart from their formulations. In the *Brown Book*, he commonly identified rules used in language games with tables and inscriptions (*BRB* section 3 f.), and in distinguishing rule accord from rule involvement in the *Blue Book*, he considers only cases in which the 'expression' or 'symbol' of a rule forms a part of the language activity (*BB* p. 13). It is possible that he would have disallowed the kind of distinction between a rule and its expression this objection appeals to.[13]

However, Wittgenstein could allow the distinction between a rule and its expression without weakening this argument. Even if the rule is quite distinct from its expression, the application of the rule still requires that cases to which the rule is applied be recognized as falling under it. It is essential to the correct application of a rule that each piece of behaviour it is appealed to to certify be relevantly similar to those the rule is intended to certify, and relevantly dissimilar from those it was intended to preclude. What will actually be called relevantly similar or relevantly dissimilar depends upon the way in which the rule is grasped or understood by those who apply it (*PI* 201). *When understood* as requiring that two performances be called similar (or that a given feature or features of a performance be taken in a certain way as determining whether the performance is or is not similar to those the rule allows or disallows) a rule tells us what performances are and what performances are not relevantly similar for the purposes of its application. But Wittgenstein holds that the rule cannot tell us how it itself is to be understood. This is the principle which underlies the argument that rules cannot determine their own applications. If it holds at all, it holds just as well for rules as for their expressions, and so the distinction between a rule and its expression drops out of consideration.

(2.3) We have seen that Wittgenstein's rejection of the calculus theory depends upon the thesis that a rule (or its expression) cannot itself determine what will or will not count as its correct application. His argument for this rests on the contention that a rule or its expression can be understood in different ways. There is, I think, a serious objection to this. If I read Wittgenstein correctly, his contention that taken by itself a rule or its expression can be understood in different ways is supposed to imply or entail that there is no single way of understanding a rule such that

(1) it is *the* (one and only) correct understanding of the rule, and

(2) its correctness is established by the rule itself without supplementation by anything outside the rule. I take Wittgenstein to have assumed that a rule determines its own application only if there is a way of understanding it which meets conditions (1) and (2). But does the premise that a rule or its expression can be understood in different ways establish this? The objection I want to consider is that, for example, the man who follows the hand in Wittgenstein's example by walking in the direction of its wrist simply does not understand the signpost. What underlies this is the idea that a rule (or its expression) has only one correct application and provides enough to establish what this application is, taken by itself—abstracted from the 'natural historical facts' to which Wittgenstein eventually appealed to explain the notion of the correct way to follow a rule. Suppose that a rule is or entails what can figure as a premise or premises from which it follows that a given application is correct and that others are incorrect. That is a natural way of interpreting conditions (1) and (2) above. It would seem to be compatible with this supposition that a man should fail to realize which application the rule calls for, or fail to realize that his own application is incompatible with the rule. If so, it is compatible with Wittgenstein's contention that men might understand the rule in different ways. Alternative understandings of the rule need only be taken to be failures in applying the rule owing to stupidity, inattention, carelessness, insanity, or whatever else we choose to explain someone's permanent or temporary inability to grasp the consequences of the premises the anti-Wittgensteinian supposes the rule to provide.

People of normal intelligence can usually understand a rule and experience no difficulties in seeing how it is to be applied. Such questions as 'am I to follow the rule for moving a bishop by moving it straight across the squares or on the diagonal this time?' or 'is moving this way (see (i)): or this way (see (ii)): the same as moving this way (see (iii)):?' do not occur

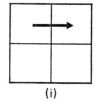

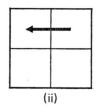

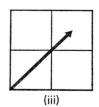

(i)   (ii)   (iii)

to chess players of average intelligence, even when they encounter the rules for the first time. The anti-Wittgensteinian would say this is so because the rule determines precisely what is to be done in each case leaving no room for a man who understands it to doubt how it is to be applied and that most men can understand it. If so, all that is shown by Wittgenstein's examples is that there could be men too stupid or too crazy to understand a rule well enough to see what it does determine as its own correct application.

One answer to this objection is that even if a rule did determine its own application if properly understood, it does not itself guarantee that we understand it properly. Thus we still have to appeal to something outside rules to explain how a rule can govern a linguistic practice—including the practice of following that very rule. But Wittgenstein has a more interesting reply (*RFM* I, 113):

> 'But am I not compelled then to go the way I do in a chain of inferences?'—Compelled? After all I can presumably go as I choose! 'But if you want to remain in accord with the rules you *must* go this way.' Not at all, I call *this* 'accord'.—'Then you have changed the meaning of the word "accord", or the meaning of the rule.' —No;—who says what 'change' and 'remaining the same' mean here?

To see what is involved in this exchange, consider the following example from the *Investigations*.[14] A pupil is trained to construct a series of numbers according to rules of the form '+n' (*PI* 185):

so at the order '+1' he writes down the series of natural numbers. . . . Let us suppose we have done exercises and given him tests up to 1000. Now we get the pupil to continue a series (say +2) beyond 1000—and he writes 1000, 1004, 1008, 1012. We say to him: 'Look what you've done!' He doesn't understand. We say: 'You were meant to add *two*: look how you began the series!'—He answers; 'Yes, isn't it right? I thought that was how I was *meant* to do it.' . . . Or suppose he pointed to the series and said: 'But I went on in just the same way.'—It would now be no use to say: 'But can't you see . . . ?'—and repeat the old examples and explanations. In such a case we might perhaps say: It comes natural to this person to understand our order with our explanations as *we* would understand the order: 'Add 2 up to 1000, 4 up to 2000, 6 up to 3000, and so on.' Such a case would present similarities with one in which a person naturally reacted to the gesture of pointing with the hand by looking in the direction of the line from finger-tip to wrist, not from wrist to finger-tip.

If the rule or its meaning determined that the pupil did not do the same thing after 1,000 as he did before, and that what he did before was the correct way to follow the rule, then we ought to be able to *prove* that the pupil had followed the rule incorrectly. But the pupil can no more accept our criticism of his continuation of the series than we can accept his continuation, and Wittgenstein claims there is no absolute standard by which to settle the dispute (*PI* 186). This doesn't mean that *we* do not have an answer to the question 'did the pupil apply the rule correctly?' It seems clear to us that the pupil was wrong. The point is that the pupil has an answer too, that it conflicts with ours, and that this conflict (between what is clear to us and what is clear to him) cannot in principle be resolved. If this is so, it cannot, *a fortiori,* be resolved by any appeal to rules. 'However many rules you give me—I give a rule which justifies *my* employment of your rules' (*RFM* I, 113; see also *RFM* I, 116, 147–151; *PI* 198, 215–242). Wittgenstein provides no examples of this. However, we can see what an example would have to include. A challenges B's application of a rule, claiming that he is not doing the same thing he did in the cases in which we say he applied it correctly. B replies that the move under criticism is relevantly similar to those A had previously accepted. A replies that they are different, citing whatever feature of the move he thinks establishes the difference. B is then supposed to be able to discount this, either by exhibiting some similarity between the allegedly distinguishing features of his moves or by offering an interpretation of the rule which legitimizes what A took to be a departure from its previous application. It is essential that neither A nor B should be able to prove the other wrong. If they could, there would be room to say the rule can be applied in only one way, any departure from which can be demonstrated to be a mistake or misunderstanding. Furthermore, A and B must disagree over the application of *one and the same rule* to the *same* move in the *same* activity. If the pupil who wrote '1,004' after '1,000' were really applying the rule 'add 2 up to 1,000, 4 up to 2,000, etc.' instead of the +2 rule, his disagreement with his teacher would only show that *different* rules call for different steps or moves, not that a single rule fails to determine its own application. Finally, we must not be able to say that A and B are doing the same thing with different signs (for example, that B's '1,004' means the same thing as A's '1,002'). Otherwise the example would involve a terminological misunderstanding instead of a genuine disagreement over B's application of the rule. If these conditions are met, the example would rule out the objection that anything except what we call its correct application can be proved to be a mistake or a misunderstanding solely by appeal to the relevant rule.

Assuming, for the time being, that such examples can be given, why *do* we say that such and such is the correct application of the rule, and that so and so is not? Our saying so, thinks Wittgenstein, is the result of psychological, sociological and physical facts which make it *natural* for us to see the rule as calling for such and such, and impossible for us to take seriously the kinds of alternative application which would be open to creatures of a different kind (*PI* 189, *RFM* V, 15, I, 118, *PI* 466–480). Eventually we reach a point at which we cannot *justify* our calling this instead of that the correct application of the rule in the sense of providing a deductive argument, a further rule, or any other sort of demonstration that what we take to be its correct application is in fact correct (*Z* 301, *RFM* V, 46). All we can do is explain the practice or custom which constitutes what it is for us to apply the rule (*PI* 202, 206, 211, 217, etc.). The custom itself is neither correct nor incorrect, true or false. It consists of regular responses to the rule, the regularity established by training (*PI* 206), by the actions of the society in refusing to allow or encourage alternative responses (*Z* 499, *RFM* I, 116), together with the physical or psychological makeup of the speakers of a language (*BRB* section 40, 30). On the basis of our applications of a rule, we may call certain performances (for example, in adding, multiplying, containing a mathematical series, etc.) correct or incorrect. But the possibility of such assessments depends upon the consistency and generality of the behaviour patterns which constitute our ways of applying rules (*PI* 240–241). This account has two consequences which are wholly incompatible with the claim that 'the co-ordination of the sentence with reality ceases to be arbitrary' only as the sentence belongs to a rule-defined projection system.

(1)   The *content* of a rule (what the rule calls for, permits, excludes, etc.) is determined by the customary behaviour which constitutes the way we apply the rule, and this behaviour cannot be proved correct or incorrect, let alone so proved by appeal to rules (cp. *PI* 219). As a result, even in cases where speakers follow rules in employing signs, the distinction between arbitrary and non-arbitrary performances ultimately rests upon the behaviour which constitutes the practice of rule application. *Relative* to a given practice (including the content of the rule constituted by it) a performance may be called arbitrary if it ignores or violates a rule. But beyond this, non-arbitrariness is to be explained in terms of facts about the speakers which make it 'natural' for them to behave as they do and to engage in the practices which characterize their linguistic behaviour.

(2)   If in applying a rule we ultimately act 'without reasons' (*PI* 211, 219) there is no need to think rules are always necessary to prevent arbitrary and insignificant uses of language. As a result, there is no longer any point in claiming that every use of language must be rule-bound. Rules can secure regularity in the use of language (assuming that we apply them in regular ways). What kinds of regularity are required may depend upon

the purposes for which the language is being used—in cases where there is a clear purpose. For example, the purposes of the builders require that "slab" always be used to call for a slab, but not that it be pronounced always with the same inflection, volume, etc., etc. When regularity is needed it does not follow that rules are required to establish it. In the case of the builders' language, for example, the training of the speakers is enough to establish crucial regularities without the employment of rules. A builder's employment of "slab" is no less regular than it would have been if he had had a rule to consult to guide and correct his use. But more importantly, it is established by essentially the same kinds of custom (to be explained in terms of the same kinds of causes) as those required for the regular and non-arbitrary application of a rule.

This makes it possible for Wittgenstein to reject the notion that every use of language must be bound by rules in favour of the more modest and correct doctrine that rules occur only when required to correct irregularities which are not precluded by the existing (non-rule-governed) practices to which they are added (*PI* 83, 84, 85). In this connection rule use turns out to be just another linguistic practice, no more fundamental or essential than any other to the use of language. If the use of rules is just as dependent on practices, forms of life, and natural history as the uses of other kinds of linguistic apparatus, it would clearly be wrong to think that language in general must be underpinned by a system of rules. Such an underpinning would be no more secure than an underpinning by any other linguistic machinery.[15]

(2.4) I want to revert to the examples of series continuation Wittgenstein needed to establish that a rule does not determine its own application. We saw that Wittgenstein provided no details of the kind of conversation by which the pupil who applied the + 2 rule differently from the way we do would try to support his application. I believe Wittgenstein's failure to produce convincing examples is symptomatic of an incoherence in his later discussion of rules. My argument in support of this contention is bound up with the later Wittgenstein's rejection of conventionalism. The following digression on Wittgenstein and conventionalism will be necessary to introduce it.

Wittgenstein's examples of allegedly irreconcilable disagreements over the application of a rule occur in the *Remarks* as part of an attack upon the view that 'all necessity is imposed by us not on reality but on our language; a statement is necessary by virtue of our having decided not to count anything as falsifying it'.[16] The kind of conventionalism with which Wittgenstein was chiefly concerned was the theory typically embraced by the logical positivists.[17] Following Dummett, I label it 'modified conventionalism'. The modified conventionalist holds that all necessary truths are either expressions of rules by which we have decided to conduct our linguistic behaviour, or more or less remote logical consequences of these rules.[18]

Wittgenstein's examples of disagreement over the application of rules are intended to attack this view. Our adoption of a rule could not *necessitate* our saying something, 'p', if it were possible to invoke the rule to justify the assertion of any proposition 'q' which is logically incompatible with 'p'. A positivist would have to say that the assertion '1,004 is the successor of 1,000 in the +2 series' is incompatible with '1,002 is the successor of 1,000 in the +2 series', and that the latter assertion is necessarily true in virtue of the rule for generating the series. But (if Wittgenstein is right) someone could write '1,004' after '1,000' without our being able to prove that he had violated the rule for generating the +2 series and without our being able to discount his invocation of this rule to justify his own continuation of the series. If this is so, determination to follow the rule does not establish the falsity of '1,004 is the successor . . .' or any other substitution instance of 'n is the successor of 1,000 in the +2 series', and hence does not account for the necessity of '1,002 is the successor of 1,000 in the +2 series'.[19]

At the same time, Wittgenstein's 'natural historical' account of our use of rules attacks another aspect of the conventionalist theory. If necessity were *simply* a matter of our determination to follow certain rules, then it should be possible for us to determine otherwise—to change the rules and thereby render what used to be necessary truths contingent, false, or even nonsensical. On Wittgenstein's account, only creatures with a radically different kind of natural history, leading a radically different kind of life, could have practices under which what we consider necessary truths would be contingent, false, or nonsensical (*PI* p. 230). *We* cannot seriously envisage such alternatives to our own conceptual systems; our natural history prevents it. Thus the truth of our necessary truths is not a matter of our having *chosen* or agreed to linguistic conventions, for choice presupposes that we can envisage and understand alternatives from which to choose (*RFM* I 149, III, 29, *PI* 230, 236, etc.).

Wittgenstein's views on necessity have often been compared to Kant's. Like Kant he eschews Platonism and attempts to explain necessity on the basis of the way we think. And like Kant he holds that certain assertions are called necessarily true because we have no choice but to conceptualize our world in such a way as to make them true. However, it is more illuminating to compare Wittgenstein to Hume on this point. Unlike Kant, Wittgenstein maintains that the limits of our thought and language depend upon *psychological, physical,* and *sociological* facts about ourselves, our environment, and our ways of adapting to it (*RFM* I, 118, V, 15).

> Thinking and inferring (like counting) is of course bounded for us, not [as a modified conventionalist would say] by an arbitrary definition, but by natural limits corresponding to the body of what can be called the role of thinking and inferring in our life. (*RFM* I, 116).

As an example of what can be called the role of thinking and inferring in our lives, consider what Wittgenstein has to say in the *Investigations* about our grounds for 'believing' that past experience can tell us what to expect in the future (*PI* 472):

> The character of the belief in the uniformity of nature can perhaps be seen most clearly in the case where we fear what we expect. Nothing could induce me to put my hand into a flame—although after all it is *only in the past* that I have burnt myself.

We do not weigh evidence for or against the belief that we'll get burnt if we stick our hands in a fire. Nor do we test it as we would a hypothesis, or try to deduce it from other beliefs. It is a fact about human nature that we expect to get burnt the next time. 'The belief ... is of the same kind as the fear that it [the fire] will burn me' (*PI* 473). That is why, 'If anyone said that information about the past could not convince him that something would happen in the future, I should not understand him' (*PI* 481). (Even though a different kind of creature might find what he says perfectly natural and find himself unable to understand us.) Such facts about us as the fact that given certain past experience we simply do not, or are unable to consider the possibility that the fire might not burn us the next time are—together with our needs and the features of the environment and of ourselves which determine how we will be able to go about fulfilling them—among the kinds of fact which determine what role thinking and speaking will play in our lives. At bottom, the facts about human nature which determine what we take to be necessary about our rules and applications of them in logic and mathematics are essentially similar to these. Wittgenstein discusses our fear of the fire in connection with thinking in general. He does not restrict the discussion to 'inductive' as opposed to 'deductive' thought (*PI* 466–468). Thus logical necessity (like our belief in the relevance of the past to the prediction of the future) rests not upon Kantian facts about pure reason, but upon facts about human nature reminiscent of the psychological facts Hume invoked to explain our belief in and idea of a necessary connection between cause and effect, as well as other non-deductive modes of thought and reasoning.[20]

(2.5)   Now we can see why Wittgenstein did not produce more convincing examples of what the pupil would say in order to justify his application of the rule for generating the + 2 series. The pupil's reply must be convincing enough to prevent us from discounting it as stupid, mistaken, or irrelevant to the application of the rule. He must be able to 'reply like a reasonable person and yet not be with us' (*RFM* I, 115).[21] Otherwise, the example will not establish that the rule does not carry with it an absolute standard of correct application. But at the same time, the pupil's reply cannot justify his application of the + 2 rule to the point where we could treat it as a genuine alternative to our own. If it did, the example would work against Wittgenstein's account of how our natural history and form of life establish the application of a rule. Thus in some sense, we must be unable to understand the pupil or his application of the rule (*RFM* I, 116). If we could understand the pupil clearly, we should have to be able to say that in writing '1,004' after '1,000' he is applying the rule differently from us (or that he is applying a different rule) and then we should, I take it, be able to accept or reject his reason for doing so.[22]

This confronts Wittgenstein with the following dilemma. If he filled in the example in such a way as to leave the disagreement between the pupil and his teacher unintelligible, that would support his contention that alternative applications of the +2 rule are not open to us. But then what the pupil says in the example would not be convincing enough to establish that rules do not determine their own application. On the other hand, if he provided an example which made the pupil perfectly intelligible to us the example would show either that we are or the pupil is mistaken (thus supporting the conventionalist contentions that a rule determines its own correct application), or that the pupil is right and there are available to us intelligible and acceptable alternatives to our way of applying the rule. Dummet holds that Wittgenstein embraced this last alternative. According to him, the arguments which show that a rule does not determine its own application thereby show that we are free to devise new methods for the application of a rule and to apply it in any of the ways we have devised. This means that in constructing or following a mathematical or logical proof, we are free to accept or reject each step as we choose without any constraint from previously established rules or conventions. Each step in a proof establishes a fresh convention and no convention so established is binding on us or anyone else for any further step in the proof, or in any other proof or argument.[23] This view is implausible, and there is no convincing evidence that Wittgenstein held it. From the premise that no rule taken by itself determines its own application, it does not follow that *nothing* determines how a rule or convention is to be applied. We have seen that in appealing to 'natural history' and 'forms of life' Wittgenstein was trying to provide an account of what does constrain us in our application of rules.

Wittgenstein cannot embrace any of the alternatives presented by the dilemma just sketched, and I do not think he can avoid facing the dilemma. The only defence of Wittgenstein's position which seems promising is suggested by Stroud who distinguished between (S1) the intelligibility of the *claim* that there could be alternative practices (for example, alternative ways of counting, continuing the + 2 series, etc.) and (S2) the intelligibility of *practices* which differ as greatly from ours as does the pupil's way of continuing the + 2 series. Stroud suggests that Wittgenstein should be able to establish (S1) *without* establishing (S2). If he can show us that alternative ways of applying a rule are possible and that they cannot be ruled out as incorrect, he will have established that the conventionalists are wrong. But at the same time, he cannot show that the alternatives are intelligible to us without supporting the extreme conventionalist position that we are free to choose at will between alternative conventions and ways of applying rules. According to Stroud, (S1) does not imply or entail (S2). In order to establish that there *could* be alternatives to our own ways of applying a rule, calculating, etc., we need only realize that our practices are shaped by contingent facts about our world and ourselves, and that we and our world could have been different (cf. *PI* p. 230). But since our realization of this will not change our natural history, it will not make intelligible to us the pupil's continuation of the series, or the adoption of alternative conceptual schemes which a change in natural history could make possible. Thus Wittgenstein can have his cake and eat it too; he can establish (S1) in a way which actually rules out (S2).[24]

The trouble with this is that where øing is an activity or practice whose performances can be assessed as correct or incorrect, our concept of what it is to ø (to engage in that particular activity) is essentially bound up with our concept of what it is to ø correctly or incorrectly. (This does not hold for activities like walking or eating to which the terms 'incorrect' and 'correct' do not straightforwardly apply, but Wittgenstein's examples are of things we can be said to do correctly or incorrectly.) Part of what it means to say that two performances are instances of the same activity is to be explicated in terms of what counts as their being correctly or incorrectly performed. If two performances, P_1 and P_2, are such that P_2 can be proved to be neither correct nor incorrect by appeal to the standards by which P_1 is judged, we cannot call them instances of the same activity or practice. Where the performances have a purpose whose description is logically independent of the description of the practices to which they belong, we may be able to call them the same in the sense of having the same purpose or accomplishing similar ends. But this is only to say they are different ways of accomplishing the same end, or instances of different practices with a similar point.

Now what is unintelligible about the practices which Stroud grants are unintelligible to us because of our natural history? At least part of what is unintelligible is that performances which are instances of the alien practices would be correct (for the aliens) even though we could not understand how they could be considered correct. That is to say that they would be performances to which our standards of correctness do not apply. But if the identification of a practice is bound up with standards of correctness as I suggested, that would show that the alien practices are not the same as ours. Performances which the aliens call continuing the $+2$ series are not assessible by our standards, and therefore, what they call continuing the $+2$ series cannot be the same activity or practice we call continuing the $+2$ series. Similarly, what they call applying the rule for generating the series cannot be what we call applying the rule for generating that series. Thus even if we can understand how there could be different practices we cannot understand how there could be different ways of doing the *same thing* (for example, continuing the same series, following the same rule) in this kind of case unless 'same' only means, for example, that what they do achieves the same purpose as what we do. Recall that Wittgenstein was not just trying to show that people with different natural histories might have different practices. In order to defeat conventionalism he had to show they might do the *same thing* (apply the same rule at the same point in the generation of the same series) differently.

Suppose we follow Stroud's suggestion and consider that our natural history need not have been as it is. If our practices are shaped by our natural histories we can grant that if our natural history had been different, we might have called writing '7' after '2' a correct application of something called the rule for generating the $+2$ series. But it does not follow from this that the rule would then be the *same* rule we apply by writing '4' after '2'. And it does not follow that I can have a concept of 'same rule', 'same activity', or of 'adding two' under which it would make sense to say that (given a different natural history) writing '7' after '2' could be an application of the *same* rule I now apply by writing '4'—or that writing '7' could be a different way of doing the *same* thing I now do when I write '4'.

The difficulty, then, is this: the claim that different applications of the same rule are possible presupposes that we can think of the different applications as applications of the *same* rule. But Wittgenstein's doctrine of natural history rules out the possibility of such an identification. It is essential to his account of necessity that we be unable to see how anything *but* our application of a rule can be a correct one. Since using a rule means applying it, I think that Wittgenstein's account of necessity makes the claim that the same rule could be applied in different ways unintelligible.

Notice that it will not help to import an external observer (a philosopher) into Wittgenstein's examples. Suppose we do and he can recognize '1,002, 1,004, 1,006' and '1,000, 1,004, and 1,008' as continuations of the same series involving different applications of a single rule, neither of which need be called incorrect. I think we would have to conclude that what the observer calls the '+2' rule allows for two different performances and therefore that it is not the same as what we (or the pupil) call the '+2' rule because our rule allows no such choice. I do not see how Wittgenstein can rule this out. Unless it is ruled out, the addition of a hypothetical observer who reports that the pupil and his teacher are applying the same rule will not help the argument.

As Stroud has shown, we can distinguish the later Wittgenstein's *position* from Platonism and conventionalism, the two views he opposed. The Platonist maintains that 'our present ways of counting, calculating, and so forth ... are the only possible ones' because they correctly reflect facts about numbers, etc., which are independent of our language and ways of thought and which could not have been otherwise.[25] Against this, Wittgenstein maintains that our ways of calculating, etc., are as they are because of contingent facts about our natural history; had our natural history been different, our ways of counting and calculating would be different. The conventionalist maintains (1) that our adoption of a rule determines what results we must get if we follow it without making a mistake, and (2) that our adoptions of rules are *decisions* and therefore that we could adopt alternative rules and customs. Against this, Wittgenstein holds (1′) that what determines our application of a rule is a practice which rests on our natural history and (2′) our natural history determines our linguistic practices by ruling out alternatives to them and therefore we cannot be said to have chosen them or to be capable of doing so. Although this may be a coherent position, I do not think Wittgenstein has a coherent argument for it. The Platonist might claim the laws governing what those with a different natural history would call counting describe a different set of eternal objects from those which figure in the activity we call counting. Though implausible, this is tenable if what they call counting is something entirely different from our counting. Wittgenstein must say that there could be different ways *of counting* (doing what we do), not just that there could be different activities which could be labelled with the sign "counting". He must claim that *one and the same* activity could be carried out in different and incompatible ways. In order to oppose conventionalism, he must say that the *same rule,* decision or determination of language use could be applied in different ways which though incompatible can be called wrong or right only relative to a natural history or form of life. But in order to maintain (2′) he must also say that alternatives to our practices cannot be understood by us as being correct. The trouble is that what should not be called correct or incorrect øing, should not be called øing either.

Analogous difficulties infect Wittgenstein's rejection of the calculus theory of language. Here he must oppose the theory that a system of rules determines the distinction between arbitrary and non-arbitrary uses of signs by showing that the application of rules is not itself rule-determined. In order to do this, he must establish that a rule does not determine its own application by showing that there could be an application of a rule quite different from ours which could not be proved to be incorrect. But he wants also to block the inference from this to the thesis that we are free to apply a rule in any way we happen to choose, and so he argues that alternatives to our uses of signs are unintelligible or inaccessible to us. His attempts to invoke the theory of natural history and forms of life for this purpose confront him with essentially the same dilemma as that which arose from his opposition to conventionalism.

3 IS THERE A LATER ACCOUNT OF USE?

(3.1) The features of the early Wittgenstein's account of language with which we have been concerned were

(1) the account of the Tractarian proposition as a picture essentially connected to a putative fact, and

(2) the account of the use of a sign as projection carried out according to strict rules.

In chapter II of this book, I argued that Wittgenstein abandoned (1) (and as a result, the Tractarian ontology) on the grounds that two numerically different, existentially independent individuals cannot be essentially connected in the way required by the *Tractatus* picture theory. In this chapter I have been arguing that Wittgenstein rejected (2) on the grounds that the application of rules cannot itself be determined by rules.

In place of (1) the later Wittgenstein treated the proposition as a *sign* (*BRB* section 7) contingently connected by our use of it with the things it is used to talk about. This helps explain his emphasis in the later work on the investigation of how signs are actually used by native speakers. In place of (2) he argued that the use of signs (including signs which express rules) should be described in terms of practices and customs shaped and given their significance by what he called 'natural history' and 'forms of life'. It is now time to ask what if anything he had to offer in the way of a positive account of use during the later period.

(3.2) I am inclined to think that Wittgenstein's later thought provides not so much a theory of use as a sort of metatheory— the rejection of various different kinds of account of use, together with a *very* rough indication of how a philosophical investigation of use should proceed. This should not be surprising. The methodological remarks in the *Investigations* (particularly in the 100s) expressly eschew the attempt to explain philosophically the foundations of language use, and tend to be uncongenial to the notion that any general account of use is possible or desirable. However, it is tempting to ascribe to the later Wittgenstein at least two quite definite accounts of use.

(A) Wittgenstein took very seriously the fact that in speaking meaningfully we do things with words. This, together with the historical coincidence of our readings of Wittgenstein and Austin, has made it tempting to say that Wittgenstein espoused a 'speech act' account of meaning and use.[26]

(B) Wittgenstein often appealed to what he called 'language games' to illustrate and expound facets of the use of language. This has led many readers (particularly Malcolm, Rhees, and Pitcher) to think Wittgenstein intended to explain the use of a word or sentence in ordinary language as its 'role in a language game'—on the analogy of the role of a piece in a game like chess.[27]

I believe against (A) that although Wittgenstein's later work is generally compatible with 'speech act' theories, it does not include a theory of speech acts. I think (B) is a seriously distorting interpretation. I shall take up (B) first, since some of what I have to say about it also bears on (A).

Wittgenstein's language games are parts of the customary behaviour of societies or tribes (usually fictitious ones) on a par with behaviour which a cultural anthropologist might include in his description of the community's way of life. Like the builders' games, most of the language games are engaged in because of, and gain their importance from, the part they play in some practical or cultural activity characteristic of the lives of the members of the community (see *PI* 2 ff.; *BRB* sections 1–11, 58, 47–48, etc.). The games consist of utterances of signs together with the activities into which they are woven (*PI* 7). In most (though not all) cases the game has as its point the furthering of some practical activity (for example, getting stones moved about so that the interminable building of the builders can proceed).

The games are always presented as very clearly marked off from other practices and pieces of customary behaviour. Wittgenstein's fullest descriptions of a game tell us precisely what words can occur in it, what combinations are possible, and what is to be accomplished by the utterance of each combination (see *PI* 8, 48). We are told on what occasions and for what purposes a given utterance would be made and what the appropriate response to it would be. As Rhees remarks, Wittgenstein's descriptions of the games and the activities (building, for example) with which they are connected make them sound suspiciously mechanical and stereotyped, remarkably free from the surprises and improvizations which mark most of our practical activities and the talk they involve.[28] To describe the use of ordinary language words in terms of language game roles would presuppose that ordinary language is a collection of equally discrete and stereotyped activities and that these activities exhaust our uses of words.

Had Wittgenstein given such an account of ordinary language, it would have been susceptible to the following methodological objections.

(1) Wittgenstein provides no account, not even a rule-of-thumb one, of identity or individuation conditions for discrete language games. Neither does he tell us what distinguishes instances of the same from instances of different moves in a language game.

(2) Wittgenstein says that 'one could imagine sounds being emitted for purposes now served by language which sounds yet did not form a language' (*RFM* V, 24; cf. *PI* 528). He suggests he has in mind sounds which serve their purpose by producing conditioned responses whose production does not involve knowing or understanding a language, but he does not provide a clear distinction between such responses and those to which the builders' assistants have been trained. By now he has given up the calculus theory's appeal to rules to distinguish between meaning and understanding and causing a response and responding to a stimulus (in the form of a mark or sign). A language game theory of meaning would somehow have to distinguish linguistic use of signs from stimulus-response mechanisms by appeal to the kinds of practice which constitute them. This in turn presupposes a distinction between linguistic and non-linguistic practices, and the later works do not tell us how to draw this distinction. They do not tell us the difference between a language and a non-language game (cp. *Z* 320–326).

(3) An adequate account of use would have to provide for the classifications of signs as words, sentences, and phrases. The closest we come to finding this in the later writings is an account given in connection with the *Brown Book* versions of the builders' games (*BRB* 1–7). Here Wittgenstein defines

'sentence' as meaning 'a complete sign in a language game' and 'word' as meaning a constituent part of sentence (*BRB* p. 82). Since the criteria for the 'completeness' of a sign depend upon the notion of a complete language game performance, we must explain 'complete sign' in terms of 'complete performance' or 'move in a game'. But Wittgenstein says nothing whatever about what constitutes a complete performance.

(4) We could not give an account of the use of any particular sign unless we could explain how instances of it are identified. It might look from *BRB* p. 82 as though this could be accomplished via the identification of specific language game performances in which a sign occurs (if only Wittgenstein had provided for *their* identification) but in fact it could not. If we undertook to identify the word 'slab' as the mark or sound used in calling for slabs without providing for an independent method of identification in terms of physical properties, we could not distinguish between it and other signs used for the same purpose. At the same time, we cannot rely upon physical features because their relevance to the identification of words would depend upon the games to which the sign belongs, and Wittgenstein leaves us in the dark about how these are to be distinguished or identified.

(5) Use is apparently to be explained and characterized at least in part in terms of what a speaker accomplishes or intends to accomplish by his utterance. But all sorts of different things may be accomplished by a single utterance, and Wittgenstein does not tell us how to decide what purposes and achievements belong and in what sense they belong to a language game. By uttering the word "salt", a native speaker of English could succeed in asking for salt, making a listener aware that he wants salt, obtaining salt, offending a chef, showing that he doesn't know that French cooking isn't supposed to require the addition of salt at table, showing that he knows (or knows how to pronounce) the word "salt", that he is awake, etc. Some of these accomplishments are irrelevant to an account of the meaning (use) of the word "salt" and those that are relevant are relevant in different ways. Wittgenstein is of no help in sorting these out. At best, his remarks on this are hopelessly general (see *BRB* p. 103, for example).

These difficulties would be enough to prevent Wittgenstein

from giving an informative account of language use in terms of language games, but in addition, there is the fundamental objection that ordinary language simply does not consist of discrete activities which fix the uses of our words in the way that the language games fix the uses of the words used by the builders. We can think of commonly repeated kinds of activities in which certain words are frequently used, but the speaking of our language does not consist merely of repetitions of set combinations of words uttered in the course of routines as stereotyped as those of the builders.[29] For many theoretical purposes the comparison of the use of a word to the role of a piece in a game loses its force unless we are able to think of words as having more or less fixed employments in discretely delimited activities. But consider the different ways in which the word "cow" might be used in true or fictitious anecdotes (some of them about cows, others about things compared and connected in different ways to cows in the stories), in poetry, in judging animals at agricultural fairs, in buying and selling livestock and animal figurines, etc., and in leisure-time conversations which ramble on without any fixed direction. Or consider Wittgenstein's example of the question 'is Tuesday leaner than Wednesday?' (The answer, says Wittgenstein, is that Tuesday is lean and Wednesday, fat (*PI* p. 216).)

To show how unnatural it is to think that every use of words is bound by rules, Wittgenstein suggests that we compare language to games by imagining (*PI* 83):

> people amusing themselves in a field by playing with a ball
> so as to start various existing games, but playing many
> without finishing them and in between throwing the ball
> aimlessly into the air, chasing one another with the ball and
> bombarding one another for a joke, and so on.

It would be absurd to think that 'the whole time they are playing a ball game and following definite rules at every throw' (ibid). It would be equally misleading to say that every throw in their play must belong to an existing game in which the ball plays a definite pre-established role. This shows what is wrong with thinking that in every conversation the use of words can be assimilated to the use of pieces in a pre-established game in which the roles of the pieces are clear and can be given ahead of time.

And finally, there is the difficulty of understanding how the same word can have the same meaning in different contexts if we assume that each context is a separate language game. How, for example, could we explain how "Tuesday" in "Tuesday is my birthday" and "Tuesday is lean" means the same thing if these are considered sentences belonging to different language games and if the meaning of a word is constituted by its use and hence by its role in language games?

Did Wittgenstein really think the use of a word is its role in a language game? Although he sometimes refers to our ordinary use of words as language games (for example, *PI* 654–656, 640, 217, 244, 23; *OC passim*) he does not explicitly claim that our language is a collection of discrete language games. In fact, he denies it. 'The picture we have of the language of the grown up is that of a nebulous mass of language, his mother tongue, surrounded by discrete and more or less clear cut language games, the technical languages' (*BRB* p. 81). As examples of 'technical languages' he cites 'the use of charts and diagrams, descriptive geometry, and chemical symbolism' (*BRB* p. 81). Many areas of higher mathematics and the logician's use of the truth-functional calculus would probably qualify too (*PI* 136). Outside these abnormally well-determined uses of language, the analogy between words and pieces whose roles are clearly fixed by the practices and rules of a game becomes far-fetched and misleading. What then does the study of language games have to do with understanding the 'nebulous mass of language' from which the 'technical languages' spring?

We can get an answer to this by considering why the methodological difficulties ((1) to (5) above) do not obstruct Wittgenstein's own appeals to language games. Notice that many of Wittgenstein's language games are wholly fictitious. They are simpler and more clearly defined than most areas of our language (*BB* p. 17, *BRB* p. 81, *PI* 17, etc.) because Wittgenstein has deliberately constructed them that way. He has simplified them so that it is easier to 'command a clear view of the aim and functioning of the words' in his examples (*PI* 5). The reason Wittgenstein does not worry about how to decide whether two of his fictitious linguistic activities are instances of the same or different games, etc., is that instead of picking out distinct games from real languages he simply stipulates whatever delimitations are necessary for his purposes. When he refers to existing linguistic practices as language games, he usually abstracts bits of ordinary use from simple contexts (see, for example, *PI* 654–656, 633, 640). In so doing, he does not claim that the language actually comes divided up into the bits he abstracts from it.

Since Wittgenstein realized that ordinary language is nebulous, and since his language games are either imaginary examples or simplified instances of use artificially abstracted from our own language, it is unlikely that he thought our language actually consists of language games. He employed language games as artificial models which illuminate features of our language *by comparison*: 'The man who is philosophically puzzled sees a law in the way a word is used, and trying to apply this law consistently, comes up against cases where it leads to paradoxical results' (*BB* p. 27; cp. *PI* 125). The cure for this is to 'make up several different usages which will more or less agree with the ways the word is actually used' (*BB* p. 27). These will show to what extent the putative law is correct and to what extent it is not, but we are to bear in mind that there is not one exact use for the word in question (ibid). The invented uses, tailored to cure the philosopher's puzzlement, are called language games, and although the *Blue Book* makes language games sound more like notations than the activities of the *Brown Book* and *Investigations,* this much of Wittgenstein's conception of the therapeutic purposes to be served by using language games in philosophy did not change greatly after the *Blue Book* ;(cf. *PI* 81, 125, and Rhees's Preface to *BB*).

In the *Investigations* Wittgenstein says that his language games are 'objects of comparison ... meant to throw light on the facts of our language by way not only of similarities but of dissimilarities' (*PI* 13). In connection with this, he warns us that (*PI* 131):

we can avoid ineptness or emptiness in our assertions only by presenting the model as what it is, as an object of comparison—as, so to speak, a measuring rod; not as a preconceived idea to which the reality *must* correspond. (The dogmatism into which we fall so easily in doing philosophy.)

One piece of dogmatism he wanted to avoid was the idea that our language actually does consist of discrete language games related to one another in the same ways as Wittgenstein's own models. 'We want to establish an order in our knowledge of the use of language: an order with a particular end in view; one out of many orders; not *the* order' (*PI* 132).

Thus it is incorrect to say that Wittgenstein thought the uses of words in ordinary language are their roles in language games. Instead, he thought that *aspects* of the nebulous mass of language which comprises most of a mother tongue could be illuminated for philosophical purposes by comparing ordinary usage to language games. Language games belong to a *technique* for examining uses of words and sentences in ordinary language, and not to a *theory* (that is, that ordinary language is a collection of language games) of use.

This saves Wittgenstein from a number of serious objections, but not without cost. For example, in chapter II.2 of this book, I argued that if (as may not be the case) the later Wittgenstein had an account of truth, it would have to have equated conditions of truth with conditions for asserting and maintaining an assertion relative to the departments of language in which a given sentence is put forth as true. This account may fit the notion of truth in formal systems like *PM,* but its application to contingent ordinary language assertions presupposes that here, too, we can find discrete linguistic practices with well-laid-out conditions for asserting and maintaining. Its applicability would be secured if (as is unfortunately not the case) ordinary language really were a collection of language games. If instead it is 'nebulous', it is difficult to see how—using Wittgenstein's methods—we could give a clear enough account of the notion of conditions of assertability to develop a theory of truth along the lines suggested by Wittgenstein's later remarks on truth.

The other account (A) sometimes ascribed to Wittgenstein is that to use a word is to perform a speech act of the kind discussed by Austin, Grice, and others. I suggested that although nothing in the later works seems clearly opposed to such accounts, a theory of speech acts is not to be found in Wittgenstein. My reasons for saying this have to do with the methodological complaints to which Wittgenstein would have been susceptible had he defined the use of a word in ordinary language as its role in a language game. Two examples will suffice to illustrate this.

(1) It is characteristic of the speech act theory developed by Grice to define the meaning of a word or sentence in terms of the purpose which speakers intend its utterance to secure.[30] This would be untenable unless we could distinguish between the kinds of aim and purpose we illustrated earlier in connection with the utterance of the English word "salt", ruling out those which are irrelevant to meaning in the sense of that word to be explicated by a speech act analysis. Wittgenstein fails to provide any means for doing this.

(2) The Austinian kind of speech act theory which emphasizes conventions and rules governing such performances as promising, stating, etc., depends for its success upon the distinction between perlocutionary and illocutionary effects of an utterance.[31] Wittgenstein provides no machinery for drawing this distinction.

(3.3) Instead of a general definition or account of use, the later Wittgenstein offers a discussion of what it is to investigate uses of words and sentences. His aim was to rule out inappropriate and wrong-headed questions about language use by showing us what the subject-matter of its investigation should be.

His most general doctrine concerning this is that to study the use of language is to study (1) the natural history of human beings (*PI* 25, 415, etc.) and (2) forms of life (*PI* 19). The former invites a comparison between the study of language use and natural historical accounts of the life of the bee or the ant having to do with the standard behaviour by which an animal adapts itself to its environment. The latter invites comparison with a cultural anthropologist's examination of the customary behaviour which is characteristic of a culture, community, or society.

In an extremely helpful discussion, K. W. Rankin draws the following analogy between the later Wittgenstein's approach to the study of language and the anthropological studies of Evans-

Pritchard, Lévi-Strauss, and others whom he characterizes as 'descriptive analysts':[32]

> The descriptive anthropoligical school might be interpreted as holding that the 'meaning' of a social form of behaviour lies . . . in the functional interdependence between it and different forms of behaviour within a spatio-temporal extended area. Similarly, but in a more literal sense of 'meaning', Wittgenstein . . . [holds] that the meaning of language behaviour lies in its interdependence with other forms of behaviour within the total way of life of the community.

Wittgenstein held that 'the common behaviour of mankind is the system of reference by means of which we interpret an unknown language' and hence that to say that the speakers of a strange language give orders, understand them, obey them, etc., etc., is to locate various pieces of their behaviour within this 'system' (*PI* 206; see also *BRB* p. 103). The reason for this is his belief that 'ordering', 'understanding an order', etc., as well as 'describing', 'asking', 'answering', etc., are descriptions of pieces of behaviour based on their place in a way of living. The identification of a performance as the giving of an order depends in part upon our ability to recognize the behaviour of a man who wants something (wants to get another man to do something) and who is speaking. It depends also upon our ability to see connections between the speaker's utterance and other pieces of customary behaviour, together with its place in what is going on when the speaker gives his order. These last are analogous to the insights upon which an anthropologist depends in order to classify a piece of behaviour as, for example, part of a conventional activity constitutive of a marriage ceremony, fertility dance, or other tribal practice. The former is analogous to a natural historian's identification of a piece of behaviour as an expression of desire, pain, dissatisfaction, expectation, etc., etc., in an animal (cp. *PI* 647).

What is of interest about this is that it is not *simply* a doctrine about how we go about determining what the speaker of a strange language is doing. It is a doctrine about *what it is*, for example, to order, ask a question, describe, etc., and by extension, what it is to perform the acts (for example, referring, predicating, etc.) we ascribe to a speaker who orders, asks, or describes. What makes a performance the giving of an order, the asking of a question, etc., is its place with reference to the natural behaviour of a human being together with its inter-dependence with the conventional behaviour which consti-tutes a form of life or culture. Similarly, what makes the cor-relation of a mark or sound with a thing a *reference* to that thing is the place of the correlation in a performance which belongs to a linguistic practice and which (together with the practice) is shaped by a system of customary behaviour.

This goes together with Wittgenstein's view about what kinds of inquiry can constitute a study of language use. First and most importantly he thinks there is an investigation whose aim is to *describe* linguistic performances and their interconnections with each other and with extra-linguistic institutions and activi-ties. The following examples fall under this heading.

(1)   Unpacking such terms as 'referring', 'naming', etc. (*PI* 37):

> What is the relation between name and thing named?—
> Well, what *is* it? Look at the [builders'] ... language game
> or at another one : there you can see the sort of thing this
> relation consists in.

The later Wittgenstein hears the question 'what is the relation between name and thing named?' on analogy with 'what is the relation between such and such tool and the thing to which it is applied?' An answer would be a description of the ways in which activities in which things are named and their names used are carried out, and what is done with the names in these activities. Aspects of this are illuminated by the construction of language games which isolate or exemplify specific features of the practices under investigation.

(2)   The dissolution of philosophical problems resulting from misdescriptions of activities which comprise the uses of langu-age. Philosophical problems, Wittgenstein claimed, arise from 'grammatical illusions', misinterpretations of 'our forms of language' (*PI* 110, 111).

An example is Wittgenstein's suggestion (*PI* 654) that in trying to understand how a man can report his intentions 'our mistake is to look for an explanation where we ought to look at what happens as a 'proto phenomenon'. This is where we

ought to have said: *this language game is played.'* The suggestion comes at the end of a discussion of a case in which a man
tries to remember what he was going to go on to say when
interrupted in the middle of a remark (*PI* 633 f). This becomes difficult to understand when we consider that what he
will remember are specific feelings, sensations, thoughts, etc.,
together with details of the situation in which he was going to
speak. It is essential to the intention to say such and such,
that it be the intention to say just that and nothing else,
while a connection with saying such and such is *not* essential
to any of the specific incidents, feelings, etc., he will remember.
If we think that in order to recall his intention, the man
must find a remembered event, feeling, etc., essentially connected to the remark he was going to make before he was
interrupted, we will be perplexed by the fact that nothing he
remembers is so connected to the interrupted remark. But,
thinks Wittgenstein, our perplexity arises from an incorrect
assimilation of recalling an intention to such things as recalling
a feeling or event. A man who has trouble recalling what he
was going to go on to say may try to remember *by* recalling
what he was feeling or what was going on. We mistake this
fact for evidence that the intention he tries to recall *is* one of
the feelings or happenings which occurred before he was interrupted. This mistake is due partly to similarities between what
the man does and what we do when we are simply trying to
remember a past feeling or event, and partly to superficial
grammatical similarities between the language with which we
recall what we intended to do and the language with which
we recall past feelings, etc. (*PI* 664). The mistake is to be
remedied by sorting out the various linguistic performances
which have thus become conflated. To do this, we use language
games to point out dissimilarities between them, and also perhaps, the similarities which led to our original confusion in
order to get clear about what went wrong.

It is helpful to compare this to a kind of mistake which an
anthropologist might make in describing the customs of a community under observation. An anthropologist who mistakenly
identifies an observed practice with one which he is already
familiar with (from his own or from a foreign culture which he
has observed) will become perplexed in roughly similar ways.

The cure for his perplexity will be a correct classification and description of the practice in question.

A simpler and rather different example is Wittgenstein's discussion of simplicity in connection with Socrates' dream and the Tractarian doctrine of simple objects (*PI* 48 f.; Chapter I, 4 of this book). Part of Wittgenstein's investigation of the notion of simplicity consisted of noting that a thing is called simple or complex only in connection with the application of a definite standard for complexity and a method for division or description. His intention was to avoid mistakes which arise from our ignoring this fact about the way we use the words "simple" and "complex", and in particular, the mistake of thinking that there is such a thing as absolute simplicity.

(3) Rejecting questions about the 'foundations' of language. Suppose we had a complete description of a characteristic use of language (for example, cursing or begging) or of a language game like one of the builders' games. By 'complete', I mean a description which tells us what words are uttered and in what circumstances, for what purposes, etc., and which tells us what behaviour, feelings, and thoughts normally accompany their utterance. Someone might then ask: 'In order to curse X, a speaker must refer to him. We have observed that he does this by uttering the word "X". How is it possible for the utterance of this word in the course of this activity to accomplish a reference to X?' The question asks for something which underlies and makes possible the linguistic activity which has already been described. As answers, this question may get an account of a method of projection and the way in which it meshes with an ontology, a theory of mental acts (intending and meaning) whose performance is supposed to accompany and give significance to the observed linguistic performance, the postulation of symbols said to mediate between the spoken or written words and things talked about, etc.

Wittgenstein wanted to reject such questions by pointing out, for example, that referring to a man and cursing him *is* (*consists of*) the behaviour, etc., which has already been described. Suppose what has been observed *is* what it is to use words to refer and curse. Then the question 'how can one refer and curse by uttering such and such words in such and such circumstances?' becomes analogous to 'how can a man eat by doing *that?*' where *that* is the behaviour which constitutes eating, or to 'how can a man run by moving his legs in that way?' where *that way* is what we call running.

The question 'how can he refer to X by uttering the word "X"?' assumes that referring to X is one thing, while the linguistic practice which has been fully described is something else which presupposes the accomplishment of the reference by some other means or somehow brings it about. Wittgenstein's point is that since the activity and the referring are one and the same thing, there is no room for the question how the activity (uttering the word, etc.) can accomplish the reference. The question amounts to no more than a question of the form 'How can a speaker ø by øing?'

(4) Determining what is essential to a use. In order to assess the claim that something is essential to the meaningfulness or use of a form of words, Wittgenstein suggests we consider the 'point' of the utterance or the linguistic practice to which it belongs (*PI* 562–570). By 'point' he means (very roughly) the way an utterance fits into the conversation or the extra-linguistic activity (if any) in which it occurs, or the significance which a linguistic practice gains from its connection with other aspects of a form of life. To show that a feature of language or its use is essential would be to show that without it, a use of language would become 'pointless'—would lose its significance. Thus Wittgenstein objects to the suggestion that the occurrence of a mental picture is essential to the use of a common name by pointing out that the builders' use of "slab!" to call for slabs can achieve its purpose without the occurrence of a mental image (*PI* 6).

The foregoing examples are illustrations of what Wittgenstein thought could be accomplished by *descriptions* of linguistic practices and their places in a form of life. The second kind of investigation of use is one which the later Wittgenstein held to be legitimate but philosophically uninteresting. This is the investigation of causes. The development of an actual practice or use of words depends upon physical, physiological, and psychological regularities which characterize the speakers and their environment: 'To invent a language could mean to invent an instrument for a particular purpose on the basis of the laws of nature (or consistently with them)' (*PI* 492). If so, in order to understand what makes possible a linguistic practice we should have to know something about the relevant natural regularities. As an example consider the training by which we teach someone an activity by giving him examples and encouraging him to go on in a certain way. Wittgenstein observes that a pupil's capacity to learn (for example, to continue a mathematical series) from such training may 'come to an end' (*PI* 143), and describes a tribe in which children who are unable to respond to gestures which encourage them to go on are separated from the others and treated as lunatics (*BRB* section 30; cp. *Z* 371–372). If our capacities to learn regularly came to an end in such a way as to frustrate this kind of training, the linguistic practices whose teaching depends upon it would become impossible for us to engage in. Therefore, in order to understand what makes these practices possible, we might look for psychological and physical (causal) explanations for the responses upon which training by example depends.

Part of what Wittgenstein meant by saying that a philosophical problem requires description instead of explanations of language use is that such causal accounts are not what a philosopher needs. Philosophical perplexities arise from confusions about linguistic practices themselves (*PI* 122, 123). Causal explanations presuppose an understanding of the linguistic phenomena—the uses of language—which the causes underlie. And that, Wittgenstein thought, is precisely what the philosopher who is confused about language lacks.

In arguing that philosophical questions about language require descriptions rather than explanations of language use, Wittgenstein does not tell us what in general we shall find when we successfully describe it, or what we must look for. What we must look for will depend upon the philosophical needs which drive us to look, and these are various (*PI* 127). He holds that the multiplicity of kinds of language use makes it impossible to say what we are bound to find when examining the uses of particular words—either *a priori*, or by extrapolation from what examinations of other uses have revealed (*BB* pp. 17–18). Accordingly I think it incorrect to say that Wittgenstein wanted to provide a single positive theory of language use. It is not surprising that the doctrines he presents which centre on the idea that language use is part of our natural history are too

P

general and ill-defined to comprise a specific theory of use. They are more satisfactory if treated as guides to the philosophical study of use.

Whether the later Wittgenstein's failure to provide a detailed positive theory of use is justified by his idea that our employment of language is too diversified to make a general theory possible is debatable. Current work in structural linguistics suggests, for instance, that very general theories of syntax may be possible.[33] However, Wittgenstein's own therapeutic interests make it understandable why he himself did not attempt to provide a detailed theory. He saw his task as 'assembling reminders' to aid philosophers who are perplexed about particular features of language use (*PI* 123–127). To accomplish this, he needed to describe specific aspects of language use and to tell philosophers how they had been mistaken in their understanding of them. This kind of work requires the methodology provided by Wittgenstein's remarks about natural history, the technique of using language games as models, etc. It is not clear that it also requires the development of a full-blown theory or definition of language use.

(3.4) Although I do not think Wittgenstein's later philosophy contains a well-worked-out theory of use, its pronouncements concerning the philosophical study of use have consequences which rule out some of the more characteristic doctrines of the *Tractatus*.

The most important contrast between the later and the earlier discussions of use stems from the Tractarian characterization of the use of language as the application of signs according to the rules of a projection system which accomplishes the expression of agreement and disagreement with truth possibilities of elementary propositions. Given this characterization, asserting can be seen as an activity which could be successfully carried out by speakers who never did anything else. Although a speaker could produce a Tractarian proposition in order to further some extra-linguistic activity, it is not *essential* to asserting (as described in the *Tractatus*) that it have any connection whatever with any other practice or activity. According to the *Tractatus,* to assert is simply to use signs as models of reality— nothing more. In contrast to this, we have just been observing that on the later theory, the significance of an utterance depends upon its place in a form of life (*PI* 25, *RFM* V, 2, V, 26, *BRB* 134, etc.).

As an example of the difference between these two accounts of use, consider the difference between the following (superficially similar) remarks:

> I want to say: it is essential to mathematics that its signs should also be used in civil life. It is their use outside of mathematics, in other words, the *meaning* of the signs that makes the sign game mathematics. Just as it is not a logical conclusion if I change one configuration into another (say one arrangement of chairs into another) unless these configurations have some use in language *besides* the making of these configurations. (RFM p. 133.)
> In real life a mathematical proposition is never what we want. Rather, we make use of mathematical propositions only in inferences from propositions that do not belong to mathematics to others that likewise do not belong to mathematics.
> (In philosophy the question, 'What do we actually use this word or proposition for?' repeatedly leads to valuable insights.) (*TS* 6211.)

The passage from the *Tractatus* claims it is essential to the meaningfulness of mathematical symbols and sentences that they be used in connection with non-mathematical assertions. But that is not to say that they must have a role in what the later Wittgenstein meant by 'civil life'. The non-mathematical propositions of the *Tractatus* are connected with 'civil life' accidentally, if at all.

The distinction between the early and later views to which this points is that the former treats use as characterizable in terms of systems and techniques of projection describable without reference to a form of life, while the latter treats use as constituted by features of a form of life. The following are ramifications of this contrast.

(1) According to the *Tractatus*, the limits of language are determined *a priori* by the form of reality which determines— quite apart from any considerations having to do with human nature and institutions—what must be done with words in order to construct projections of reality. On the later theory, what

can be done with words and how the significant use of signs can be accomplished depends upon contingent facts about speakers and the world they live in. That is why nothing like a general requirement for the multiplicity of a sentence or assertion is given in the later period. Earlier, Wittgenstein would have to have called a one-word utterance either elliptical or meaningless (*TS* 4032). But in the *Investigations* Wittgenstein can say that the question whether an utterance can consist of a single word is to be answered relative to a specified linguistic practice, and that practices with different requirements are possible (*PI* 19–20).

(2) The *Tractatus* classifies uses of signs under such headings as 'referring', 'signifying', 'describing', etc. On the later theory, these terms cannot be understood except as shorthand characterizations of practices involving language use. On the early theory, they are treated as if they could be understood by appeal to a scheme of projection without consideration of what might actually be done with a projection in real life.

(3) The *Tractatus* treats the meaning of an utterance as determined completely and unambiguously by the standard uses of the signs it contains. Once we are told how each of the words in a sentence functions in a system of projection, we can understand the sentence without any further explanation of its sense (*TS* 4025–403).

In contrast with this, the later Wittgenstein's examples of the diviner who says 'I feel water three feet underground' and the man who says 'it is five o'clock on the sun' are intended to show:

(a) that our understanding of a sentence on the basis of explanations of the individual words it contains presupposes an understanding of the context in which the sentence is uttered and what the speaker is doing in uttering them, and

(b) familiar words combined into sentences in unusual contexts can be unintelligible until we discover what function the utterance of the sentence has in the context in which it occurs (*PI* 350–352; *BB* pp. 9–10).

In the *Tractatus,* signs are instruments (or counters) used for the purpose of constructing projections which *show* us something. In the later work, sentences (as well as words) are often (but not exclusively) compared to tools or instruments whose use furthers an activity from which their utterance gets its point (*PI* 199, 206, 241, 325, 569, and p. 226, etc.). It follows from this that in order to understand a sentence, we need to understand what a man (the speaker) is doing. An enumeration of conventions governing the specific words he uses may not tell us this, and so we may need to have the sentence as a whole explained to us.

This reflects the difference between the earlier conception of the proposition as a projection of reality and the later idea that the utterance of a sentence is to be considered a performance which gets its significance from the activities and institutions with which it is connected. We can think of what is shown by a projection as a function of the projective uses of its elements, and the assimilation of a sentence in use to a projection accounts for the early notion that an understanding of each word must guarantee the understanding of a connection of words. Wittgenstein had this conception in mind when he said that 'one would like to speak of the function of a word in *this* proposition. As if the proposition were a mechanism in which the word had a particular function' (*PI* 559). On the later view, this picture of language involves the mistake of thinking that the significance of an element in an activity is independent of the context in which it occurs (*PI* 584):

> suppose I sit in my room and hope that N. N. will come and bring me some money, and suppose one minute of this state could be isolated, cut out of its context.... Think ... of the words which you ... utter in this space of time. They are no longer part of this language. And in different surroundings, the institution of money doesn't exist either. A coronation is the picture of pomp and dignity. Cut one minute of this proceeding out of its surroundings: the crown is being placed on the head of the king in his coronation robes.—But in different surroundings gold is the cheapest of metals, its gleam is thought vulgar. There the fabric of the robe is cheap to produce. A crown is a parody of a respectable hat.

This does not give us a theory of use or meaning. But it puts limits on a theory; it secures that if a theory could be constructed to meet the specifications of Wittgenstein's later work, it would have to be different from the Tractarian theory, and it shows what the differences would have to be. I do not believe much more in the way of a theory of use is to be found in the later work.

4 SIMPLES AGAIN

(4.1) By way of a conclusion I want to consider briefly what effects the changes in Wittgenstein's thought I have considered have upon the arguments against the doctrine of simple objects and symbols which were considered earlier. The point of reverting to this discussion is to give an example of the effect of the developments we have been considering upon the conduct of a traditional philosophical inquiry.

I have already suggested (in ch. I.4) why the *Investigations* arguments concerning simples might seem unconvincing and inconclusive from the standpoint of the *Tractatus*. If my interpretation of the *Tractatus* (ch. I.2 and 3) was correct, Wittgenstein postulated the subsistence of absolutely simple objects in order to secure the determinacy of sense and the continuing existence of the bearers of *Tractatus* names. All of this seemed necessary in order to explain how a proposition could be a representative picture of every possible reality. The *Investigations* arguments seemed to ignore Wittgenstein's early reasons for postulating simple objects and so appeared to be directed against caricatures of Tractarian theory. Wittgenstein argued, for example, that it was not essential to the language game of *PI* 48 (the description of combinations of coloured squares) that the individual coloured squares be absolutely unanalysable, immutable, or indestructible. The difficulty with this was that pending a refutation of the Tractarian arguments for simples, all this could show was that the coloured squares were not *bona fide* examples of simples. Wittgenstein argues that we often use sentences which do not meet Tractarian standards for determinacy and that ordinary proper names are used to name bearers which have ceased to exist. A Tractarian would object that the examples of allegedly indeterminate uses were unanalysed ordinary language locutions, and that ordinary proper names are not genuine names. Finally, there was the question of the legitimacy of treating traditional philosophical doctrines as though they had been intended as descriptions of language games on a par with descriptions which field linguists observing the tribes which play the games might give.

The later Wittgenstein's failure to feel such qualms can now be explained as follows:

(1) The assumptions that appeared to make necessary the postulation of simple objects (the assumptions that the meaning of a genuine name is its bearer and that sense must be determinate) were abandoned during the transitional period as the result of Wittgenstein's consideration of the intentionality of assertions. When Wittgenstein gave up the Tractarian thesis that facts are real individuals which obey the laws of identity, he had no more need to assume that sense must be determinate. And when he gave up the picture theory, he had no more need to assume that the bearers of names must be their meanings. This assumption had served to justify the contention that what is represented by a proposition is reality and what is presented, a possible fact. The erosion of the ontological elements of the picture theory together with Wittgenstein's growing belief that the intentionality of the assertion had to be explained in terms of what a speaker does with a sentence made this assumption unnecessary.

It is to be observed that the arguments which I claim Wittgenstein had in hand to direct against the picture theory and the Tractarian ontology are 'traditional' in kind; they come before the development of the later views on use and the language game method for its investigation and thus do not involve what seemed to be problematical in the style of the *Investigations* arguments.

(2) The objections that what seemed to be primary elements in the language game of *PI* 48 could not *really* be primary elements, that ordinary names could not possibly be *genuine* names, etc., on the basis of which we were able to imagine the early Wittgenstein rejecting his later arguments against simples were based on the Tractarian theory. For example, what seemed fishy about calling the coloured squares simples in the *Investigations* was the fact that we could analyse them. This seemed to beg the question against the *Tractatus* assumption that the possibility of picturing depends upon the unanalysability of simples. But Wittgenstein had rejected the

crucial features of the picture theory *before* embarking on the later investigation of Socrates' dream and so he had no further need to think there *must* be unanalysable simples.

(3) A consequence of Wittgenstein's later views on use is that apart from the investigation of the laws of nature which make the uses of language physically, psychologically, and physiologically possible, the subject-matter of an investigation of use is exhausted by a description of linguistic practices and their places in a form of life. It follows from this that a philosophical account of use *must* be treated as a putative description of a real or artificially conceived linguistic practice; there is nothing else left for it to be treated as. If this is correct, it legitimizes the features of the language game method for assessing a philosophical theory whose application to the theory of simples originally seemed questionable. The method is to try to invent a language which could be described by the theory of simples, explicating the theory in terms of features of the invented language, and then comparing the invented language to areas of the language we actually speak. The answer to the objection that our description of the invented language must be incomplete because its simples are not *absolutely* simple is that Wittgenstein had no reason at this point to think there *must* be absolutely simple objects. To show the necessity of the subsistence of Tractarian objects we should have to argue that the purposes served by language and the natural-historical limitations of its speakers make it impossible for a speaker to use language without simples. The possibility of imagining a language game like the game of *PI* 48 shows that no such argument can be given.

The moral of this is that the cogency of the language game arguments against the theory of simples depends upon arguments which do not involve an appeal to language games and which are necessary to support a view of language under which considerations raised from the study of language games become admissible. Thus the language game method does not, as many commentators have supposed, stand on its own as a replacement for 'traditional' methods in the philosophy of language; it presupposes them.

NOTES

INTRODUCTION

1 See RLF, *PASS*, IX, 1929, in C.

2 C. D. Broad, *The Mind and its Place in Nature*, Patterson, N.J., 1960; p. vii; Bertrand Russell, *Portraits from Memory and Other Essays*, Allen & Unwin, 1956, pp. 24, 166–72; and *My Philosophical Development*, Allen & Unwin, 1959, pp. 214–17.

3 For a typical example of this kind of commentary, see George Pitcher, *The Philosophy of Wittgenstein*, Englewood Cliffs, N.J., 1964, chs. 8, 9. The quotation is from p. 7.

4 It is debatable what the *Sätze* of *TS* were supposed to be and whether they were the same as what Wittgenstein later called *Sätze*. I translate *Satz* 'proposition', the word Wittgenstein used when writing or lecturing in English. 'Proposition' has the virtue of having been used in so many different ways that the reader is unlikely to rely heavily on it as an attempt at interpretation. For a discussion of the Tractarian *Satz* see chapter 3 below.

5 G. E. Moore, 'Wittgenstein's Lectures in 1930–1933' in Moore, *Philosophical Papers*, New York, 1962, p. 247 f.

6 I do not believe an intellectual biography is possible at this time, and doubt whether it ever will be possible to produce a very satisfactory one. Crucial documents from the transitional period are missing. Many were destroyed by Wittgenstein, and others may still be lost. Some documents from the early period are held by persons who have been unwilling to release them to Wittgenstein's literary executors or to the public. The chronology of the unpublished works which have survived is often uncertain. To add to the confusion, Wittgenstein made it a practice to return to the same topics over and over again, often starting afresh as though earlier work had not been done. This blurs the chronological and sometimes the logical development of his thoughts. It also requires a great deal of guess-work (in which I have freely indulged) on the part of a commentator who wishes to identify the doctrines to which a given discussion in the notebooks

applies. On the whole the corpus of Wittgenstein's surviving work allows for reconstruction of the kind this discussion engages in, but I do not think it allows for the kind of chronicling of philosophical development one would wish for in an intellectual biography.

7 John Buridan, *Sophisms on Meaning and Truth*, trans. T. K. Scott, New York, 1966, pp. 64, 85, 97.

8 This distinction is reflected in the Tractarian doctrine that what must be so if we are able to assert at all and is therefore shown to be so by asserting cannot itself be asserted to be the case. (*TS* 41212, etc.). For Austin on 'verdictive' uses of language, see John L. Austin, *How to do Things with Words*, Cambridge, Mass., 1962, pp. 88, 140, 159–61.

9 Cp. *BB* pp. 31–2, 36–7; *PI* 461, 428.

10 Plato, *Theaetetus*, 188d. Plato's own discussion is in part a response to Parmenides' doctrine that what is not is unspeakable or unthinkable. See John Burnet, *Early Greek Philosophy*, New York, 1957, pp. 174–5.

11 Cp. W. E. Johnson, *Logic*, New York, 1964, part I, ch. 1; G. E. Moore, *Some Main Problems of Philosophy*, New York, 1962, pp. 277–8; Bertrand Russell, *The Problems of Philosophy*, New York, 1959, pp. 36–8 (first published by William & Norgate, 1912). See also Plato, *Sophist*, 262e–263d.

12 Recall that 'fact' is another word, along with 'object' and 'exists', whose misunderstanding leads to trouble according to *BB* p. 31.

13 Is this a genuine problem? Following Donald Davidson (see, for example, 'Actions, Reasons, and Causes' in *Free Will and Determinism*, ed. Bernard Berofsky, New York, 1966, p. 234) someone might argue that it is not on the following grounds. Under appropriately chosen descriptions, connections between things we usually think of as accidental or contingent may be given by analytically true statements, and purportedly necessary connections may be stated by contingently true statements. For example, most people think the connection between a cause and its effect holds contingently, but statements of the form 'the cause of such and such is the cause of such and such' are necessarily true. Similarly, even if " 'p' is true iff p* exists" were necessarily true, a statement of the form " 'p' is true iff what John thinks to be the case is the case' is only contingently true when 'what John thinks to be the case" is used to identify what would be a fact if 'p' were true. On the basis of this, it could be suggested that the truth of " 'p' is true iff it is the case that p" does not imply that 'p' is necessarily connected with p* even on the assumption that 'p' and p* are real individuals, because necessary connections *never* hold between individuals of any kind. In other words, 'necessary' applies properly to assertions of the obtainings of connections, not to connections between individuals. Whether or not this argument is cogent, I believe that Wittgenstein did believe that the theory that 'p' and p* are real individuals commits its holder to the claim that an essential connection holds between them, and this is my chief concern. However, the cogency of the argument is questionable. It depends upon the assumption that a necessary connection cannot be said to obtain between two things, X and Y, unless the assertion of its obtaining is necessarily true under any true descriptions of X and Y. This in turn assumes that all necessity is *de dicto*. This view of necessity is far

from self-evident, and we have no conclusive arguments for it. There are possible worlds in which (assuming that 'p' and p* are real individuals) the existence of what John believes to be a fact does not make 'p' true. From this we can conclude that 'what John thinks to be the case is not that 'p'' is not a necessarily true proposition. It is not clear how or why this should lead to the further claim that it is not essential to 'p' that it be made true by the existence of p* and that it is not essential to p* that it make 'p' true, etc.

14 Cp. Frank P. Ramsey, 'Facts and Propositions', *PASS*, VII (1927), reprinted in Ramsey, *Foundations of Mathematics*, Routledge & Kegan Paul, 1931, pp. 138–56; P. F. Strawson, 'Truth', *A*, IX, No. 6 (1949), pp. 83–97; and 'Truth' *PASS*, XXIV (1950), pp. 129–56.

15 Until sometime during or just after assembling *PI* part I, Wittgenstein held that to think is to talk to oneself (*PI* 32, n. p. 16).

I THE PICTURE THEORY AND THE *TRACTATUS* ONTOLOGY

1 The label 'name-theory' is borrowed from Erik Stenius, *Wittgenstein's Tractatus*, Ithaca, N.Y., 1960, p. 118 f.

2 J. N. Findlay, *Meinong's Theory of Objects*, Oxford University Press, 1933, pp. 60, 66 f.

3 W. V. O. Quine, 'On What There Is', in *Semantics and the Philosophy of Language*, ed. L. Linsky, Urbana, Ill., 1952, p. 191.

4 In discussing the ontology of the *Tractatus*, I reserve 'object' for use in connection with simples. 'Thing' is used broadly to include simples as well as other sorts of individual. Occasionally 'thing' in the translation by D. F. Pears and B. F. McGuinness (Routledge & Kegan Paul, 1961) is replaced by 'object' in my quotation from *TS*. Wittgenstein himself did not reserve any special term for use in connection with simples. For example, '*Ding*' refers to simples at *TS* 201, but not at *TS* 31431 where it is used in connection with tables and chairs. '*Gegenstand*' is used here for things which are spatially extended and hence complex; but later in the same passage it refers to what can occur in *Sachverhalte* and hence to simple objects.

5 I know of no wholly satisfactory way of translating '*Sachverhalt*' as it occurs in *TS*. In the translation by C. K. Ogden and F. P. Ramsey (Routledge & Kegan Paul, 1922; corrected reprint, 1933), it is rendered as 'atomic fact', but Wittgenstein speaks of the obtaining and non-obtaining of *Sachverhalte*. It sounds redundant to talk about obtaining facts, and faintly contradictory to speak of non-obtaining ones. This is not an overwhelming difficulty, but it makes the translation uncomfortable. (But cp. Max Black, *A Companion to the Tractatus*, Ithaca, N.Y., 1964, pp. 38–45.) Pears and McGuinness translate '*Sachverhalt*' as 'state of affairs'. But 'state of affairs' is a non-technical term while Wittgenstein's employment of '*Sachverhalt*' is highly technical. Its etymological meaning is 'relation of things'. Wittgenstein uses it only in connection with simples and in this way departs from the ordinary German use which I am told is much closer to

our use of 'state of affairs'. Since '*Sachverhalt*' is etymologically more informative and since little is gained by replacing a technical term with a deceptively familiar non-technical phrase in English, it might have been best to leave it untranslated. However, I shall use 'state of affairs' as a translation in the hope that the context will make it clear that this phrase is used as a technical term.

6   David S. Shwayder, 'Critical Notice', *M*, 72, 1963, p. 284.

7   Ibid., pp. 284–5.

8   Compare Wittgenstein's example of a picture and his comments on it, *NS*, p. 7.

9   Stenius, *Wittgenstein's Tractatus*, p. 89.

10   This notation, though similar to that employed by Wittgenstein at *TS* 4012, is not faithful to the *Tractatus*, for elementary propositions should contain no terms signifying relations—see ch. I, 1.4 below. The signs 'R', 'R'', etc., are used for convenience; the argument could be presented without them.

11   Stenius, *Wittgenstein's Tractatus*, ch. 9.

12   Notice that the conclusion that a certain state of affairs does not obtain *does not* follow from a premise of the form 'such and such states of affairs obtain' unless the premise is conjoined with 'such and such comprise the totality of obtaining states of affairs'. Unless this is borne in mind *TS* 111, 112 will appear to contradict *TS* 2061.

13   H. R. G. Schwyzer, 'Wittgenstein's Picture Theory of Language', in *C*, p. 31f. The technical use of 'present' and 'represent' is suggested by Schwyzer's commentary on *TS* 215. The distinction is well founded in *TS* even though Wittgenstein does not use special terms to mark it.

14   This point is taken up in ch. II.2 below.

15   And yet Wittgenstein does at one point appear to be talking about senses of propositions as if they were entities of some kind with Meinongian lives of their own. See ch. II.1 below.

16   For a discussion of the difference between 'p & q' and the pair of assertions, 'p', 'q' see Peter Geach, 'Assertion', *PR*, 74, Oct. 1965, pp. 453–4.

17   Although the doctrine that all of the truth functions of the elementary propositions can be produced by joint negation depends upon Sheffer's discovery that the truth-functional connectives can be reproduced in a notation whose only logical constant is 'neither . . . nor . . .', two departures from Sheffer should be noted. First, Sheffer's stroke is a binary sentential connective while Wittgenstein's method for generating truth functions employs an operation of joint denial performed upon arbitrarily large sets of propositions. Second, Wittgenstein treated existentially and universally-quantified propositions as truth functions; Sheffer did not (*TS* 552–5525, 426–4427; H. M. Sheffer, 'A Set of Five Independent Postulates for Boolean Algebras', *Transactions of the American Mathematical Society*, 14 (1913), pp. 481–8). Sheffer's discovery was an independent rediscovery of a result first obtained by Peirce (William and Martha Kneale, *The Development of Logic*, Oxford University Press, 1962, p. 443). For a discussion of the first difference noted above between Sheffer and Wittgenstein, see

David S. Shwayder, '*Gegenstände* and Other Matters', hereafter *Gegenstände, I* (Winter 1964), p. 392.

18 E. Daitz, 'The Picture Theory of Meaning', in *Essays in Conceptual Analysis*, ed. A. G. N. Flew, Macmillan, 1956, pp. 56–7.

19 Wittgenstein could have meant something much less interesting by *TS* 2151. The text reads: '*Die Form der Abbildung ist die Möglichkeit, dass sich die Dinge so ʀu einander verhalten, wie die Elemente des Bildes.*' This could mean that like picture elements, pictured things too can combine and that the Form of Representation makes combination in general possible—not any particular kinds of combination. But it is difficult to give a literal translation which fits this interpretation, and if this is all that Wittgenstein had in mind, it is doubtful whether he would have bothered to say it. In any case, what I interpret this passage to mean is said explicitly later on (at *TS* 2203) and so my interpretation does not ascribe to Wittgenstein anything he wouldn't have said.

20 But suppose, as is possible, that none of the objects mentioned in a proposition stand in any relation to any other objects or to each other—that they are not constituents of any obtaining states of affairs. In this case they do not occur in the world at all. If this were so, how could we call the proposition a representational picture? The answer is that any object which does not belong to an obtaining state of affairs belongs to the fact presented by the assertion that such and such a state of affairs does not obtain. Thus, if the assertion 'aRb' is false, the assertion ' – (aRb)' is true and it is a fact that *a* is not related to *b*. Accordingly, when an object is not to be found in the world (when it is not the constituent of a positive fact), it must be in reality as a constituent of a negative fact. This shows the importance of the doctrine that the proposition represents *reality* (and not just the world).

21 The Pears-McGuinness translation, 'it is laid against reality like a ruler' (*TS* 21512) is ruled out by *TS* 21511. If the proposition 'reaches right out to' reality, nothing *lies* it against it.

22 G. E. M. Anscombe, *An Introduction to Wittgenstein's Tractatus*, Hutchinson 1959, ch. 2; James Griffin, *Wittgenstein's Logical Atomism*, Oxford University Press, 1964, ch. 6.

23 This account of the indeterminacy of propositions which mention complexes depends, of course, on the assumption that such propositions are existential. This assumption would seem to be warranted by *TS* 324.

Against this, Griffin suggests that the Tractarian analysis proceeds along the lines of the example given in *PI* 60; he argues that an analysis of this kind should never get us to existentials (Griffin, *Wittgenstein's Logical Atomism*, pp. 51–65). I submit that whereas he offers this account of analysis in order to show how assertions about complexes are indeterminate, the kind of analysis he describes allows for no indeterminacy whatever.

Griffin suggests following *PI* 60 that 'the broom is in the corner' should be analysed in terms of 'the stick is in the corner and the brush is in the corner, and the stick is attached to the brush' (op. cit., p. 47). In the next step, we eliminate the complex 'brush' to get 'the stick is in the corner and the back is in the corner and the bristles are in the corner and the bristles and the back are attached to the stick' (op. cit., p. 48). Griffin insists that this analysis must proceed by repeating the same kind of move at each stage (op. cit., p. 44). If we follow his instructions, I think we should have to arrive eventually at an analysis of the form 'aRb&cRb& dRb&cRa& . . .' in which each conjunct asserts the obtaining of a state of affairs. Conjunctions do not seem to be indeterminate in any sense. They do not have the kind of indeterminacy which is characteristic of disjunctions or existentials, and if the conjuncts are all elementary propositions, they do not allow for border-line cases or fail to set out their truth conditions completely. Since Griffin's account of Tractarian analysis does not provide for indeterminacy, it would seem to be incompatible with *TS* 324.

24 David S. Shwayder, '*Gegenstände* and Other Matters', *I* (Winter 1964), p. 399.

25 David S. Shwayder, 'Critical Notice', *M*, 72, 1963, p. 283.

26 Ibid., pp. 283–4.

27 An alternative suggestion is hinted at in Shwayder, '*Gegenstände* and Other Matters', *I* (Winter 1964), pp. 410–12.

28 Cp. Max Black, 'The Semantic Definition of Truth', *A*, 8, no. 4 (1948), pp. 49–63.

29 Shwayder, '*Gegenstände* and Other Matters', *I* (Winter 1964), p. 399.

30 Must the expression of the truth conditions for 'the cat is on the mat' really include a specification of *every* positive C–M situation if *TS* is correct? Perhaps only a few need to be explicitly indicated in order to secure the identification of the fact which verifies the proposition. There are two ways of elaborating on this suggestion, but neither stands up under examination.

(1) In order to identify something like a building you need to know *some* of its features, but not *all* of them. Why not treat positive C–M situations as features of the fact that the cat is on the mat and say the same thing about the identification of the fact? The answer is that unlike the identifying features of a building, positive C–M situations exclude each other; the cat can't stand in the middle of the mat in the same reality in which it is sitting in the corner. Hence unless we specified all of the positive C–M situations, there would be worlds (those containing unspecified positive C–M situations) in which the fact that the cat is on the mat couldn't be identified.

(2) A more attractive possibility is suggested by John Austin. According to him, conventions governing the use of a sentence to make an assertion determine that the assertion will be verified by a situation of a particular type. A situation is of the right type if it is 'sufficiently like' other situations of that type (John L. Austin, 'Truth', in Austin, *Philosophical Papers*, Oxford University Press, 1961, n. 2, p. 90).

This account might be grafted on to the picture theory by supposing that 'the cat is on the mat' presents a possible fact by picturing one or more standard or paradigm positive C–M situations to which other C–M situations are to be compared for likeness. The proposition would then be verified by any C–M situation 'sufficiently like' the paradigms, and falsified by any C–M situation 'sufficiently unlike' the paradigms. The proposition would explicitly specify only a few and not all of the situations whose obtaining would verify it.

This account gives a highly unnatural picture of the way we verify an assertion. Someone who finds the cat sitting on the mat does not consult a paradigm cat-on-the-mat situation to determine whether this counts as the cat being on the mat. The only cases in which it would be natural to go through the procedure Austin's account suggests are border-line cases. If someone found the cat straddling two mats, or perched on the edge of the mat in a very peculiar way and if he were forced to decide whether this verified the assertion, he might compare the situation to others which would clearly verify it. He might say, 'I would have said the cat was on the mat if I'd found it in such and such a position, and this is a bit like that, so I might as well say he's on the mat here too.' The only excuse for going through this kind of rigmarole is that in this case, the assertion *isn't* flatly true or false. Normal cases of verification (where the assertion *is* flatly true or false) cannot be assimilated to border-line cases like this without distortion. It is also worth noting that this picture of verification is antipathetical to the spirit of a non-truistic correspondence theory of truth. Accounts like the Tractarian version of the correspondence theory maintain that when an assertion is true it is true because reality contains what the assertion presents as a fact. In the border-line cases which Austin's account fits, the speaker who pronounces an assertion true is not so much *acknowledging* the existence of a certain fact as *stipulating* or *deciding* that if any decision about truth value is to be made, the assertion is to be called true. It is as though his decision to count the obtaining situation as verifying 'the cat is on the mat' *makes its obtaining into* the fact that the cat is on the mat. This grates against the correspondence notion that facts are given independently of our decisions to call a given assertion true or false.

Finally Austin's account breaks down when we try to fill in the details of the story about comparing a given situation to a paradigm to see if they are 'sufficiently like one another' to be called situations of the same type. Suppose we take as a standard positive C–M situation the one in which the cat is sitting in the middle of the mat. Call this situation 'CS', and call the cat is lying on the upper left-hand corner, 'CL'. The obtaining of CL verifies 'the cat is on the mat' and so it must be 'sufficiently like' CS. But in what way are they like one another? The relevant features of the two situations are the cat, the mat, and the cat's position. If the situations are sufficiently alike, this cannot be due simply to their involving the same cat and the same mat, and so the likeness must be due to a similarity between the positions of the cat in the two situations. But in what respect does lying on a corner resemble sitting in the middle of the mat? There is no relevant similarity except for this: a cat in either of these positions is on the mat. Apart from this, standing isn't much like sitting, and being on the corner isn't much like being in the middle. But if the only relevant similarity between CS and CL is that in both cases the cat is on the mat, we cannot establish 'sufficient likeness' *in order* to determine whether CL verifies 'the cat is on the mat'; instead we verify the assertion in order to justify saying that CS is like CL.

Since Austin's account (2) and the attempt to treat some positive C–M situations as identifying features of the fact fail, I submit that there is no way a picture theorist can avoid the conclusion that every situation whose obtaining could possibly verify a proposition must be explicitly permitted by the proposition's expression of its truth conditions.

31 Bertrand Russell, *Introduction to Mathematical Philosophy*, Allen & Unwin, 1919, p. 174.

32 It is likely that if Wittgenstein had provided an explicit type/token distinction, he would have classified a sign as a *type* of mark or sound. This is suggested by his remark that "A" and "A" are the same sign, (*TS* 3203).

33 H. R. G. Schwyzer, 'Wittgenstein's Picture Theory of Language', in C, pp. 54–5. Stenius objects to this in a reply to Schwyzer, *I*, 6, Summer 1963, 184–95. His arguments are unconvincing.

34 This fits Wittgenstein's complaints about superficial grammatical features of the natural languages. The reason that everyday language 'disguises thought ... so much so that from the outward form ... it is impossible to infer the form of the thought beneath it' (*TS* 4002) is that the number of signs used in an ordinary language sentence does not correspond to the number of symbols, and that typal differences between symbols are not registered by clearly perceptible sensible features of the signs. For example, the same word may belong to different symbols, and the same symbol may be associated with different words (*TS* 3323). More importantly, two signs which are superficially similar may actually signify in different ways (*TS* 3322). What looks like a name may really be a contraction for a string of symbols; what seems to be a word which refers to a thing or property, may really function to accomplish some of what would be accomplished by various stages in the marking of the Ultimate Truth Table or by the successive joint denial of sets of propositions generated from the elementary propositions.

35 *TS* 33411. Cp. H. R. G. Schwyzer, 'Wittgenstein's Picture Theory of Language', in C, p. 54.

36 H. H. Price, *Perception*, Methuen, 1932, p. 15.

37 Plato, *Theaetetus*, 201c–208b. Cp. *PI* 46, and ch. I.4 of this discussion.

38 The explanation of a great deal that went on at Cambridge during its golden age would be greatly furthered by an account of just what appeal this theory about describing had for Moore, Russell, Wittgenstein, and others. Cf. G. E. Moore, *Principia Ethica*, Cambridge University Press, 1959, p. 7f.

39 G. E. M. Anscombe, *An Introduction to Wittgenstein's Tractatus*, p. 25f.

40 I am indebted to Shwayder for this point.

41 Again, there can be *worlds* in which a given object does not figure. That is because a world is a collection of obtaining *Sachverhalte*, and it could be that none of the *Sachverhalte* in which the object could figure actually obtain. Thus we must say the *Satz* is a picture of every *reality*.

42 Russell, *Introduction to Mathematical Philosophy*, pp. 177–9; Russell and Whitehead, *Principia Mathematica, Volume I*, Cambridge University Press, 1910, part I, section B/*14.

43 Russell, *Mysticism and Logic*, Garden City, N.Y., 1918, pp. 211–12 (first published by Longman in 1918).

44 Ibid., pp. 208–9.

45 This point was suggested to me by David Pears.

46 *Translations from the Philosophical Writings of Gottlob Frege*, trans. P. Geach and M. Black, Blackwell, 1952, p. 15. For a valuable discussion of connections between Frege's objections to piecemeal definitions and Wittgenstein's requirement that sense be determinate, see James Griffin, *Wittgenstein's Logical Atomism*, pp. 9–13.

47 From a paper read to the Aristotelian Society at Aberystwyth, 7 July 1956.

48 Wittgenstein uses a German translation of *Theaetetus* 201d which emphasizes the necessary existence of the primary elements more heavily than the Greek text.

49 Cp. Ramsey on universals (Frank P. Ramsey, *Foundations of Mathematics*, Routledge & Kegan Paul, 1931, ch. IV). Presumably Ramsey's account represents the doctrine of the early Wittgenstein, and if this is so, the *Tractatus* ontology does not distinguish between universals and particulars with regard to objects. For example, two of the classical distinctions between a universal and a particular do not apply to the *Tractatus*. Universals are sometimes treated as fundamentally incomplete and incapable of existence without particulars to complete them. But it is essential to a Tractarian object that it cannot occur in the world except as the constituent of a state of affairs and so each object is every bit as 'incomplete' or 'unsaturated' as every other. A second (linguistic) test to distinguish universals from particulars derives from the distinction between subject and predicate; what is predicated is said to be a universal and what it is predicated of, a particular. But the elementary propositions of the *Tractatus* are not of the subject-predicate form. If we assert the obtaining of the state of affairs *a b*, it is no more true to say that 'b' predicates something of *a* than that 'a' predicates something of *b*. Wittgenstein's grounds for saying it is indifferent whether we think the elements are individual squares or kinds of square are quite different from these considerations. But it is of interest to observe that the early Wittgenstein would probably have rejected the question whether objects are universals or particulars—even though he would not have given the same reasons for his rejection of the question. See also G. E. M. Anscombe, '*Retractation*', *Analysis*, 26, 1965, pp. 33–6.

50 This is of interest in connection with Wittgenstein's more familiar doctrine that a physical sample can always take the place of a memory sample.

51 Ch. III.3 of this book.

52 George Pitcher, *The Philosophy of Wittgenstein*, p. 183.

II THE ABANDONMENT OF THE PICTURE THEORY

1 If one spoke the language described by the *Tractatus*, the 'p*' notation

would be impossible and the problem of intentionality could not be formulated. That is because a fact can only be given by a proposition—by asserting it, and cannot be referred to by a name or a description (*TS* 41272, 3144). Indeed, since a proposition is a fact, it is not clear that a Tractarian language should include the machinery used by Wittgenstein himself to mention propositions by enclosing them in single quotes. Strictly speaking, the contention that 'p' and p* are individuals which are internally connected should be considered something which can be shown by the language but not said in it. However, the question about intentionality must be asked in assessing the success of the *Tractatus* and the *Tractatus* provides ample precedent for talking about what on the Tractarian theory is unspeakable.

2   It may be objected that in order to say that p* has the property that its non-existence falsifies 'p' we must ascribe a property to a non-entity. But suppose that 'p' is true and, therefore, that p* is a fact. Then we can say of it that its existence (its being a fact) is what makes 'p' true and that if reality contained no fact identical to p*, 'p' would be false.

3   See Introduction, p. 10, n. 13.

4   The connection of this remark with the rest of the passage becomes a bit clearer if '*teilt uns . . . mit*' is translated 'presents (shows) us' instead of 'communicates'.

5   See also *TS* 4021. Here Wittgenstein argues that a proposition must be a picture of reality because we can understand a proposition—know what it presents as a fact—without having its sense explained to us. This argument (like that of *TS* 403) assumes that a proposition is essentially connected to its sense.

6   Cp. Bertrand Russell, *Analysis of Mind*, Allen & Unwin, 1921, pp. 32–65.

7   G. E. Moore, *Philosophical Papers*, p. 260. Cp. W. E. Johnson, *Logic*, part I, ch. 1.

8   Cp. *PI* 441; *BB* p. 30f.

9   The term 'satisfy' is a translation of '*erfüllen*', frequently used by Wittgenstein in talking about intentionality during the transitional and later period. See, for example, *B* 16, *PI* 437–439, etc. *PI* 437–439 are versions of passages dating from 1930–1 notebooks.

10   A cautionary (and disclamatory) note. This account of the analogy between assertions and other mental acts is a crude one, refined only as far as necessary to establish the relevance of Wittgenstein's considerations of expectation and other non-assertive mental acts to the picture theory of assertions. Because I believe it will serve this purpose, I leave it in its present crude form. However, it is obvious that without considerable refinement, the analogy could not be pressed beyond the point I wish to press it. In particular, I have not considered the often-discussed and important point that a true statement of the form 'X øs O' can be falsified by replacing 'O' with a different true description of the same object. For example, a man who wants to eat a strawberry does not necessarily want to eat a poisoned strawberry. If he does not know that this is a poisoned strawberry, he may want to eat this under the description 'a strawberry' but not under the equally true description 'a strawberry shot with arsenic'. In considering examples of mental acts, the reader is to assume that the object of the

mental act is always given in the description under which it is asserted, wished, wanted, etc.

11   G. E. Moore, *Some Main Problems of Philosophy*, p. 184; W. E. Johnson, *Logic*, part I, ch. 1; J. N. Findlay, *Meinong's Theory of Objects, passim*.

12   '*Zum Satz gehört alles, was zur Projektion . . .*' (*TS* 313). Griffin thinks this passage shows that a proposition is a sentence or dummy sentence which does not have a sense until it is used to say something. On this reading, all Wittgenstein meant by saying the proposition does not contain its sense is that a sentence says nothing until we use it as a projection. But this is untenable, for the proposition contains everything needed for projection, and so it cannot require anything additional to make it into a projection (*TS* 313, line 1). What Wittgenstein meant by 'sinnvoller Satz' was simply a contingent assertion—in contrast to tautologies and contradictions which he says are *sinnloss* (*TS* 4461). He did not mean a dummy sentence waiting for use to breathe a sense into it. Cp. James Griffin, *Wittgenstein's Logical Atomism*, p. 132.

13   Useful and fascinating examples to consider in this connection are Rauschenberg's 'portrait' of Iris Clert, a telegram that reads 'This is a portrait of Iris Clert if I say so', and a notarized certificate in which Robert Morris withdraws content from an earlier work of his (Barbara Rose, 'Didactic Art', *Art Forum*, 5, no. 8, April 1967, p. 32).

14   My assimilation of Moore, Johnson, and Meinong is, of course, an oversimplification. Their accounts of what a fact has which a proposition (or 'objective') lacks are different. Moore held that p* is 'p' plus a simple and unanalysable property, truth (G. E. Moore, *Some Main Problems of Philosophy*, pp. 284–5). Johnson's account appears to have been that the proposition and the fact differ with regard to the kinds of connection which obtain between their constituents. With some hesitation, I would suggest that the doctrine of *Logic*, part I, ch. 1, sections 5 and 6, and ch. 2 is that the elements of the proposition whose connection is described in terms of the 'characterizating tie' (*Logic*, p. 10) are connected in an additional way in case the proposition is true. Meinong's account has to do with a distinction between the existence and subsistence of an 'objective'. These differences between the three theories do not affect the point at present under discussion so far as I can see.

15   But isn't the behaviour a *criterion* for expectation? (cf. *PI* 580). If so, is it logically possible to have the behaviour without the expectation? We all know that it is possible and so did Wittgenstein. Wittgenstein may have wanted to hold that it is necessarily the case that what exhibits criteria for something, X, has the *appearance* of (being) X, but not that it is necessarily the case that what exhibits the criteria *is* or *has* X (*PI* 354). Thus, even if 'X exhibits such and such behaviour' were necessarily connected with 'X expects so and so', because the behaviour is a criterion for expectation, it does not follow that it entails 'X expects so and so'. Furthermore, if the behaviour I mentioned is a criterion for expectation, it would show favouritism to deny that it is a criterion for other 'states' as well. And it is highly implausible to say that pacing up and down, etc, etc., comprise the criteria

for expecting just *this* (an explosion) and nothing else—even if it did comprise criteria for expecting *something*.

16 P. F. Strawson, 'Truth', *PASS*, XXIV (1950), pp. 129–56. A much earlier (and perhaps the first published) version of this theory is Frank P. Ramsey, 'Facts and Propositions', *PASS*, VII (1927), reprinted in Ramsey, *Foundation of Mathematics*. This predates Wittgenstein's return to Cambridge, but it is to be expected that Ramsey had been conversing with Wittgenstein in, if not before, 1927.

17 In 1931 Wittgenstein explicitly suggested that 'fact' should be used 'only in the complete proposition which asserts the obtaining of this fact' (i.e., in assertions of the form 'it is a fact that. . . .') (UPN).

18 John L. Austin, 'Unfair to Facts', in Austin, *Philosophical Papers*, p. 104.

19 This does not mean that the account was intended only for application to mathematical and logical truths. At *PI* 136 the equation appears as a pronouncement about the truth of assertions in general, not assertions of any specified kind.

20 Cp. Michael Dummett, 'Truth', in *Truth*, ed. George Pitcher, Englewood Cliffs, N.J., 1964, p. 100.

21 I have been considering Wittgensteinian criteria because Wittgenstein mentions them (and little else) as conditions which under a speaker is entitled to make an assertion. But Wittgenstein did not give any general account of conditions for assertability, let alone an account which identifies them exclusively with what he calls 'criteria'. He emphasizes that some assertions are made without criteria or the need for them (*BB* p. 14f.; *PI* 289, 290). Although many commentators (e.g. Rollins and Malcolm) claim that the locutions in question are not genuine assertions, I have been unable to find support for this in the texts.

22 For a representative example of the most prevalent interpretation of these passages see Norman Malcolm, 'Knowledge of Other Minds' and review of *PI* in *The Philosophy of Mind*, ed. V. C. Chappell, Englewood Cliffs, N.J., 1963. See also Rogers Albritton, 'On Wittgenstein's Use of the Term "Criterion" ', pp. 231–51. As a corrective, see John Cook, 'Human Beings', in *Studies in the Philosophy of Wittgenstein*, ed. Peter Winch, Routledge & Kegan Paul, 1969, pp. 117–51.

23 That it is not the doctrine of *BB* has been argued by Stanley Cavell (in an unpublished dissertation on deposit at the Harvard Library), to whom I am indebted on this point. Cp. John Cook, 'Human Beings'.

24 The example is Shwayder's.

25 I do not wish to give the impression that the distinction between meaningless and ungrammatical strings of words is easy to draw in any hard and fast way. Noam Chomsky's early grammars (e.g. his difficulties with passives in *Syntactic Structures* (*Janua Linguarum*, IV), the Hague, 1957, sections 5.4, 7.4, 7.5) show how difficult the distinction is to draw and suggest (against Chomsky's intentions at that time) that any precise distinction will probably be relative to a particular grammar to which alternatives are possible.

26 Although it is not clear that Austin would concur, I am inclined to classify what I call asserting as a locutionary rather than an illocutionary

act. But in using the term 'assertion' here I do not intend to imply advocacy of Austin's or any other particular account of assertion. I should perhaps add 'and commits himself to its truth' to 'says what is true or false' to distinguish the assertion of 'p' from the occurrence of 'p' in 'if p then q', 'pvq', etc. I omitted this condition because there is at least one use of the verb 'to say' under which it is incorrect to claim that a man who said 'if p then q' *said* 'p'. In any case, the 'entertaining' of 'p' and its inclusion in hypotheticals, disjunctions, conjunctions, etc., is to be distinguished from the assertion of 'p'.

27 Aristotle (Theophrastus?), *Magna Moralia*, 1211b 30 ff.

28 In this chapter and elsewhere I make frequent use of the phrases 'use of a sentence' and 'use of a word'. I am indebted to Richard Bosley for an interesting point concerning this. Using a hammer to drive a nail involves taking an existing thing (a hammer) and hitting a nail with it. If this kind of example is taken over-seriously as a paradigm, we may be bothered by the fact that a sentence or word isn't there lying round waiting to be used before its use. The tokens I am now producing didn't exist until I produced them to say what I am now saying. The types of these tokens seem odd sorts of things to think of as lying round waiting for use. It is worth noting that although Wittgenstein's talk of use probably does involve analogies between the use of a word or sentence and the use of a pre-existing thing like a tool, the analogies are not pressed at the point which Bosley's observation shows to be problematical. When he held the calculus theory, using a sign meant producing (or exhibiting) a token according to a rule, conformity with which secures a sense or meaning for the sign produced in accordance with it. Later, Wittgenstein could mean producing or exhibiting a token for a certain purpose (e.g., saying something, asking a question, etc.) in the context of a practice or activity in which its production or exhibition can accomplish the purpose. So understood, Wittgenstein's talk of use does not presuppose the pre-existence of what is used. It is also worth noting that one way of using a sentence or word is to read it to find out what someone said. In this case the token does exist before it is used.

29 John L. Austin, *How to do Things with Words*, p. 98.

30 Ibid., pp. 101–31, 138, 144.

31 *Translations from the Philosophical Writings of Gottlob Frege*, ed. P. Geach and M. Black, Blackwell, 1952, p. 118f.

32 Although the discussion which follows departs in various ways from theirs, I am heavily indebted to Shwayder and Schwyzer on so many points that it would be unreasonably cumbrous to cite them point by point. The reader is urged to consult Schwyzer and Shwayder ('Critical Notice', *M*, 72, 1963). However, the bulk of Shwayder's discussion of this topic occurs in his unpublished dissertation on deposit at Oxford in the Bodleian Library.

33 James Bogen, 'Was Wittgenstein a Psychologist?' *I*, 7 (1964), pp. 374–8.

34 Although Wittgenstein presents this as though it applied to *all* pictures, it is incompatible with crucial Tractarian doctrines (e.g., that the logical constants do not stand for things) unless restricted to elementary propositions.

35 H. R. G. Schwyzer, p. 54.

36 I am indebted to Shwayder for pointing out that there are cases to which the application of this doctrine is problematical. For example, does a man who asserts that Tabby is on the mat by saying 'yes' when asked, make reference to the cat and the mat? It would seem more natural to say that if anyone makes reference to them, it is his questioner. However, the doctrine appears plausible in many cases and (plausible or not) seems to follow from the Tractarian accounts of analysis and the essential features of the proposition.

37 Schwyzer, p. 61.

38 But cp. Schwyzer, pp. 54–6, for an opposing view.

39 G. E. M. Anscombe, 'The Intentionality of Sensation: A Grammatical Feature', in *Analytical Philosophy, 2nd Series*, ed. Ronald J. Butler, New York, 1965, pp. 158–68.

40 Sraffa is supposed to have made a (possibly obscene) gesture and asked 'What is the logical form of *that*?' And Wittgenstein is said to have been struck by how little the gesture had in common with its spoken or written equivalent (Norman Malcolm, *Ludwig Wittgenstein; a Memoir*, Oxford University Press, 1958, p. 69). See George Pitcher, *The Philosophy of Wittgenstein*, ch. 9. Incidentally, it is worth noting that Wittgenstein did *not* think that all classification can be explained on the family resemblance model. The aroma of coffee is a universal which cannot be so treated (*PI* 610). And there can be no family resemblance account of why we call various things red (*BB, BRB*). The family resemblance account requires distinguishable, discrete features in the thing classified, on the basis of which classification is made. Red and the aroma of coffee lack appropriate features which are sufficiently distinguishable.

41 I ascribe this doctrine to Wittgenstein with some hesitation. *TS* 42211 suggests that there might be an infinite number of simple objects; if so, we could not name them all. *TS* 555 says that 'we are unable to give the number of names with different meanings' and, therefore, that 'we are . . . unable to give the composition of elementary propositions'. This could be because there is an infinite number of names with different meanings, or because it cannot be determined *a priori* what the objects are or whether they are exhausted by a given collection of names.

If Wittgenstein really did mean to say that we cannot give the names of all of the objects *a priori*, he was maintaining a doctrine which cannot be easily accommodated to the rest of the *Tractatus*. His analysis of general assertions is incoherent unless we are given all of the elementary propositions, and we cannot have these unless we can name all of the objects. Furthermore, the simple objects determine the forms of elementary propositions, and of reality. As Shwayder observes, 'if . . . familiarity with the forms of *Elementarsätze* and *Gegenstände* were contingent and empirical, then apparently knowledge of necessary truth would depend upon knowledge of contingent truth—perhaps true, but contrary to the whole spirit of the *Tractatus* conception of necessary truth (e.g. 2012, 547, 5551) ('*Gegenstände* and Other Matters', *I* (Winter 1964), p. 402). And finally, Wittgenstein's use of the variable p to stand for the elementary propositions in giving the general form of the proposition is scarcely comprehensible if we cannot be given the names of all of the objects. Lacking these, we could not know the values of the variable.

There is a bare possibility of reconciling *TS* 42211, 555 with the rest of the *Tractatus* by treating *TS* 555 as a special instance of the doctrine of *TS* 41272. As an example of what he means by saying we cannot give the forms of the elementary propositions *a priori*, Wittgenstein says that it makes no sense to ask whether 'I can get into a position in which I need the sign for a 27 termed relation in order to signify something' (*TS* 55542). A reason for saying this could be our inability to say whether or not there are 27 objects to be related. And this is something we cannot say because it makes no sense to say 'there are objects' as one might say 'there are books', or to say 'there are 100 objects', or 'there are n objects' (*TS* 41272). This suggests the possibility of taking *TS* 555 to mean that we cannot *say* how many objects there are (and hence how many names the largest possible elementary propositions might have) even though we *can name* all of the objects. But this interpretation is strained, and it may be more plausible to say that *TS* 555, etc., does contradict the Tractarian accounts of generality, the general form, and necessity. If this is so, the latter must take precedence, and we shall have to ignore *TS* 555, 42211 on the grounds that they undermine fundamental elements of the Tractarian doctrine. That is why I advance the thesis that all the objects can be named, despite these passages.

42   Neither the joint denial operation nor the series supposed to be generable from the elementary propositions by means of its successive applications is well defined in the *Tractatus*. Cp. Anscombe's attempts to generate the truth functions of two elementary propositions, *An Introduction to Wittgenstein's Tractatus*, pp. 132–4.

43   This is a cardinal feature of Wittgenstein's later philosophy which Pole studiously ignores. Many of his most vigorously-pressed objections to Wittgenstein depend upon his ignoring it (David Pole, *The Later Philosophy of Wittgenstein*, Athlone Press, University of London, 1958, p. 55 f., ch. IV). As a corrective, see Stanley Cavell, 'The Availability of Wittgenstein's Later Philosophy', in P, pp. 153–65, and Barry Stroud, 'Wittgenstein and Logical Necessity', in P, pp. 477–97.

III   USE

1   RLF citations are page numbers in C. The term 'atomic proposition' probably comes from Russell, but it appears to have been approved by Wittgenstein as a translation of '*Elementarsatz*' for the Ogden–Ramsey edition of *TS* (1922).

2   For what appears to be a faithfully-reported and representative exposition of this, see G. E. Moore, 'Wittgenstein's Lectures, in 1930–1931', in *Philosophical Papers*, p. 252.

3   See Norman Malcolm, 'Wittgenstein's *Philosophische Bemerkungen*', *PR*, 76 April 1967, p. 224.

4   Moore, 'Wittgenstein's Lectures in 1930–1931', in *Philosophical Papers*, p. 252.

5   Russell, *Analysis of Mind*, p. 198 f.: *B* 22.

6 'Desire, like force in mechanics is of the nature of a convenient fiction for describing shortly certain laws of behaviour. A hungry animal is restless until it finds food; then it becomes quiescent. The thing which will bring a restless condition to an end is said to be what is desired. But only experience can show what will have this sedative effect, and it is easy to make mistakes. We feel dissatisfaction and think that such and such a thing would remove it; but in thinking this, we are theorizing, not observing a patent fact. Our theorizing is often mistaken, and when it is mistaken there is a difference between what we think we desire and what in fact will bring satisfaction' (ibid., p. 32).

'On this theory desire and purpose involve "behaviour cycles". A behaviour cycle is set in motion by a state of discomfort or dissatisfaction and it tends to cause and terminate in a state of satisfaction (or at least cessation of dissatisfaction). "The purpose of a behaviour cycle", says Russell, "is the result which brings it to an end, normally by a condition of temporary quiescence—provided there is no interruption." ' (Malcolm, 'Wittgenstein's *Philosophische Bemerkungen*', *PR*, April 1967, p. 233).

7 Cp. Russell, *Analysis of Mind*, p. 199.

8 Wittgenstein says nothing about unexpressed thought in the *Tractatus*. He could have treated it as silent speech in which images of words and things take the place of written or spoken signs. See James Bogen, 'Was Wittgenstein a Psychologist?' *I*, 7 (1964), pp. 374–8.

9 It has been objected that a man could hear what comes out of the speaker without realizing that it is a symphony. But whether what results from playing the record is a symphony does not depend upon whether anyone actually recognizes it. The same holds for assertions. My failure to recognize that a man is saying something does not entail that he failed to make an assertion.

10 Cp. Gottlob Frege, *The Foundations of Arithmetic*, trans. J. L. Austin, New York, 1960, sections 26, 59. I suspect Wittgenstein's opposition to psychologistic theories of meaning derives from Frege. If so, there is little he got from any philosopher which turned out to be as fruitful and permanently influential as this from Frege.

11 W. V. O. Quine, *Word and Object*, Cambridge, Mass., 1960, ch. 2.

12 Presumably the reason field linguists do not worry about such possibilities is that instead of simply collecting a corpus of utterances and trying to make them fit a set of rules, they begin to learn the language they are studying before trying to find a grammar for it. If so, what rules out the possibility of accidental accord is the linguist's understanding of and success in speaking the language, not the mere circumstance that a corpus of utterances can be described as according with a system of rules.

13 This possibility together with an interesting alternative interpretation is developed by Robert Fogelin in a forthcoming book. A hint of the drift of the interpretation is given in Fogelin, 'Wittgenstein and Intuitionism', *APQ*, 5, October 1968, p. 272f.

14 The discussion of continuing a series in *PI* 142f. overlaps the discussion in *RFM* section I; the two ought to be read together.

15 Notice that the view that language requires no underpinning of rules

is compatible with what may sound like appeals to rules by which Wittgenstein sometimes corrected accounts of the use of particular words in the later works. On what, for example, did he base his pronouncement that 'I' is not the name of a person, 'here', of a place, etc., if not on rules of language? (*PI* 410). And what are the 'conventions' he calls the bedrock of language in *BB*, *PI*, and *RFM* if not rules? The conventions are practices constitutive of uses of languages. They are what we do when we use language. In trying to get clear about the use of a word we may give a rule (e.g., ' "I" is not the name of a person . . .'). But the rule, if correct, is a *description*, or part of a description of what we do and what we expect others to do. It is not what underlies and shapes the practice. Thus Wittgenstein's appeals to rules and conventions in this connection do not commit him to the view of rules which he rejected.

16 Michael Dummett, 'Wittgenstein's Philosophy of Mathematics', in *Philosophy of Mathematics*, ed. Paul Benacerraf and Hillary Putnam, Englewood Cliffs, N.J., 1964, p. 494.

17 For example, see A. J. Ayer, *Language, Truth and Logic*, New York, 1946, p. 78.

18 Michael Dummett, 'Wittgenstein's Philosophy of Mathematics', in *Philosophy of Mathematics*, ed. Paul Benacerraf and Hillary Putnam, p. 494.

19 In this discussion I am heavily indebted to Barry Stroud. On this point see his 'Wittgenstein and Logical Necessity', in P, pp. 484–5.

20 David Hume, *A Treatise of Human Nature*, ed. Sir L. A. Selby-Bigge, Oxford University Press, 1958, book I, part III, sections iv-xv.

21 This departs from the editors' translation of '*mit uns nicht spielen*'. I am indebted to Stuart Friebert and Peter Spycher here.

22 Cp. Charles S. Chihara, 'Wittgenstein and Logical Compulsion', in P, pp. 448–69. Chihara's explication fails to bring out the unintelligibility of the pupil's procedure and justifications. His description of the Myonese practice leaves no doubt over whether it could be called a correct application of the rule in the example. This is an instance of a rare phenomenon: an account which is objectionable because it makes things too easy to understand.

23 Michael Dummett in *Philosophy of Mathematics*, ed. Paul Benacerraf and Hillary Putnam, pp. 495–6. For a detailed argument against this interpretation, see Barry Stroud, 'Wittgenstein and Logical Necessity', in P.

24 Stroud, op. cit. pp. 485–6.

25 Stroud, op. cit. p. 480.

26 Pitcher, *The Philosophy of Wittgenstein*, ch. 10.

27 It is curious to note how nationalistic an interpretation this is. On the whole, Wittgenstein's English students appear to have been less inclined towards it than his American students and readers.

28 Rush Rhees, 'Wittgenstein's Builders', *PAS*, LX (1959–60), p. 178f.

29 Ibid.

30 H. P. Grice, 'Meaning', *PR*, LXVI (1957), pp. 377–88.

31 John L. Austin, *How to do Things with Words*, pp. 91, 99, 101–31, 138, 144.

32   K. W. Rankin, 'Wittgenstein on Meaning, Understanding, and Intending', *APQ*, 3, 1966, p. 3.

33   See, for example, Noam Chomsky, *Syntactic Structures*, chs. 2, 5; and *Aspects of the Theory of Syntax*, Cambridge, Mass., 1965, ch. 1.

BIBLIOGRAPHY

ALBRITTON, ROGERS. 'On Wittgenstein's Use of the Term "Criterion" ', reprinted in P.

ANSCOMBE, G. E. M. *An Introduction to Wittgenstein's Tractatus*, London: Hutchinson, 1959.

——'Retraction', *A*, 1965.

——'The Intentionality of Sensation: a Grammatical Feature' in Ronald J. Butler (ed.), *Analytical Philosophy; 2nd Series*, New York: Barnes and Noble, 1965.

ARISTOTLE. *Magna Moralia*. Included in Aristotle. *Metaphysics II, Oeconomica, Magna Moralia*, translated by H. Tredennick, G. C. Armstrong. London: Heinemann, 1935.

AUSTIN, JOHN L. *How to Do Things With Words* (J. O. Urmson, G. J. Warnock, eds), London: Oxford University Press, 1962.

——'Truth', reprinted in John L. Austin, *Philosophical Papers* (J. O. Urmson, G. J. Warnock, eds), 1st edition, London: Oxford University Press, 1961.

——'Unfair to Facts', reprinted in John L. Austin, *Philosophical Papers* (J. O. Urmson, G. J. Warnock, eds), 1st edition, London: Oxford University Press, 1961.

AYER, A. J. *Language, Truth and Logic*, New York: Dover Press, 1946.

BLACK, MAX. 'The Semantic Definition of Truth', *A*, 1948.

——*A Companion to Wittgenstein's Tractatus*, Ithaca: Cornell University Press, 1964.

BOGEN, JAMES. 'Was Wittgenstein a Psychologist?', *I*, 1964.

BROAD, C. D. *The Mind and its Place in Nature*, Littlefield, Adams, Patterson, 1960.

BURIDAN, JOHN. *Sophisms on Meaning and Truth*, translated by T. Kermit Scott, New York: Appleton, Century, Crofts, 1966.

BURNET, JOHN. *Early Greek Philosophy*, New York: Meridian, 1957.

CAVELL, STANLEY. 'The Availability of Wittgenstein's Later Philosophy', reprinted in P.

CHIHARA, CHARLES. 'Wittgenstein and Logical Compulsion', reprinted in P.

Bibliography

CHOMSKY, NAOM. *Syntactic Structures, Janua Linguarum* IV, The Hague, 1957.
——*Aspects of the Theory of Syntax*, Cambridge, Mass.: MIT Press, 1965.
COOK, JOHN. 'Human Beings', in Peter Winch (ed.), *Studies in the Philosophy of Wittgenstein*, London: Routledge and Kegan Paul, 1969.
COPI, IRVING M., and BEARD, ROBERT W. (eds). *Essays on Wittgenstein's Tractatus* (C) London: Routledge and Kegan Paul, 1966.
DAITZ, EDNA. 'The Picture Theory of Meaning', reprinted in A. G. N. Flew (ed.), *Essays in Conceptual Analysis*, London: Macmillan, 1956.
DAVIDSON. 'Actions, Reasons and Causes', reprinted in Bernard Berofsky (ed.), *Free Will and Determinism*, New York and London: Harper & Row, 1966.
DUMMETT, MICHAEL. 'Truth', reprinted in George Pitcher (ed.), *Truth*, Englewood Cliffs: Prentice Hall, 1964.
——'Wittgenstein's Philosophy of Mathematics', reprinted in Paul Benacerraf, Hillary Putnam (eds), *Philosophy of Mathematics*, Englewood Cliffs: Prentice Hall, 1964.
FINDLAY, J. N. *Meinong's Theory of Objects*, London: Oxford University Press, 1933.
FOGELIN, ROBERT J. 'Wittgenstein and Intuitionism', *APQ*, 1968.
FREGE, GOTTLOB. *Translations from the Philosophical Writings* (Peter Geach, Max Black, eds), Oxford: Blackwell, 1952.
——*Foundations of Arithmetic*, translated by John L. Austin, New York: Harper, 1960.
GEACH, P. T. 'The Law of Excluded Middle', *PAS*, 1956–7.
——'Assertion', *PR*, 1965.
GRIFFIN, JAMES. *Wittgenstein's Logical Atomism*, London: Oxford University Press, 1964.
HUME, DAVID. *A Treatise Concerning Human Nature* (Selby-Bigge, ed.), London: Oxford University Press, 1958.
JOHNSON, W. E. *Logic, Part I*, New York: Dover Press, 1964.
KNEALE, WILLIAM, and KNEALE, MARTHA. *The Development of Logic*, London: Oxford University Press, 1962.
MALCOLM, NORMAN. *Ludwig Wittgenstein; a Memoir*, London: Oxford University Press, 1958.
——'Knowledge of Other Minds', reprinted in Vere Chappell (ed.), *The Philosophy of Mind*, Englewood Cliffs: Spectrum, 1963.
——'Wittgenstein's *Philosophische Bemerkungen*', *PR*, 1967.
MOORE, G. E. *Some Main Problems of Philosophy*, London: Allen and Unwin, 1953.
——*Principia Ethica*, Cambridge: Cambridge University Press, 1959.
——'Wittgenstein's Lectures in 1930–33', reprinted in G. E. Moore, *Philosophical Papers*, London: Allen and Unwin, 1959.
PITCHER, GEORGE. *The Philosophy of Wittgenstein*. Englewood Cliffs: Prentice Hall, 1964.
——(ed.). *Wittgenstein: The Philosophical Investigations* (P). Garden City: Doubleday Anchor, 1966.
PLATO. *Theaetetus and Sophist*, translated by H. H. Fowler, London: Heinemann, 1921.

POLE, DAVID. *The Later Philosophy of Wittgenstein*, London: Athlone Press, 1958.

PRICE, H. H. *Perception*. London: Methuen, 1932.

QUINE, W. V. O. 'On What There is', reprinted in Leonard Linsky (ed.), *Semantics and the Philosophy of Language*, Urbana: University of Illinois Press, 1952.

——*Word and Object*. Cambridge, Mass.: MIT Press, 1960.

RAMSEY, FRANK P. 'Facts and Propositions', reprinted in Frank P. Ramsey, *The Foundations of Mathematics and Other Logical Essays* (R. B. Braithwaite, ed.), London: Routledge and Kegan Paul, 1931.

RHEES, RUSH. 'Wittgenstein's Builders', *PAS*, 1959–60.

ROSE, BARBARA. 'Didactic Art', *Art Forum*, 1967.

RUSSELL, BERTRAND. *The Problems of Philosophy*, New York: Holt, 1912.

——'Knowledge by Acquaintance and Knowledge by Description', reprinted in Bertrand Russell, *Mysticism and Logic and Other Essays*, New York: Longmans and Green, 1918.

——'Mysticism and Logic', reprinted in Bertrand Russell, *Mysticism and Logic and Other Essays*, New York: Longmans and Green, 1918.

——*Analysis of Mind*, London: Allen and Unwin, 1921.

——*Portraits From Memory and Other Essays*, London: Allen and Unwin, 1956.

——*My Philosophical Development*, London: Allen and Unwin, 1959.

——and WHITEHEAD, A. N. *Principia Mathematica, Vol. I*, Cambridge: Cambridge University Press, 1910.

SCHWYZER, H. R. G. 'Wittgenstein's Picture Theory of Language', reprinted in C.

SHEFFER, H. M. 'A Set of Five Independent Postulates for Boolean Algebras', *Transactions of the American Mathematical Society*, 1913.

SHWAYDER, D. S. 'Critical Notice of Stenius, *Wittgenstein's Tractatus*', *M*, 1963, reprinted in part in C.

——'*Gegenstände* and Other Matters: Observations Occasioned by a New Commentary on the *Tractatus*', *I*, 1964.

——'Wittgenstein's Tractatus': A Historical and Critical Commentary, unpublished thesis on deposit in the Bodleian Library, Oxford University.

STENIUS, ERIK. 'Wittgenstein's Picture Theory: A Reply to Mr. H. R. G. Schwyzer', *I*, 1963, reprinted in C.

——*Wittgenstein's Tractatus: A Critical Exposition of its Main Lines of Thought*, Oxford, Blackwell, 1960.

STRAWSON, P. F. 'Truth', *A*, 1949.

——'Truth', *PASS*, 1950.

STROUD, BARRY. 'Wittgenstein and Logical Necessity', reprinted in P.

WITTGENSTEIN, LUDWIG. *Remarks on the Foundations of Mathematics* (G. E. M. Anscombe, Rush Rhees, G. H. Von Wright, eds), Oxford: Blackwell, 1956.

——*Preliminary Studies for the 'Philosophical Investigations' Generally Known as the Blue and Brown Books*, Oxford: Blackwell, 1958.

——*Zettel* (G. E. M. Anscombe, G. H. Von Wright, eds), Oxford: Blackwell, 1958.

Bibliography

——*Philosophical Investigations* (G. E. M. Anscombe, trans.), 2nd edition (revised), Oxford: Blackwell, 1958.

——*Notebooks, 1914–1916* (G. E. M. Anscombe, G. H. Von Wright, eds), Oxford: Blackwell, 1961.

——*Tractatus Logico-Philosophicus*, translated by D. F. Pears and B. F. McGuinness, London: Routledge and Kegan Paul, 1961.

——*Philosophische Bemerkungen* (R. Rhees, ed.), Oxford: Blackwell, 1964.

——*On Certainty* (G. E. M. Anscombe, G. H. Von Wright, eds), Oxford: Blackwell, 1969.

——'Some Remarks on Logical Form', Oxford: reprinted in C.

INDEX